CAPITAL

CAPITAL

*The Story of Long-Term
Investment Excellence*

CHARLES D. ELLIS

WILEY

John Wiley & Sons, Inc.

Published by John Wiley & Sons, Inc., Hoboken, New Jersey.
Published simultaneously in Canada.

For general information on our other products and services please contact our Customer Care Department within the United States at (800) 762-2974, outside the United States at (317) 572-3993 or fax (317) 572-4002.

Wiley also publishes its books in a variety of electronic formats. Some content that appears in print may not be available in electronic books. For more information about Wiley products, visit our web site at www.wiley.com.

Library of Congress Cataloging-in-Publication Data:

Ellis, Charles D.
  Capital : the story of long-term investment
excellence / Charles D. Ellis.
    p. cm.
  Includes bibliographical references and index.
  ISBN 0-471-56704-3 (CLOTH)
  1. Capital Group—History. 2. Investment advisors—History. I.
Title.
HG4621.E45 2004
332.6—dc22

                                        2003020207

Printed in the United States of America.

10 9 8 7 6 5 4 3 2 1

With admiration and affection, this story of global
professional excellence is dedicated to
Richard C. Levin,
Yale University's great and twenty-second President,
exemplary servant-leader, pragmatist-scholar,
native Californian, and baseball fan.

ACKNOWLEDGMENTS

LINDA KOCH LORIMER, my beloved wife and best friend, encouraged me with penetrating questions and helpful suggestions—some on trips to China, some on vacation in Europe, and some in New Haven. Heidi Fiske, my friend over 35 years, uncovered historical sources of information and gave generously her keen editorial skills and her journalist's knowledge of Capital. Randy Whitestone combined good humor and discipline to help clarify and tighten the text—significantly. Jack MacDonald and David Rintels gave numerous useful suggestions. Kimberly Breed cheerfully converted the complexities of various pieces of text collected into complex paste-ups with extensive handwritten annotations, arrows, and codes into draft after draft in the ungainly process of struggling toward clarity. Dozens of Capital Associates gave me great help and a first-hand experience with the Capital process of making decisions—generosity in support and assistance *and* the clear understanding that all final decisions were entirely mine to make.

C. D. E.

CONTENTS

FOREWORD

IT IS ALWAYS a treat to welcome a new book by Charley Ellis, and I am honored to provide an introduction. The practice of investment management owes Charley an enormous intellectual debt. He is one of the titans of finance. A seminal thinker, a keen observer of financial markets, a writer who combines intellectual rigor and common horse sense, and an influential consultant, Charley Ellis has made a profound and lasting impression on the landscape of the investment business. The firm he founded, Greenwich Associates, and his many articles and books have improved investment decision making for literally thousands of institutional and individual investors. Charley's writings have become investment classics. "The Loser's Game" is mandatory reading for anyone entering the investment business. *How to Win the Loser's Game* provides institutional and individual investors with an indispensable guide for effective asset allocation. *Classics: An Investor's Anthology* (Volumes I and II) brings together the major pieces in the literature that have helped change the practice of investment management from an art to a science. *Wall Street People* (Volumes I and II) profiles Wall Street luminaries from Warren Buffett to George Soros. And now comes *Capital,* the story of one of the largest and most successful investment organizations in the world—The Capital Group Companies.

For many reasons, Charley Ellis is the perfect person to tell the story of this remarkable firm. The building of Capital and the values that sustain the firm are not dissimilar to the development of Charley's own firm, Greenwich Associates. The factors that made Greenwich the premier global financial strategy consultancy firm bear a close relationship to those that made Capital a firm described by Charley as "among the best at everything it does." Perhaps the most important factors are absolute integrity and "what's good for the client" as the essential driving principles of both firms. In these days of tainted research, insider trading, obscene compensation arrangements, and mutual fund complexes that put the profits of the firm above the interests of the shareholders, it is reassuring to be reminded that successful firms do flourish by holding fast to fundamental values: sticking to the right path; taking the long-term view; and insisting always on quality and excellence. And finally, it is clear that both Capital and Greenwich have been led by men of vision, tenacity, and inspiration, who know what it takes to bring a start-up to grandeur.

Indeed, this book represents a perfect pairing of one of the most astute observers of the investment scene with one of the most outstanding investment firms ever created. Not only is Charley smart; he is a professional listener. In preparing this volume, he interviewed the people involved in the building of Capital, and he has an ability to make everyone he talks with believe that what they have to say is of the utmost significance. He recognizes the importance of molding a set of enormously capable colleagues into a community and of continually raising the bar to define excellence. There could not be a better person than Charley Ellis to tell the story of Capital with such finesse and critical understanding.

In another sense, however, Charley is a very unlikely person to write this book, and I am a very unlikely person to provide its Foreword. Charley and I are soul mates in believing that stock picking is a losing game and that the most useful function of professional investment advice is in selecting an appropriate asset allocation consistent with the needs, circumstances, and preferences of different investors—not in trading from one stock to another on the basis of perceived differences in valuation. Indeed, winning the loser's game is accomplished by using investment funds that simply buy and hold the stocks (as well as bonds and real estate investment trusts) that comprise a very broad-based market index. On a foundation investment committee where Charley and I served, he once chastised me for my only lukewarm espousal of indexing. (I recommended that we start by indexing only half of the portfolio. Charley wanted to go much farther.) Why, then, would Charley Ellis—a man who believes that our stock markets are so dominated by talented and dedicated institutional investors that it is virtually impossible for anyone "to do significantly better than the others, particularly in the long run"—write a book praising a firm whose raison d'être is active portfolio management?

There are at least two justifications for a book about the virtues of Capital—even for such confirmed indexers as Charley and me.

The first reason to extol at least some active managers stems from a basic paradox in the theory of efficient markets. If markets were always perfectly efficient, there would be no incentive for any professionals to uncover the information that so quickly gets reflected in market prices. Markets need some professionals to ensure that information is quickly incorporated into market prices, and those professionals have to earn above-market returns to compensate them for the time and effort involved in doing fundamental research. I firmly believe that too much effort is put into finding mispriced securities and that few investors actually gain from the effort. But the market could not be efficient if everyone simply invested in index funds. Paradoxical as it may sound, markets need firms such as Capital to ensure that low-cost indexing is, in fact, a winning strategy.

The second justification is that Capital is one of those very rare investment managers to have achieved superior long-run investment returns. The records of the mutual funds managed by Capital are publicly available, and we can examine the long-run results of these funds compared with broad-based index funds. In the table below, I compare the results of the general domestic equity mutual funds managed by Capital with the returns from the S&P 500 and the Wilshire 5000 indexes. The S&P and Wilshire returns are shown for the same 30-year period over which the fund returns are measured. The table shows that investors would, in fact, have been better off by investing in those mutual funds managed by Capital. Capital has indeed produced above-average and even well-above-average market returns for investors.

What is Capital's secret? Why has this organization excelled in the investment race while most others have played the loser's game—at least where investment results are concerned? In these pages, Charley Ellis tells the Capital story and shows how the organization of the firm has been designed for sustained success.

Of the many factors explaining Capital's success, three stand out. The first is Capital's unusual way of organizing its "knowledge workers" in an industry that typically celebrates individual "stars" and where hubris is common. An unusual amount of effort and care is taken in recruiting, coaching, and developing Capital's exceptionally talented investment analysts. There is no room for egotistical

AVERAGE ANNUAL RETURNS, JUNE 30, 1973–JUNE 30, 2003

Indexes (before expenses)

S&P 500	11.46%
Wilshire 5000	11.58

Domestic Equity Mutual Funds Managed by Capital (after expenses)

AMCAP Fund	14.71%
Growth Fund of America	15.33
American Mutual	13.36
Investment Company of America	13.25
Washington Mutual	14.02
Income Fund of America	12.28

Sources: Lipper and CRSP.

stars, and hierarchical symbols are removed that would interfere with individuals working effectively together in groups. The organization has been successful in creating a pervasive tone of trust, mutual respect, and interpersonal enjoyment.

A second—and related—unique feature of the Capital organization is its innovative "multiple counselor system" of portfolio management. Each portfolio is assigned not to an individual manager but instead to several individual managers (which might include some of the firm's research analysts), each of whom is responsible for one part of the overall fund and each make direct investment decisions. The system ensures that there will be no star managers, and it effectively copes with a problem endemic to investment organizations: As the size of the assets to be managed increases, the flexibility of an individual portfolio manager is often severely constrained.

Finally, Capital has managed to maintain a long-term focus in the face of changing fads and the changing popularity of investment styles. In inevitable periods of underperformance, Capital's answer to the question, "what are you going to change?" is "nothing." When popular faddish products (such as new Internet or high-technology funds) have been brought to market by competitors, Capital has refrained from bringing out similar products. Capital eschews publicity. Capital's leaders are not interested in promoting stories about their funds—especially those that are "hot"—because they know that investors invariably tend to put their money in such funds at just the worst time, when investment results are likely to revert to the mean. Capital does not even use the term "performance" to describe investment results—in its view, performance should be used only to describe what actors do in Hollywood or New York.

In these pages, you will find some wonderful stories about the people who made Capital the outstandingly successful investment organization that it is. Occasional failures are recounted as well as the more frequent successes. And *Capital* is written with grace, wit, and eloquence. Charley Ellis has an anti-Midas touch. If he touched gold, he would bring it to life. I can't imagine another writer who could make a discussion of custodial services and the transfer agency function interesting. And all this from a writer whose comprehension of the investment business is unexcelled. You are about to embark on some delicious reading—*bon appétit!*

BURTON G. MALKIEL
Author, *A Random Walk Down Wall Street*

INTRODUCTION

NOTES FOR READERS

While dozens of Capital Associates have made themselves available for candid interviews and several have helped on factual accuracy, this is certainly not an authorized biography. Out of all the information provided to me, only four small, factual deletions were requested and made. All along, it's been understood by everyone at Capital that I would tell it as I see it, and I have done just that.

NO INVESTMENT ORGANIZATION in the world has ever done so well for so long for so many clients as The Capital Group Companies. It is one of the world's largest investment management organizations, consistently earns the admiration of clients and competitors, and decade after decade achieves superior long-term investment results. Yet most people, even its own customers and clients, know very little about Capital.

This is no accident. Capital is a very private organization—both financially and philosophically—and sees no benefit to its clients from organizational recognition or individual fame.

As an organization, Capital is *designed* for sustained success. No other investment organization is so well organized, staffed, and motivated to continue striving to be among the best at everything it does while achieving superior long-term results for clients around the world.

Capital does not advertise and avoids the media. Its largest division, one of the world's largest mutual fund organizations, even uses a completely different name: "The American Funds." That's why most people do not realize that Capital is:

- One of America's three largest managers of mutual funds—serving over 20 million shareholder accounts and managing four of the nation's 10 largest mutual funds. With the best long-term record of investment results, it is gaining market share.

- A leading institutional investment manager, serving 35 percent of America's large institutions and 65 percent of those very large funds with assets over $10 billion.

- One of the largest independent investment research organizations in the world—repetitively identified as having the most capable research analysts.

- One of the most respected investment managers in *each* of the world's large national markets: America, Japan, the United Kingdom, Australia, Canada, and continental Europe—and gaining market share.

- The world's leading international investment manager.

- The largest investor—by far—in the emerging markets.

Much more important to the company and to its investors, Capital achieves superior long-term investment results. Over the past 5 years—*and* 10 years, 20 years, 50 years, and longer—Capital's investment results rank in the Top Quartile. No other investment manager has done so well for so long. Not nearly. And no other organization is so well resourced and so well organized to succeed in the future.

Unsurprisingly, Capital is where most investment professionals would most like to work *and* is the firm they would most frequently recommend as long-term investment managers for their family and friends. Capital is also the one investment organization senior corporate executives would most like to have owning their company's common stock.

Finally, Capital is both the one organization most likely to fulfill favorable expectations over many years into the future *and* the least likely to say or even acknowledge such prospects. As Jon Lovelace, who has been central to Capital's development, says, "Nothing wilts faster than laurels rested upon." Modesty is pervasive at Capital, where people are far more interested in what lies ahead than in past achievements.

Investors—both individuals and institutions—seeking to understand why Capital is such an admired organization will find in this book many important lessons in organization design, management of professional people, and strategic development. These lessons will not only inform other investment firms, they also have application for other types of professional organizations. Capital may well be the world's best-designed organization of what Peter Drucker so wisely calls "knowledge workers." The major factors that make Capital the world's most admired investment organization include:

- *Long-term focus.* Capital is creatively conservative and comfortable saying "No" to currently popular and apparently profitable ideas that, in the long run, might harm investors. Capital comfortably defers action on new mutual funds until the market is truly attractive for long-term investment commitments, even though this will often be the very same time the market for that particular type of investment seems *least* attractive. Capital is comfortable absorbing significant operating losses—for many years—to support strategic commitments that can prove rewarding over the long run.

While most investment organizations try—and many try too hard—to keep up with changing fashions in investing, Capital has shown that over the long term, faithfully serving investors' true long-term interests will build a remarkably strong, growing, and profitable franchise.

- *Consistent objectivity.* Rational thought and behavior are paramount at Capital. Investment results are reported quite frequently and compensation is carefully linked to long-term results to assure consistent objectivity.

- *People-centered operations.* With all its systems and consistently rigorous rationality, Capital's operations—both daily and long term—are remarkably humane and sensitive to each individual. Capital is unusual in the time and care it invests in recruiting exceptionally talented people who will work well together and produce superior services and results for investors.

  Capital is even more remarkable in the continuing investment it makes in helping each individual develop her or his capabilities *and* in designing the organization in ways that enable each person to contribute most. Jobs are designed, and continuously redesigned, around specific individuals to match and capitalize on their particular strengths.

  Capital is not so much in the investment business as it is in the business of developing individuals and groups who can and will make superior investment decisions and deliver superior service to clients. At this, it excels.

- *Seminal organizational innovation.* Capital's seminal organizational innovation—which perhaps only Capital itself can fully utilize—is the multiple-counselor system of portfolio management. This system deals effectively with the formidable "asset-size barrier" that eventually confounds most growing investment organizations. The problem of size cannot be eliminated, but it can be made manageable by dividing large portfolios into several segments. The manager of each segment invests in her or his "highest conviction" ideas—with full accountability for rigorously measured results.

- *Flexibility in the organization.* Capital's overall organization is flexible and fluid. (To outsiders, it often appears vague or amorphous.) The firm disperses decision-making power widely and keeps strategic options for future development open as long as possible. Since stable *structure* is all too often the dangerous enemy of dynamic *strategy,* Capital avoids such tangible indicators of organizational status as vested titles, different size offices, and hierarchical reporting. Corporate titles change frequently and have little real significance.

- *Flexibility in compensation.* Capital's compensation policy is both very flexible and based directly on the objective measurement over several years of each individual's long-term contributions to Capital's long-term goal to serve three equally important and ultimately complementary groups: investors, Associates, and owners.

- *Private ownership.* The broad and equitable distribution of private ownership is considered essential.

- *Recognition of the need for ego strength.* Although egotistical manners and negative remarks are *verboten,* each individual needs quiet ego strength to flourish professionally and personally when surrounded by skilled and dedicated professional colleagues who work closely together and continuously compete to achieve superior long-term investment results.

As an organization, Capital has made serious mistakes, particularly back in the 1970s, but it has made fewer major mistakes and has corrected those mistakes sooner than its competitors. And individual people at Capital make mistakes: Feelings get hurt, tempers flare, and of course, mistakes are made in investments every day. If making mistakes is the inevitable cost of striving, correcting mistakes—and learning how to avoid repeating them—is the best measure of a learning organization that will continue to get better and better. The people inside Capital Group Companies would be first to say that Capital is not and never has been perfect—*and* hopefully never will be because the drive to do better and better creates the dynamic tension in the pursuit of excellence that keeps Associates focused on the future and on continuous improvement.

Hard as it is to *become* a champion, the hardest task is always to *stay* a champion. The longer an organization has been successful, the harder it is to sustain the creativity and competitive commitment required to continue improving—and Capital has been more successful for longer than any other investment organization in the world. Each year of success adds to the cumulative challenge to prevent the conventional and insidious diseases of "success": complacency, insularity, and overconfidence. If the Lovelaces, father and son, represent two generations of leadership, then the third generation of leaders— Shanahan, Fisher, Rothenberg, and others—is already devolving major responsibility to the fourth. To succeed with success, as the many leaders within Capital Group Companies know and understand, is a forever challenge.

A view toward the future raises more generalized questions: Has Capital overinvested in talent for the incremental rate of return actually earned? Will success lead to inbreeding or cult culture? Should Capital have been much more successful in developing its business in bond management or in serving wealthy families? Will Capital's complex and subtle corporate culture flourish in *each* of the many nations around the world? Can Capital maintain consistency across all those very different nations and business cultures? Will successive generations of leadership continue to develop a stronger and stronger organization that is able to do more *and* better for Capital's three great constituencies? As institutional investors increasingly dominate the world's capital markets, can even as strong a research-based investment organization as Capital achieve results that are consistently superior to passive investing? To what extent will Capital's professionals use their understanding of investing to work with clients as investment counselors, helping each client develop the appropriate investment program to meet its long-term and interim objectives? Although Capital is likely to develop superior answers to these questions, the questions remain challenging—even for Capital.

CHAPTER 1

THE FOUNDING

NOTES FOR READERS

An investment management organization—like any professional organization—is profoundly dependent on the capabilities, character, motivations, and values of its people. And the attributes of the early joiners primarily determine the kind of professionals the firm will attract in future years. Once the die is cast, upgrading an organization is very hard. For an organization to upgrade itself at a later date is almost impossible. So, the founders and early joiners matter greatly.

Hundreds of investment management firms have been launched during the past 50 years. Collectively, their behavior in recruiting professionals confirms the grim validity of David Ogilvy's caution: "Only giants will hire giants. Ordinary men will hire men who are less than they are—and then those will go on to hire men of even less stature until the whole organization is replete with *pygmies!*"[1] Creating and building and then sustaining a superior professional firm is always deliberate, continuous, and "unnatural"—unnatural in the

[1] *Confessions of an Advertising Man* by David Ogilvy, NTC Publishing Group (March, 1994).

sense that something new and different is being brought to life *and* built to last.

Jonathan Bell Lovelace[2] and his son Jon Lovelace repeatedly demonstrated leadership in reaching out to bring exceptional people to Capital. By their persistent searching for strong people—repetitively taking the initiative to exploit "lucky" opportunities—they assembled a collection of talented professionals who worked well together. Capital became increasingly recognizable as a firm of unusually capable and congenial professional people: a good group to join.

The core group of individuals illustrates one obvious lesson and one not so obvious. The obvious lesson is that attracting and keeping highly motivated and talented individuals is essential in building a superior professional firm. The familiar keys to success are (1) persistent and imaginative recruiting; (2) consistently high standards for acceptance into the group; (3) uncompromising search for meritocracy in the distribution of rewards and responsibilities according to real contribution; (4) devotion to professional excellence and superior service to clients; and (5) genuine collegiality. In sad contrast, when hiring people, many start-up firms make expedient compromises that they later learn to regret and recruit too few real leaders to ever become a truly superior firm.

The less obvious lesson—but no less critical to success—is how deeply new firms depend on pursuing very thin threads of possibility to identify and then bring aboard those individuals who will later prove to be their exceptional and indispensable people. Although the retrospective view of history, with the outcome known, may make the steps along the way seem natural or even preordained, those who have led in the development of great organizations know how uncertain and fragile the early stages always are. As key people appear in the Capital story, readers might enjoy imagining the consequences for

---

[2] Founder of Capital in 1931.

Capital if, among many other coincidences, Coleman Morton's father had not expanded his cement business into Alabama where he met Jonathan Bell Lovelace *or* Coleman Morton had not been sold insurance by Jim Fullerton *or* Bob Egelston had not agreed to see Jim Fullerton *or* Bob Cody had not gotten to know Jonathan Bell Lovelace in an aborted merger *or* Bill Newton hadn't noticed, in the Post library on Okinawa, how well investment managers were paid *or* Bob Kirby had not cracked his ribs racing cars *or* Howard Schow had not looked in through a window at Harvard *or* Ned Bailey had not decided to go to Virginia to follow Charlie Abbot *or* if Bill Hurt had not included Jon Lovelace in his luncheon group *or* if Bob Kirby and Dick Barker had not been flying across the United States on the same plane *or* Nilly Sikorsky had not needed a part-time job while in graduate school *or* Jim Rothenberg's classmate had not mentioned his name, and so on, and on. *And* what if individuals who were determined to find strong people had not pursued slight possibilities? As Madam Curie so shrewdly and famously observed, "Chance favors the prepared mind!"

In addition to organizing a core group of mutual fund investment managers, a set of significant decisions are made in this chapter: Jon Lovelace overcomes his thoughtful reluctance and accepts the leadership of Capital, where he then promulgates a three-way organizational mission of serving investment clients, Capital Associates, and Capital's owners—and begins a career as Capital's servant leader that will continue for four decades. Capital establishes itself as an important mutual fund manager, and the American Express and Anchor Group funds are taken over on what prove to be very favorable terms. The separately owned and managed mutual fund sales organization is brought into Capital. So is a faltering East Coast investment operation. Venture capital and international investing are initiated—the first outside the organization, and the second deeply within it—even though many at Capital would have thought international investing had no real place in a West Coast mutual fund organization struggling financially in a depressed investment market.

EVEN THE MOST thoughtful observer would not have imagined the future in store for the modest 34-year-old in the brown business suit, gazing out at the uninterrupted prairie of the Great Plains from the window of his room on the Santa Fe Super Chief. It was 1929, and he was on his way to Los Angeles with his wife and 2-year-old son, where he would soon start a small firm that, by the end of the century, would become the world's leading professional investment management organization: the Capital Group Companies.

Jonathan Bell Lovelace[3] had a rendezvous with the emerging profession of investment management. Raised in southern Alabama, where his family was active in timber, Lovelace trained to become an architect in two years' study at Alabama Polytechnic, later renamed Auburn University. One year later, showing a special aptitude for mathematics, he earned a master's degree while serving as instructor in architecture and mathematics, and as manager for a championship football team—and developed an enduring interest in team sports.

Enlisting in the U.S. Army for European duty in World War I, Lovelace encountered new concepts and new technologies. Because he knew trigonometry, he went into the artillery. A whiz at mental arithmetic, Lovelace joined a group that pioneered antiaircraft artillery, by solving the problem of hitting fast-moving targets.[4]

---

[3] Known as JBL to identify him separately from his son Jon Lovelace, who was baptized Jonathan Bell Lovelace Jr. and later changed to the shorter name and is known by his associates as JL. (Initials were originally used on office memoranda to save space as more and more people were to receive copies.) Today, Capital Associates are routinely identified by their respective assigned initials.

[4] Lovelace contributed to the writing of the Army's *Manual of Anti-Aircraft Artillery* and coached Edward MacCrone, who had never gone to college, but was very bright, on the use of tangents, sines, and cosines.

Lovelace provided the necessary calculations, and his was the first American artillery unit in France to shoot down a German plane.[5] He mustered out as a captain.

During his service, Lovelace met new people with interesting new ideas, including Edward MacCrone. With their last names coming in alphabetical sequence, Lovelace and MacCrone had adjoining bunks in officer training camp[6] and then on the troopship that took them to Europe. Their friendship, which began with this alphabetical accident, flourished during their service in the same combat unit.

Earlier, MacCrone had split from a firm that was a predecessor of Merrill Lynch to form E.E. MacCrone & Co., a small stockbrokerage in Detroit—then the equivalent in industrial creativity to today's Silicon Valley. He had the support of important clients like Walter Chrysler, W.C. Durant, and Stuart Mott of General Motors. Eddie MacCrone urged his thoughtful friend to get into the new and exciting field of investments as his firm's research statistician. MacCrone's proposition: "You'll pick the stocks for our customers' men to sell!" Lovelace had other plans, so he demurred. Jauntily, MacCrone assured him that such a position[7] would be open if and when Lovelace were ever interested.

Noting that only one major building was constructed in the state of Alabama during the year he graduated, Lovelace resolved to leave architecture and make his future elsewhere. After the Great War, Lovelace ventured a brief stint in California: He and his brothers, Jim and Jay, bought a date ranch near the town of Indio. But the war's end also ended the sugar shortage that had contributed—temporarily—to the higher demand and favorable price level of

---

[5] For many years, he kept a large chunk of wood from the fuselage of that plane in his Beverly Hills basement as a souvenir.

[6] Fortress Monroe in Virginia housed two training units before they shipped out to Europe: one from Chattanooga, Tennessee, and one from Battle Creek, Michigan.

[7] At a salary of $150 per month.

dates. With a return to peacetime and normal pricing, the Lovelace brothers' venture in date growing soon faded.[8]

In 1919, Lovelace decided to join Eddie MacCrone[9] and moved East to Detroit. Lovelace quickly established himself as an "idea man," organized a small but effective research unit, and was one of the early pioneers in securities research. No GNP data was available; public companies disclosed very little data and only at their convenience; Moody's and Standard & Poor's did not yet publish; and the Dow Jones Average included only 20 industrials until October 1928. Finding the available data inadequate or out of date, Lovelace championed independent field research.

Lovelace and MacCrone had a series of disagreements over the amount of time Lovelace devoted to investment research. MacCrone wanted to concentrate on underwriting new issues—where the underwriting spread was a rich 15 to 20 percent and there were no bureaucratic delays—so he offered to pay for a new research organization[10] if Lovelace would concentrate on the firm's underwritings. They agreed on a compromise: Research would be done Lovelace's way, and the firm's new issue underwritings would get full research coverage. As part of the arrangement, Lovelace, who enjoyed designing financial structures that worked well for the companies involved, agreed to help solicit corporate finance business.

[8] Jay maintained the ranch for many years and ran The Desert Date Shop.

[9] E.E. MacCrone & Company was formed on February 13, 1919. The firm was suspended from the New York Stock Exchange for one year on October 27, 1926 for violating a section of the exchange's constitution by paying two branch managers—in addition to their salaries—one half of their offices' net profits without having obtained prior written approval from the Committee on Quotations and Commissions. Later, on February 24, 1930, the brokerage business and assets (including six offices around Michigan) were sold to EA Pierce & Company, which later became part of Merrill Lynch, Pierce, Fenner and Beane, known today as Merrill Lynch. E.E. MacCrone & Company continued in business until 1934, when it was succeeded by B.E. Hopper & Company, with Edward E. MacCrone and Bernard E. Hopper partners.

[10] Lovelace recruited Albert Hettinger and Donald Smith, from Harvard Business School; Alexander Standish, from AT&T; Ray Chambers, chief of statistics at the U.S. Treasury; and Ragnar Naess, of the New York Federal Reserve. He also set up a group of economic consultants that included Professor Lionel D. Edie, from the University of Chicago; Professor Irving Fisher, from Yale; Edmund Ezra Day, from Michigan; and Joseph Davis, from Stanford.

His real enthusiasm during this period was in developing the investment trust business for individual investors of moderate means. This almost became the very first mutual fund in the United States. Lovelace had studied the Scottish investment trusts, whose sole purpose was to invest in other companies based on the concept that individual investors would fare far better by combining their investments, spreading the risk, and retaining professional investment management instead of buying individual stocks on margin through retail stockbrokers. Lovelace wanted to organize a similar investment company for American investors, and MacCrone eventually agreed. But believing that his firm deserved half the profits above a 6 percent return on investors' capital, MacCrone designed the new investment company with heavy leverage from debt and preferred stock. For each share of common stock bought by the public, E.E. MacCrone & Co. would get a perpetual warrant to buy an equal number of shares. The new investment company was named the Investment Company of America.

Before underwriting the company, Lovelace and MacCrone agreed to obtain at least some kind of approval for their new idea from a regulatory authority. The logical choice was to get the blessing of Michigan's Commissioner of Banking. But the commissioner was a conservative regulator who felt the state's banks already faced too much competition for their own good, so he turned down the investment company idea, saying: "Gentlemen, this is a very interesting idea, but if this thing is as good as you fellows think it is, it will take money out of the savings banks and we're not going to have that here, so I will not authorize it." Trying to get any official approval and resolving various design issues took several more months, so by the time Investment Company of America came to market as a Michigan trust on March 27, 1926,[11] a Boston group's entry—Massachusetts Investors' Trust—had won the race to become the United States' first

---

[11] JBL was one of ICA's five trustees. Investment Research Corporation was organized by the Investment Company of America trustees to provide investment research to ICA and, it hoped, to a series of regional investment companies.

mutual fund. Following MIT's approval in Massachusetts, the banking commissioner in Michigan gave his approval to ICA.

The stock market was gathering momentum in the major boom of the 1920s, and Eddie MacCrone wanted to get extra gains from financial leverage by adding debt to the new fund's capitalization. Lovelace didn't want to incur the risks of financial leverage, but he lost that battle, leaving the new fund extra vulnerable to the market crash when it finally came.

MacCrone's firm did quite well at underwriting local industrial companies and organizing and sponsoring a series of closed-end investment companies—often concentrating investments in a specific industry or one region of the country. In 1928, E.E. MacCrone & Co. was prospering as a stockbroker. Most business executives anticipated a bright new era for the United States—and particularly for the stock market.

In a strong stock market environment, Lovelace prospered. He enjoyed considerable success as an investor and became a partner in E.E. MacCrone & Co. in 1924.[12] Still in his early 30s, he was financially independent.

While others might have been carried away by the euphoria of the great bull market, Lovelace thought differently. Based on his research into market *price* versus true investment *value,* Lovelace was becoming increasingly concerned about what he considered excess enthusiasm among investors. In one calculation, he found that the stock market value of a major New York bank[13] was nearly equal to its total assets—as if they didn't have *any* deposits or liabilities! Lovelace knew that this high stock market valuation was unsustainable.

In the summer of 1929, Lovelace became bearish on the stock market and sold most of his own stocks and bonds in August. He

[12] Lovelace was listed as a partner in E.E. MacCrone & Company, along with E.E. Mac-Crone, C. Collins, and C. Timewell from 1924 to 1930.

[13] First National City Bank, now Citibank, a part of Citigroup. Asked, MacCrone assured Lovelace that Charlie Mitchell would make millions underwriting Ford Motor Company, but that never happened.

tried, unsuccessfully, to persuade MacCrone to become much more conservative.[14] Unable to convince his friend, Lovelace took independent action. He withdrew from the stockbrokerage business and negotiated the sale of his 10 percent interest in E.E. MacCrone & Co. (Modestly, Lovelace would later confess he had not liquidated everything: Responding to his partner's request that he not visibly withdraw completely, he left some of his capital in the firm until year-end.) Fortunately, while the market broke sharply in September, it had recovered somewhat by year-end when Lovelace withdrew his capital. Then, over the next three years, stocks lost nearly 90 percent of their peak market value.

Having "retired" as a man of wealth at 34, Lovelace decided to move back to distant Los Angeles.[15] As usual when traveling to California, he took the Super Chief.

In 1931, to develop the information needed for his various activities, Lovelace established a small investment firm in Los Angeles—Lovelace, Dennis & Renfrew—the nucleus of what would later become Capital Group Companies.[16] Lionel D. Edie and Albert

[14] As Jim Fullerton recalls a conversation in the early 1960s, he asked, "Jon, you've always had a reputation for being a great market timer. When you got out of the stock market in 1929 just before the crash, what were the signals that you saw?" JBL replied, "Jim, I was not a market timer—not then and not now. What got me out of the market in 1929 was simply kindergarten financial research. At that time, the money center banks were in great favor in the market. Everyone wanted to own them. My kindergarten research consisted of looking at each of those banks and multiplying the number of shares it had outstanding times its market price per share. I found that each of those banks was selling in the marketplace for more than its deposits. They didn't *own* those deposits: They *owed* them. That scared me so much that I did the same simple arithmetic with a lot of other companies. I found that people were climbing all over each other to buy 100 shares or 10,000 shares of those 'hot' stocks. But no one in his right mind would buy the whole company at such a high price. That's what got me out of the market. It was a very simple lesson. Don't pay more per share for a company's stock than you'd be willing to pay if you were buying the whole company."

[15] Characteristically, Lovelace demonstrated his long-term value orientation to investing in 1930 to 1931, when he built a handsome home in Beverly Hills, employing highly skilled craftspeople who badly needed work and produced superb workmanship. He also showed his sense of humor by referring to the vacant lot he owned next door as "the tennis court."

[16] Capital Research and Management Company.

Hettinger—both had been with him in Detroit—wrote research reports for Lovelace's new firm.[17] Lovelace's business included acting as financial advisor[18] to California companies; serving as an expert witness in utility rate cases; advising on the issues that companies faced coming out of Depression-induced bankruptcy; and evaluating private holding companies as well as large blocks of stock in family-controlled businesses going through probate.

In 1931, Lovelace's new firm succeeded E.E. MacCrone & Co. as the investment advisor to two closed-end funds originally sponsored by MacCrone: American Capital Corporation and Pacific-Southern Investing Corporation.[19] Lovelace was elected president of Investment Company of America in 1932, when it was in serious trouble.[20] With all the leverage Eddie MacCrone had insisted on

[17] Later, Edie formed one of the nation's largest investment counsel firms—Lionel D. Edie & Co.—which ultimately also became part of Merrill Lynch. Hettinger joined Lazard Frères after retiring in his 60s from a distinguished academic career at Harvard Business School. Then, over 30 years, he made a personal fortune—estimated at more than $100 million—investing in "adventurous novelties" such as Japanese insurance stocks at three and four times earnings long before other investors would even consider Japan.

[18] Clients included the Gross brothers, for whom Lovelace helped raise the capital to buy control of Lockheed Aircraft; Pacific Mutual Life; Capitol Records, where he was a founding director; Muzak, where he was one of the original investors; and Walt Disney, where he served as the first outside director. He worked particularly closely with Roy Disney, who was struggling with the financing of movies and whom Lovelace introduced to a rising banker, A. P. Gianinni of Bank of America. Lovelace also helped finance the noted cartoon movie *Fantasia*. If he couldn't work on *architectural* structures, joked Lovelace, he'd work on *financial* structures. Out of the Disney connection came the Lovelace family's long-term involvement with Cal Arts (the California Institute of the Arts), the avant-garde school that aimed to do for the arts what MIT and CalTech were doing for engineering.

[19] Lovelace also set an enduring example of serving—often on investment committees—such public service organizations as Children's Hospital, the Southwest Museum, and the Huntington Library in Southern California. Today, more Capital Associates serve on *pro bono* boards in California than any other company.

[20] Lovelace had been one of the five trustees of Investment Company of America when it was organized in Detroit as a closed-end investment company or mutual fund in 1926. Lovelace was also president of American Capital Corporation, which purchased from E.E. MacCrone its controlling interest in Southern Bond & Share. Into the early 1960s, Detroit was the location for Investment Company of America's lawyers and annual meetings of shareholders.

adding to its capital structure, the trust lost over 70 percent of its value during the stock market collapse. With $3 million in long-term debt and $4 million of equity, ICA had a coverage ratio of only 133 percent: At 125 percent, the bondholders would automatically take over. So to prevent falling below the trigger point, the assets of ICA were all invested in government bonds. In 1933, a deputation of the distinguished executives on ICA's Advisory Board[21]—who had lost all confidence in MacCrone, but trusted Lovelace's investment judgment—traveled from Michigan to California to persuade him to take over the management of what remained of this investment trust.

Recapitalized as a publicly owned, closed-end investment company, the Investment Company of America had assets of less than $5 million.[22] In 1936, ICA retired its debt, and in 1939, it converted to open-end status to get away from the problems of selling in the market at a 25 to 30 percent discount from net asset value.[23]

Over the next 10 years, Investment Company of America's investment record was exceptionally favorable for three reasons: the

[21] Members included the President of Burroughs Adding Machine; the president of Parke-Davis pharmaceuticals; Roy Chapin, the chairman of Hudson Motors; Stuart Mott; Edgar A. Pierce of EA Pierce & Company; and several others. The Advisory Board had prestige, but no power—until ICA got into trouble.

[22] Southern Bond & Share and Pacific Investing Corporation were merged to form Pacific Southern Investors, which, in turn, acquired a 40 percent interest in Investment Company of America, a Delaware corporation. Reorganizing the highly leveraged complex that MacCrone had structured involved complex negotiations and exchanges. One result was a perpetual warrant that, Lovelace stated, "caused perpetual problems." Assets fluctuated in a modest range for many years. ICA grew to $22 million in 1945; but then fell under $18 million in 1948. Lovelace would live to see the fund become one of the nation's 10 largest in 1969. As one of America's best performing mutual funds, Investment Company of America is the only fund on the list of the largest funds in 1969 that has remained continuously in that group ever since. With all dividends reinvested, $10,000 invested in ICA in 1934 would have grown to be $15.2 million by the end of the century (vs. $6.6 million for the S&P Index, or just $135,000 in a bank savings account). With assets over $50 billion, the fund is now the third largest of all equity mutual funds in the United States.

[23] Pacific Investing, another closed-end investment company, had an $800,000 investment in ICA and the market discount threatened to trigger its bondholders taking over Pacific Investing and its large percentage ownership in ICA.

fund's leverage working favorably; the advantages of maneuverability given the fund's small size; and Lovelace's skill at capitalizing on the investment opportunities he found in the stock market. As the Dow Jones Average gained 7 percent annually over the decade, Investment Company of America did *twice* as well: 14 percent annual gains.[24]

Over its first 20 years—a very long period, even from today's distant perspective—Capital was, on average, only a break-even operation.[25] Today, senior executives look back and shake their heads at the daily economies that were considered necessary. To control expenses, office-to-office telephone calls (for which the first three minutes cost an initial $3—or about $25 in current dollars) were made in carefully planned sequence, with each person waiting in turn to conduct his part of the pending business. Most interoffice communication relied on mail service: After all, three-cent stamps easily beat long-distance toll charges.[26] The New York office was fitted out with used furniture. And New York received the leftover Standard & Poor's loose-leaf tear sheets on public companies from the main office in Los Angeles—but only after those reports had been replaced each year by a new set of tear sheets. If New York City was 3 *hours* ahead of Los Angeles, staffers joked, it was also a full *year* behind.

In addition to his cost-conscious manner and commitment to fundamental research, Lovelace believed in working with people he really liked, who shared a disciplined commitment to rationality in investing and to integrity in serving investors. Reserved in demeanor,

[24] The perpetual warrants continued to be a marketing nuisance, because competitors would ask darkly, "Do you really want to sell your customers a mutual fund with all that overhanging dilution?" (In the year 2000, clever brokers were still gathering responses to their advertisements suggesting investors look through their old papers for ICA warrants.)

[25] Investment results suffered in the late 1930s, perhaps because JBL was so deeply involved in the development of the Investment Company Act of 1940 that would govern the mutual fund industry. In 1939, Investment Company of America was converted into an "open-end" investment company or mutual fund and Investment Company Distributors began offering the shares of both Investment Company of America and Pacific Southern Investors.

[26] When Capital moved from Spring Street to the Statler office building, the research analysts came in on a Saturday to unpack boxes—and to keep reference books in the right order.

Lovelace was an unusually good and attentive listener—and effective as a group thought-leader. Analysts found the insights from his investment meetings helpful in developing their own judgments on companies and industries. Quiet during the investment meetings he chaired, Lovelace took extensive notes on a legal pad and would then summarize what had been said and what he understood had been agreed.[27]

Never outwardly warm or gregarious, Lovelace was certainly not effusive with praise, but he was also slow to criticize. Everyone in the organization during his tenure felt that they had a lot of elbowroom and ample time to perform before he would make any final judgments of their capabilities. "I don't know how he accomplished it," says Coleman Morton, "but you always had the feeling that he was well aware of what you were doing and how you were doing without any feeling that he was peeking over your shoulder." Lovelace understood that mistakes, even big ones, are an inherent part of investment management and that the way to judge an individual or a company is in a long-term framework.

Lovelace established an attitude toward individuals and organizations (see Chapter 13) that still pervades Capital and provides the essential basis for the organization's success in managing succession and engaging outstanding people of many different ages. "His main love was to serve as an investment banker to real entrepreneurs," says Howard Schow (see Chapter 2). "He was what the French call an 'accouché'—a midwife to ideas and the ventures that could bring them to life."

[27] "When we first met," recalls Nilly Sikorsky (see Chapter 8), "I was only 19 years old. JBL had accomplished a great deal; knew many substantial people; and was widely admired. Still, he listened to me with great care and respect, clearly listening to *learn*. He had an extraordinary ability always to respect others and never to seem superior. JBL was a real gentleman. If it weren't for my deep respect for JBL, I could never have accepted his invitation to luncheon at the old California Club when they didn't admit women or Jews—and I was both. JBL's consideration of others led him to invite Chuck Schimpff and his wife too—so I'd have the fun of being with another woman. But, of course, Mrs. Schimpff and I were nearly 50 years apart in age!"

Lovelace enjoyed serving on corporate boards with people who had Midwestern social and moral values. He cared greatly about thoughtful business strategies and conservative financial strategies—and distrusted investment bankers with breezy, big-city talk and manners. (After hearing a few New York investment bankers describe how they made deals, Lovelace murmured with quiet disdain: "That's not what *I* ever did!")

To determine the long-term *worth* of a company, JBL relied on thorough, original research into investment values that others might have overlooked—followed by purchases at reasonable market prices. Combining careful research with a long-term view on valuation, Capital's portfolio turnover was and still is far below industry norms.

"Looking at a company's numbers was never enough," recalls Bob Kirby. "JBL would only invest in guys he really believed in." "The only difference between Chrysler Corporation and its failed predecessor,"[28] JBL often said, "was Walter Chrysler."

Lovelace had a strict sense of morality and was all probity. Clearly unusual in Los Angeles, he wore dark three-piece business suits with a gold watch chain across his vest and a hat that he tipped to the ladies. Lovelace seldom took off his suit jacket or vest, even in the Spring Street office, which had no air-conditioning. He spoke softly, almost quietly, with a Southern tone of voice. Only 5 feet 7 inches tall, his slim build matched his calm, gentle demeanor. Lovelace was exceptionally modest about his considerable contributions and achievements, but he attracted many capable and powerful people because he had remarkable insight and was comfortable around smart people with ambitious ideas.[29] Lovelace was both low profile and unassuming, *and* a genuine risk taker who allowed and encouraged young people with ideas to run with them.

---

[28] Maxwell Motor Company failed and was absorbed by Chrysler.
[29] In 1955, he supported Coleman Morton's initiative to launch an early venture into international investing: International Resources Fund.

Believing in independent thinking, Lovelace combined his own contrarian view with genuine politeness, often explaining, "It's important to be accommodating. When everyone wants to sell, you accommodate them and buy. When everyone wants to buy, you accommodate them and sell. Don't try to get the last 5 percent. Don't be greedy."

A conversation with Lovelace nearly a generation ago made a lasting impression on one of Capital's current leaders—partly in the thoughtful rigor on the substance of the discussion; partly in the collegial style or tone of the discussion. Lovelace, in his early 70s, made an appointment for luncheon with David Fisher, who was 28. As usual, Lovelace wore a three-piece, dark brown suit and a hat. Deferentially, he called David "Mr. Fisher."

"What attracted you, Mr. Fisher, to this type of work?" inquired Lovelace after they were seated at their table. Fisher ventured to explain his appreciation for the marvelous operating leverage and the accelerating profitability that could come to a well-managed investment organization with relatively fixed costs if and when the stock market rose and new assets came pouring in.

Explaining that he doubted there was any real operating leverage over the long term in the investment management business, Lovelace expressed concern that any apparent leverage was more likely an indicator that not enough was being reinvested in skilled people, systems, and customer service to enable the organization to do its work well in the future. (As Jim Rothenberg explains in Chapter 9, "If the investment assets supervised by Capital are adjusted or deflated to eliminate the impact of market appreciation, the underlying growth is about 7 percent. The increase in investment people is also about 7 percent. So, just as JBL said, 'There's no major leverage in the business.'")

"Jonathan Bell Lovelace's concern about investing enough in the future continues to be a hallmark of the organization today," explains Fisher. "JBL always took a very long-term view and wanted to be sure Capital would do better and better—and *continue* doing better and better long after him."

With design innovations making seminal contributions, the little investment company that Lovelace started in an unlikely part of the country would grow in assets managed from $5 million in 1933, to $300 million in 1958 to over $1.1 billion by 1967—and then to well over $500 billion by the turn of the century. And the Capital organization grew comparably in staff: fewer than 20 in 1933; 30 in 1953; and 120 in 1967. Capital Group Companies now employs over 6,000 people.

Not only is Capital one of the largest investment managers in the world, it is also recognized as one of the very best at achieving sustained success for its three main constituencies—consistently superior investment results for investors; attractive long-term returns for owners; and fulfilling career opportunities for Associates. Also, important to those who devote their careers to Capital is a spiritual dimension. As Bob Kirby says, "Capital is a company with a soul."

CHAPTER 2

STAYING ALIVE

NOTES FOR READERS

Although seldom recognized at the time, the long-term destinies of most investment management organizations are disproportionately determined by compromising decisions made during the very early years of the organization's history. Many of these determining decisions are made almost casually.

Examples abound of investment organizations that are organized around the past performance record—and self-interests—of the leading investment managers who have the self-confidence and entrepreneurial determination to launch a new firm. The founder's name is often in the organization's name and in the way the founder talks and feels about "my firm." But in a few years, who was present at the creation will seem almost accidental.

Capital's early years were different. As founder, Jonathan Bell Lovelace was remarkably sanguine about personally absorbing all the losses—for 20 long years—because his long-term focus was on developing a superior firm. This enabled Capital to avoid making any of the ownership decisions that so often boomerang later on. Equally important and equally unusual, Lovelace was interested in sharing ownership as soon as it was worth having—and willing to arrange financing so Associates could invest in Capital.

Capital was a very small firm in a small business in 1950. It had only 28 employees and managed only $36 million. Virtually any economic or market setback could have been too much for such a marginally profitable company as Capital then was.

Time is often the most precious resource in organizational development, especially at the start-up stage when it is in such very short supply. Of all the contributions made to Capital by its founder, the most precious and productive over the long term must have been the freedom of time to develop as an organization.

LINDLEY MORTON RAN away from home at 13, worked as a lab assistant and in sales for a cement company, and then served as a Naval aviator during World War I. After the war, Morton, still in his 20s, found an abandoned cement plant in Phoenixville, Pennsylvania. He learned it was owned in foreclosure by the local bank, arranged to meet the bank's president, and boldly offered to buy the cement plant.

"What do you offer?"

"What are you looking for?"

"My bank lent the prior owners one million dollars, so that's the lowest I'll go."

"Okay! But I can only pay one dollar down—with the rest to come over the next ten years."

"Sold!"

In time, Morton expanded the business, particularly in Alabama, where he met Jonathan Bell Lovelace. Later, Lovelace asked him to join the Investment Company of America's board of directors. In 1928, Morton sold his cement company. He had seen the spectacular prices at which other company owners were selling out, and he knew competition was getting tougher and tougher. He got a good price, but soon had a problem.

Morton put one third of the proceeds into what looked like an exciting new way to invest—one of Wall Street's newly organized investment trusts. With apparently great early success, these trusts would pyramid control of operating companies through layer on layer of holding companies and holding companies *of* holding companies, fueling expectations of making highly leveraged profits. But financial leverage works both ways and Morton's main investment was in the ill-fated Goldman Sachs Trading Company, which failed very badly. From its high, the price of shares for Goldman Sachs Trading plunged a ghastly 98 percent.

But even after the total loss of one third of his fortune, Lindley Morton was still a rich man. When his son, Coleman Morton, was a senior at Yale,[1] he chose as the topic for his senior thesis in economics, a study of bank service charges.[2] While visiting California to complete his research, Morton was invited to hang his hat in the office of his father's friend from Alabama—Jonathan Bell Lovelace.

After graduating from Yale and serving in World War II, Morton joined Capital as a junior analyst in 1945. A year later, he left to join his father and brothers in the oil fields, prospecting hopefully for the Big Find. After searching for a few years without making any great discoveries, the senior Morton called his sons together: "I've been trying to teach you boys how to *win* at the $100 bettor's window, but you haven't even learned how to win $2 show bets. So you're all

---

[1] Coleman Morton likes to tell the story of how he chose to go to Hotchkiss and then to Yale: "My great grandfather was partially scalped by Indians. He prayed to God, 'If I ever escape, I will devote my life to the work of the Lord.' He did escape, of course, and took up his religious duties in Salisbury, Connecticut. Over at the Hotchkiss School, Mrs. Hotchkiss wanted someone local to represent scholarship boys; she chose great grandfather. And that's pretty much why my brothers and I went to Hotchkiss—and then on to Yale."

[2] For data, he turned to Joe Rosenberg, a family friend at Bank of America.

fired!"[3] Coleman Morton returned to Capital in 1949, worked hard, and did well. The ownership position he developed at Capital would today be appreciated as remarkably favorable: He once owned 10 percent—with an option to increase that to 25 percent.

A tall, handsome, and engaging man, Morton is intellectually gifted and was elected to Phi Beta Kappa at Yale. In contrast to the conservative dress and demeanor of most Capital people, Morton— who was stylish, confident, and outgoing—wore Savile Row suits with colorfully different mouchoirs tucked into his breast pocket each day. He traveled widely and in style, belonged to the right clubs at home and abroad, and radiated an air of great self-confidence. He *looked* like a CEO.[4] With a charismatic personality and a clear, strong voice, Morton was an effective public speaker and a highly visible portfolio manager in the otherwise low-key, conservative group at Capital. Full of bold and original ideas, Morton was the dominant personality among Capital's portfolio managers and was widely recognized by the broker-dealers selling the firm's mutual funds—and by the leaders on Wall Street. Morton, however, was not alone.

Believing strongly that the success of any management depended on finding, motivating, and backing exceptional people, Jonathan Bell Lovelace again and again attracted unusually able people to Capital—just as he had attracted unusual talents to E.E. MacCrone & Co. in Detroit.

Harleston J. "Hardy" Hall joined Capital as an analyst in 1936. As both a portfolio manager and an analyst, Hall was a major contributor, particularly in the years when he ran a solo research outpost in New York City. In addition to conducting his own research on companies all over the East Coast, he served as Capital's primary liaison with Wall Street. As an engineer from Georgia Tech, Hall was

---

[3] In future years, Lindley Morton liked to have breakfast with his two sons once each week to ask them: "Well, fellows, what have you accomplished during the past week that's *important?*"

[4] In fact, over the years, many of his "outside activities" sought out Coleman Morton to serve as their head.

certain that the stock market must have an underlying mechanism that could somehow be understood. The key, he thought, would be to know the underlying momentum of earnings, so he paid particular attention to any company that had a down quarter in earnings, seeking always to understand exactly why.

Chuck Schimpff came to Capital after several years at Dun & Bradstreet in Chicago and did most of the work required to launch American Mutual Fund—Capital's[5] second mutual fund—in 1950. Famously honest, Schimpff meticulously tallied up the sales tax he paid each day. Proud of the corporate perquisites he had earned, he expected younger men to address him as "Mr. Schimpff" and enjoyed the status of having his own reserved parking space. As he was transitioning into retirement, he did not come in every day, so the building manager began parking in Schimpff's space. Despite a warning, the manager continued to take Schimpff's space, so Schimpff took direct action: He bought a long piece of heavy-gauge steel chain, tied the offending car to a post, and padlocked it leaving a note stating that he had the key—in his office.

Jules Hoffman,[6] based in Detroit,[7] was an expert on industrial corporations, particularly the auto companies, whose increasing sales volume drove demand for rubber, steel, and all the many auto parts suppliers. Hoffman's custom was to visit three or four companies each day and write six-page reports on each of those companies that same night. Using a time-saving standardized format, he could complete and mail several reports back to the office the next day. Always comfortable with blue-collar workers, Hoffman advised,

---

[5] The full name in this era was Capital Research and Management Company.

[6] After working at the MacCrone firm, Hoffman had a successful business career and became CFO of a major construction company in Detroit that had worldwide operations. He was so successful in working out the company's financial problems that the head of the company decided his son-in-law could take over. So in 1953, Hoffman rejoined Capital on what was expected to be a temporary basis.

[7] In 1942, with a war on and assets down from $23 million in 1936 to $12 million, the Detroit office was closed and then reopened after the war.

"You can learn a very great deal of information if you're always nice to people."[8]

In 1948, Capital was a small firm with little business: only 16 employees and one mutual fund with $17.5 million in assets plus Pacific American, a closed-end fund—and little momentum.

Jonathan Bell Lovelace nicely demonstrated his skill in designing financial structures with the early 1950 creation of an initial public offering of American Mutual fund. Then, with tight security preventing any leaks that would have ruined the deal, American Mutual was merged with Security Company.[9] This closed-end investment company was selling at a substantial discount to net asset value, so its shareholders were delighted to come into American Mutual at full net asset value. The combination advanced American Mutual's assets to $10 million—and the management fees on this new fund put Capital, for the first time, safely in the black. It also gave Capital a second mutual fund that brokers (who worried about ICA's potential dilution when warrants were exercised) could sell. Capital would soon have its third mutual fund in Washington Mutual Investors Fund (see Chapter 5).

In 1954, with a strong stock market[10] and, at last, good new business in mutual fund sales, Capital was strongly in the black for the first time. Now, confident that Capital's profitability would last, JBL began selling shares in Capital to other key associates.

What later became recognized as the most important recruiting Jonathan Bell Lovelace ever did must have appeared to be the easiest: He recruited his son. This task, however, wasn't at all easy. Jon

---

[8] Professors Lionel D. Edie and Albert "Doc" Hettinger were also used frequently as consultants on the economy and investing.

[9] Security Company was the securities affiliate, organized by Security Bank during the boom of the 1920s. As was common practice then, any unsold shares left over from underwritings were placed in the affiliate's portfolio. Not surprisingly, investment results were miserable, which is why the shares sold at a major discount from net asset value.

[10] Market averages rose nearly 50 percent from September 1953 to September 1954, and in September 1954, the averages finally regained their prior peak in September 1929—after a full 25 years.

Lovelace was very reluctant to join his father's firm after graduating from Princeton[11] in 1950. He had majored in economics and social institutions, where he first became interested in industrial psychology. Although father and son had great respect for each other, they didn't always have an easy personal relationship.

Having grown up in considerable affluence as the son of a prominent man, Jon Lovelace wanted to make his own way and was concerned about being subordinated to his father *or* succeeding simply because his father made it easy. So, young Lovelace started his career with summer jobs in Personnel Administration at Lockheed and Pacific Finance and on graduation, joined Pacific Finance.[12] But, one year later, he realized he wasn't interested in a long-term career with Pacific Finance and should look for alternatives. Hearing this, his father recognized an opportunity and called to suggest coming to Capital, "This business is all about people and numbers. You're good at dealing with both. While you're thinking about your alternatives, why not try it? I think you'll like it. And if you don't, if something ever happens to me, it would be useful to our family for you to know something about the company." In October 1951, Jon Lovelace joined Capital as a statistician in Los Angeles. Still, he had doubts. He resolved to reconsider at two checkpoints: 6 months and 24 months. The first six months went well, but even at 18 months,

[11] After taking a course in summer school so he could graduate early from Beverly Hills High School, Lovelace took a year at the Hotchkiss School. In 1944, wanting to get into service, he took and passed the qualifying test to get into the V-12 OCS program, but illness prevented his going in, so after graduation, he enlisted as a radar technician. Identified as a man who had passed V-12, he took the test again, passed—but came down with scarlet fever and missed his V-12 unit again. V-J Day came in the middle of his training and, after 18 months of service, he was home. During training, Lovelace lived for a few weeks in the Honeymoon Suite at the Del Monte Hotel—in bunks with seven other seamen.

[12] The Gross brothers of Lockheed developed Pacific Finance in response to JBL's admonition that they couldn't expect to continue selling lots of airplanes after World War II ended and would need to be in businesses that would prosper in peacetime. Pacific Finance became a major West Coast consumer finance company and was subsequently acquired by TransAmerica.

he did not expect to stay much longer. Then a change in his father's health changed everything (see Chapter 4).

The traditional mother of invention came suddenly to Capital in 1953. Jonathan Bell Lovelace suffered a heart attack. He was 58 and his doctors insisted he not work for at least a full year.[13] (Fortunately, Lovelace would live another 26 years—until 1979, when he died at age 84.) The impact on organizational leadership was immediate; the impact on the investment process came a few years later.

Leadership at Capital had been concentrated in JBL, so his withdrawal from the firm was a sudden and dramatic change. Now, everyone would have to pitch in and share management responsibilities. Hardy Hall, Coleman Morton, and Chuck Schimpff would serve as a triumvirate in leadership, with Hall serving as president. (Jon Lovelace was not yet part of the inner circle.) "After JBL's heart attack," recalls Bob Cody, "we realized we should never be dependent on just *one* manager in *any* area. In this sense, the heart attack was actually fortunate because it taught us all a very important lesson."

JBL's serious heart attack was not the only confrontation with death in the Lovelace family. JL and his wife Lillian's second child died as an infant in 1954. Their grief was profound. Agreeing that a change in scenery might help them deal with their loss, they moved

---

[13] While outwardly formal, JBL was widely recognized as having an engaging and original sense of good humor. "Work was one of JBL's greatest pleasures," recalls Jim Fullerton. "So after his heart attack and retirement, I kidded him that his definition of retirement was simply no longer working every Saturday and Sunday!" Fullerton was visiting with JBL in his office one afternoon and was startled when he happened to look at the clock. "Good Lord, Jon, is it already twenty past four?" "No," came the laconic reply with a chuckle, "I keep the clock set that way so if I'm feeling a little tired, I can just glance at the clock and say, 'Oh! It's four o'clock already. Time to be going home soon!'"

Lovelace's dry humor is further illustrated by another Fullerton recollection: "He came to me while we were in New York City one day with good news: 'Jim, I have two tickets for tonight's World Series game. Would you like to go?' I explained, 'I have a longstanding business commitment with a major distributor, and I just can't join you.' JBL drew himself up and replied: 'That answer, Jim, causes me to question your business judgment!'"

to New York City in 1955 with their daughter. Lovelace would work with Hardy Hall. The New York office would become a training center, with young analysts rotated in so they could call on Eastern companies and learn firsthand the strengths and weaknesses of Wall Street's firms—and develop the requisite skepticism before rotating back to Los Angeles. (Having serious responsibilities in field offices well away from headquarters would become a characteristic learning experience for young people in the Capital organization.)

When Jon Lovelace returned to Los Angeles after a year in New York, Howard Schow succeeded him in New York. Schow grew up on Long Island, became an Eagle Scout, and served in the U.S. Navy during World War II. Mustering out in 1946, he attended Williams College and the Harvard Business School, determined to learn all he could for his intended career in investments. During his second year of business school, Schow was in a serious automobile accident and received a settlement of $6,000—after lawyers' fees of $4,000 on a $10,000 award—which gave him the stake with which to begin investing.

At Harvard, Schow took a course in finance and investment,[14] where he heard Dr. Albert Hettinger deliver a guest lecture. Impressed by the lecture, Schow later saw Hettinger at the dean's house reading annual reports, and asked his view of Capital. "Good firm" came the laconic reply—without any mention that Hettinger had been employed as Jonathan Bell Lovelace's director of research many years before in Detroit and was currently consulting to Capital.

After writing to numerous investment firms across the country with little result, Schow got an invitation to interview with Capital Research and Management Company, a firm he'd just heard of. Learning that Capital was located in Los Angeles, which Schow disdainfully thought of as "only Hollywood and movies, *not*

---

[14] With Professor Charles Abbott.

investing"—but having no other offers, yet being determined to get into investments, Schow interviewed with Hardy Hall and Jon Lovelace in New York. He received and accepted an offer to join Capital in early 1956.[15]

In the mid-1950s, Capital was managing four investment companies[16]—three open-end mutual funds, and one closed-end fund: Pacific American.[17] At Schow's first group meeting at Capital, the main speaker was surprisingly familiar: "Doc" Hettinger.

[15] Capital's regular recruiting at business schools began a year later, in 1957.

[16] Hardy Hall managed Investment Company of America; JBL managed American Mutual (together with Chuck Schimpff, who was not really an investor, but enjoyed being "involved"); Coleman Morton managed Pacific American; and JL managed Washington Mutual, which was quite small in assets and had little funds inflow. Pacific American was merged into American Mutual in 1956.

[17] Open-end mutual funds offer to buy or sell shares at the net asset value per share of the fund twice each day and so are "open" to new investors or to redeem current shares on a regular basis. Closed-end funds do not buy or sell their own shares. Their price, like that of regular companies, is determined by supply and demand.

CHAPTER 3

THE MULTIPLE-COUNSELOR SYSTEM

NOTES FOR READERS

Transformational innovations—even those that appear obvious several years later—seldom arrive like lightning bolts and even less often spring like Athena, fully developed, from a person's head. Instead, they are the product of a vague, uncomfortable awareness of the need for a better way; intuition about the general outline of the desired concept or solution; a sense of the general direction in which to move; and great personal persistence in exploration and development. There is also that magic ingredient of good luck, which is so often crucial to great successes. No wonder transformational innovations, particularly in organizational design, are so rare.

Capital's great transformational innovation was the multiple-counselor system of portfolio management. Like many great innovations—particularly transformational organizational innovations—Capital's multiple-counselor system of investment management did not arrive fully developed. It began as a tentative, pragmatic way of dealing with a specific set of circumstances, and specific prior experiences strongly influenced it. Capital's leaders persisted—through several years of cost and effort and without much evidence of progress—to work out the many details of the multiple-counselor system.

As an organizational concept, the multiple-counselor system enables Capital to deal constructively with the major problem that confronts, and often confounds, most investment management organizations: Investment success leads to asset growth that eventually overloads the organization's capacity to produce superior investment results.[1]

Great success in investments can cause such rapid growth in assets that it quickly overwhelms a manager's capacity. Ironically, when professional success produces a business success, professional disappointment or even failure often follows. And sadly, in investment management, it happens all the time. In each of the past five decades, half of the leaders at the start of the decade were no longer leaders by the end of the decade. And very few firms have been among the leaders for 30 or more years. Capital is an exception—and over the very long term, the unique exception.

In another version of the same difficulty, when an investment business is growing well because its investors are achieving good results, competitors may bid away one or more key portfolio managers—or they may decide to peel off to form a new firm. Or a star portfolio manager, with a compelling public following, can lose his touch for a year or so—or is it, perhaps, an early indication that the manager has "lost it" forever? The organization must decide between the hero's marquee value in sales versus the apparent need to replace him or restructure his role—changes that the hero may find

---

[1] If a red ant were 8 inches high, the geometrically proportional weight of its body would crush its external skeletal structure. And if an Indian elephant were 15 percent larger, its body weight would require such bone and muscle strength in its legs that its weight would make it simply too heavy for the muscles to lift and the beast, unable to move, would starve.

unacceptable. Or a rapidly developing young investor may feel personally ready for major portfolio management responsibilities, but it may not yet seem wise to turn over an entire fund to her management. Sometimes, several of these disruptive difficulties develop simultaneously.

All of these frequent growth problems have a central characteristic: They each expose the investment organization to the major risk of individual egos and business opportunities (both often dominated by short-term factors) being in conflict with the organization's long-term professional responsibilities. Capital has been almost unique in its ability to keep its priorities right, and the multiple-counselor system has been the key factor.

Astonishingly, almost no other investment organization[2] has chosen to replicate Capital's transformational innovation. This lack of replication is particularly surprising since a large majority of the world's foremost investment managers continue to produce inferior investment results because they are not designed for organizational effectiveness on a large scale. While the multiple-counselor system is difficult to replicate, the evidence continues to accumulate that it can and does work very well and that no other organizational design deals effectively with the daunting challenges of actively managing large assets successfully.

Investment management is hardly a fertile field for producing or adopting a transformational innovation in organizational structure—partly because the business is usually highly profitable as it is, so why bother?—but primarily because talented investors (who are usually dominant within their own organizations) are so deeply absorbed in investing that they can give little time or talent to managing their organizations as organizations. Therefore they are unlikely to initiate major innovative change in their firms. (The reason the business is usually so profitable is that most managers—unlike Capital—underinvest in producing service value and also tend to overcharge their clients.)

---

[2] PRIMECAP, which was formed by Howard Schow and included a group of Capital alumni.

The multiple-counselor system may only be possible in an organization like Capital that has a culture (see Chapter 9) that has largely displaced the chronic constraints of individual egotism. At most other investment organizations, each portfolio manager confronts the world daily as a hero. Capital has displaced individual heroism with a systematic commitment to personal modesty, continuous rationality, rigorous measurement of results, and organizational effectiveness.

Capital's cultural values, recruiting, management, and compensation system reinforce its explicit commitments to meritocracy—and to the primacy of successful investing.

AFTER CAPITAL HAD a few years of success having one portfolio manager for each of the four funds, the firm recognized in 1958 that it had a significant management challenge where it mattered most: investments. "Investment results were not as good as we wanted in the late 1950s," says Jon Lovelace with characteristic understatement. "We studied ourselves and concluded that committee decision-making was at fault, particularly when members of the committee genuinely disagreed."

Capital's leading portfolio managers had very different personalities and noticeably different ways of thinking about investments, so they were virtually sure to have genuine, strong disagreements. Group decisions about investments were all too often compromises, the worst kind of decision-making in investing when interpersonal accommodation muddles creative thinking, rational decisions, and decisive action; and trying to forge a consensus from competing, even conflicting, differences of opinion resulted in social and mental exhaustion. Cross-sterilization was more likely than cross-fertilization of insights and ideas. This is particularly harmful in investing where the best ideas are often tentative and "soft-shelled" at their earliest, and potentially most profitable, stage. If investing is all about creativity and making unusual, unconventional, and even unpopular decisions, great investment decisions are best made by individuals taking direct responsibility for the results of their own acts.

Capital tried having each portfolio manager manage his own fund independently, but after three or four years of experience, actual investment results seemed strangely skewed: The growth-oriented portfolio of Investment Company of America was actually more conservative than American Mutual's presumably *conservative* portfolio—even though their respective mandates were the other way around! For example, in 1957, Sputnik raised concerns about America's prospects; and the stock market, anticipating recession, started to decline. Hardy Hall, seeing a slowdown in corporate earnings, was actively selling stocks to raise cash reserves in Investment Company of America. In contrast, JBL "liked Ike"[3] and saw many opportunities for growth in the overall economy and in major industries, so he was taking a much more positive approach, boldly buying stocks in American Mutual. The differences between the managers' portfolios were not complementary; they were contradictory.

Coincidentally, JBL and Hall planned to retire soon, which meant that both Investment Company of America and American Mutual would need new portfolio managers. A choice would have to be made between Coleman Morton and Jon Lovelace—two very different people. Capital's quickly approaching need to make important decisions helped give birth to a major organizational innovation.

Capital's leaders agreed that neither of the two traditional organizational structures used in the mutual fund industry—separate and independent management of each fund by its own portfolio manager *or* collective management by committee based on consensus and compromise—would give Capital an effective solution to a serious and pressing problem. Something very different was needed.

Instead of compromising or, even worse, combining the two traditional, inherently contradictory structures, Jon Lovelace suggested

[3] President Dwight D. Eisenhower.

to his father that they might deal with the problem by taking the best components of both structures. He tentatively proposed what, in time, became an entirely new structure for an investment management organization. After a slow start, this new design—the multiple-counselor system of portfolio management—proved to be superior to either of the two traditional structures.

The multiple-counselor system of portfolio management began with a decision to divide the problem into parts and then rearrange those parts. The first step was to divide each of Capital's two large funds into four separately managed parts—one each for Hall, Morton,[4] JBL (assisted by Schimpff), and JL. Each of the four portfolio managers would manage part of *each* fund, so the results of both funds would be a blend of each manager's best efforts.

When Jon Lovelace explained his idea for dividing the funds into several separately managed components, Jonathan Bell Lovelace gave the proposition his strong sponsorship as well as its name: the "multiple-counselor system." (This terminology is used in the mutual fund business, but the conventional term "portfolio manager" is used with institutional clients.) JBL wanted to give his son full credit for the idea; but JL, who realized that this might not be helpful in gaining acceptance for what others might view as a radical idea, asked JBL to recommend the change alone.[5]

"Everyone knew that keeping perfect track of all the transactions would be difficult," explains Jim Rothenberg.[6] "But several people in

---

[4] Since Coleman Morton was the only investor with experience in natural resources or in international investing, he continued "solo" with International Resources Fund.

[5] Jon Lovelace, however, was fully prepared to take complete responsibility if his idea did *not* work out well.

[6] Jim Rothenberg went directly from Harvard College to Harvard Business School, where he took—along with three quarters of his 650 classmates—the popular course on institutional investing taught by Professor Colyer Crum. Jim Fullerton was interviewing a student in that class who was set on venture capital, so there was no fit. Then the student said: "Gee, Mr. Fullerton, you really ought to interview Jim Rothenberg. He's the smartest, best thinker in our class!"

Professor Crum had asked Rothenberg to consider staying on for a year as his Research Associate and case writer but, when asked about investment firms, suggested that one of the management recognized that if Capital was going to expand, *and* if Capital was going to move each of its mutual funds away from dependence on one individual, something had to be changed."

With all the necessary records kept by hand,[7] the multiple-counselor system began operation on April 1, 1958. (Naturally, some skeptics reminded the proponents that this was April Fool's Day.) Nine months later, the multiple-counselor system was applied to Washington Mutual.

Although it was a *de novo* innovation, developed as a pragmatic solution for a specific problem, the multiple-counselor system of portfolio management has proven to be Capital's central innovation in structuring an investment management organization. As Rothenberg explains some 40 years later, "In *developing* the concept, Jon played the central role in a father-son arrangement, while *implementing* it was made possible by JBL's strong sponsorship. This strong support was needed because, at the time, Jon had not been with Capital very long and several people opposed the idea, some because it was considered heresy and others because they simply thought it just wouldn't work."

The operational aspects underlying the multiple-counselor system have subsequently been worked out in considerable detail at considerable cost—the software used to operate the multiple-counselor system has cost over $100 million—and continues to be modified. "On one level, it is just as simple *and* profound as it was in the beginning," says Rothenberg. "On another level, it is quite elaborate, as we've learned from painful experience."

---

best outfits was Capital. At home that night, Rothenberg happened to receive a letter from Capital. He interviewed with Jan Greer and then Mike Shanahan. Having never before been west of Detroit—and that far only to play football—Rothenberg gladly went to Los Angeles, took Dr. Sanford's personality tests, and went to Shanahan's home for dinner. It was his first-ever Japanese meal. After dinner, the two men talked until 3:00 A.M.—which was 6:00 A.M. Eastern Standard time. By then, Rothenberg had given up any thoughts of being a case writer at Harvard.

[7] Adding to the managerial challenges of keeping complex records up-to-date when all were kept by hand, two separate groups in accounting—one with three members, one with two—weren't able to work effectively with each other in the early years.

"The multiple-counselor system was introduced initially as an experiment during a difficult transition period," explains Bob Egelston, who was deeply involved in working out the operational and computational complexities of the system—before it was computerized.[8] "It took several years of patient nurturing and development. Its role grew out of Jon's concern over the geometrically increasing burdens of growth in the scale and complexity of Capital's work and his desire to stay ahead of that curve."

"For several years, JBL felt the multiple-counselor system was something of a trade secret," says Coleman Morton.[9] "We knew it was unique. We knew it was not easily implemented. And we knew it worked." Some wanted to keep the multiple-counselor system a complete secret so others wouldn't catch on. But Bob Cody was sanguine, saying, "It's so complex, if any competitor tried it without *really* understanding it, they would sink!" Associates agree that the multiple-counselor system of portfolio management can be explained briefly in 30 *seconds*—or in full operational detail over 30 days.

Monitoring the multiple portfolios is a complex task that still requires a lot of time and attention by investment people to prevent frustrating errors and misunderstandings.[10] To work well, the

[8] Capital felt it could not use off-the-shelf systems that are usually considered cost-effective, because the available systems were all designed with a common assumption that one star portfolio manager would be the ultimate decision maker—the same central problem that Capital was striving to avoid with its multiple-counselor portfolio management process.

[9] Morton introduced parts of the system at Trust Company of the West, where he later worked. The "fund of funds" structure used to combine several separately managed hedge funds into one aggregate portfolio has *some* similarities and is being increasingly used.

[10] An important cushion was invented to manage the process when one of the counselors working on a fund wants to sell all or a part of a fund's holding. First, the stock is offered to the other portfolio counselors working on the fund. If they wish to take the position over, an internal exchange is made and the seller's investment performance will be measured as though an actual sale had been made into the stock market. (If other portfolio counselors do not want to take it over, the stock is sold into the market.) The difficulty comes when one portfolio counselor wants to sell and others do not want to buy *and* disagree with the decision to sell. This calls for special record keeping. (Occasionally, small amounts are held in a Committee Reserve.)

multiple-counselor system also needs at least one senior sponsor[11] who can smooth over the interpersonal rough spots that are virtually inevitable in any effort to have creative people work together closely and interactively.

As though to prove that the multiple-counselor system is hard to adopt and implement effectively without strong sponsorship, even Capital was not always successful with its introduction. Far from it, as explained in Chapters 9 and 10, in the early years of subsidiaries where portfolio managers all too often reverted to the "hero fund manager" syndrome which is the principal reason other investment organizations have not adopted the concept.

The difficulties of managing effective implementation of the system were particularly evident as the portfolio managers at Capital Guardian Trust tried it their own way. At first, they simply paired portfolio managers, but there was too much differentiation in investment styles and too little communication among portfolio managers—so when two clients with the same mandate compared their results, they could be *very* different. Naturally, such unexpected and inexplicable differences were disconcerting to clients. And in the competition for new business, the investment consultants who advise pension funds on the selection of new investment managers found such differences simply unacceptable.

"Personally and professionally," says one portfolio counselor,[12] "I like everything about the multiple-counselor system *except* trying to explain it, particularly to a client who is not very experienced or sophisticated about investing. Even for those of us who work here full time, it *is* hard to be completely on top of 90 to 100 different stocks. This is particularly true of the 'needle' stock—the stock clients will needle you about during the portfolio review meeting if performance has been disappointing."

---

[11] Provided for many years by Jon Lovelace, but now provided by several designated seniors.
[12] Dick Barker (see Chapter 8).

But as clients and their consultants got used to the system *and* as Capital Guardian's results became more consistent through a much-needed and significant increase in organizational discipline (see Chapter 10), both clients and consultants came to appreciate the multiple-counselor system's benefits more fully. Today, Capital is all about internal systems that can readily accommodate growth in size and complexity.

The multiple-counselor system has become an extraordinarily sophisticated and powerful process that enables Capital to lessen the challenges of size and complexity that accompany growth. As a mutual fund or an institutional account grows larger and larger, it can easily be divided among one or more additional portfolio counselors. Meanwhile, portfolio counselors concentrate on the kind of investing they do best, each managing a portfolio of assets that is a comfortable size. The system enables each portfolio counselor to focus on achieving Capital's primary objective: producing consistently superior long-term investment results.

Competition is always with par, never with other individual portfolio counselors. (Of course, internal comparisons can't be eliminated since everyone is compared to the same external measures.) Counselors know they will significantly increase their pay by achieving superior investment results for clients because investment results are linked directly and explicitly to each counselor's compensation over a weighted four-year moving average (see Chapter 14 for details).

For large mutual funds, Capital will have a half dozen or more separate parts with each counselor in full authority over, and fully accountable for, the investment results of his or her portion of the total portfolio. Portfolio counselors each manage portfolios for several different funds. These several portfolios are all part of the individual's measured investment results.

In the early years at Capital, investment information was not broadly shared. But now, sharing all information and reporting frequently on investment results are both integral to the multiple-counselor system. The full and prompt disclosure of all buying and all selling decisions dissipates any tendency for investors to "go it alone" and buy or sell a particular stock in the portfolio they are responsible for before sharing the idea with other portfolio counselors.

Each portfolio counselor is expected, after hearing and considering the information from peers, to act on his or her own strongest convictions with that part of the total fund for which he or she has responsibility. Bill Newton proved how much freedom each counselor has to concentrate: In his part of the New Perspective Fund—worth a total of $3 billion—he once held just nine stocks, laconically observing: "You only own what you *really* want to own."

The multiple-counselor system clarifies and simplifies communication. There is no way that additional words, particularly in a discussion among senior portfolio counselors of relative value, relative interest, and relative conviction, can compete with this simple, declarative statement: "I am authorizing the purchase of 200,000 shares of this stock—at the market—*now*."

Not only are portfolios diversified across many investments, they are also diversified across different styles and concepts of investing and across the several counselors' differing perspectives on the market. Portfolio counselors are not individually responsible for achieving optimal overall portfolio diversification. An Investment Committee oversees the whole portfolio and coordinates the component subportfolios to ensure that all investments remain within the overall objectives of the fund.

The major benefits of the multiple-counselor system are:

- Individual accountability for action, linked directly to financial and nonfinancial compensation.
- Objective measurement of results.
- Professional satisfaction and fulfillment.
- Increased portfolio diversification.

Each portfolio counselor's investment results are measured and reported frequently and regularly to all the other portfolio counselors. The Portfolio Review System reports each portfolio counselor's investment results on a daily, weekly, and monthly basis. The open flow of information and complementary compensation policies encourage portfolio counselors to help each other by sharing ideas and information, but they have no need to compromise or persuade and are expected to act independently and boldly in making their own investment decisions.

Developing consistency and continuity of results through diversity in decision making takes on an added dimension with Capital's globalization. "Major clients," explains Rothenberg, "want and expect consistency of process and results as a key indicator of quality, and that means our large, global clients look to Capital for consistency in investment objective, portfolio management process, and overall approach across all our country units. But the reality we're living with, and are working to manage effectively, is that our various local units in different countries each have their own histories and their own different experiences. So the specifics of their investment management practices do differ. Over time, we intend to work on reducing these differences. But since we celebrate individual responsibility and investment creativity, we'll move with appropriate care."

The multiple-counselor system encourages personal growth, particularly among research analysts, who manage real investments at Capital very early in their careers. An analyst typically begins investing in his or her own industry—one or two stocks at first, then more and more. Some analysts eventually manage very large amounts of money, all in the industries they know best. And there is no clearer or stronger professional and personal affirmation for an investment analyst, than to know portfolio managers are buying in size what the analyst has just recommended.

Visibility of results is also key to facilitating tough people decisions. The open information system Capital uses in investing leads naturally to open personal reviews by peers. "It's quite systematic, so if anyone has a problem, it will show up early on—so it can be addressed," explains Bob Egelston. Still, decisions about investment professionals are never made quickly, because Capital's kind of investing takes time to mature (see Chapter 15). It usually takes at least three years to move someone over and out of the investment management process, but it is always done when warranted—without emotion *and* graciously.

Capital illustrates the multiple-counselor system for mutual fund investors with Table 3.1.

In early 1962, some of the younger people in the Research Division asked at a corporate retreat, "Why not let us manage some of the money?" But after the sharp stock market break that spring, interest in the idea faded for a while. Then in 1965, after succeeding Jon Lovelace as research director, Bob Egelston worked out the details of the Research Division Account. Research analysts act directly on the portfolio, buying and selling specific securities and implementing their own best ideas and information in real-time decisions

TABLE 3.1   BENEFITS OF DECISION STRUCTURES

	Single Portfolio Manager	+	*Investment Committee*	=	*Multiple-Counselor Approach*
Highest conviction ideas	√				√
Diversity of ideas			√		√
Method of diversification			√		√
Portfolio manager accountability	√				√
Portfolio manager satisfaction	√				√
Research analyst accountability					√
Research analyst satisfaction					√
Continuity if portfolio manager leaves			√		√
Consistency of results			√		√
Benefits to client's portfolio	Value added by creative ideas		Diversification and risk control		Best of both worlds

instead of having to convince portfolio counselors to take action. The analysts' portfolio has frequently achieved superior results, and the Research Division now manages significant segments of both mutual funds and institutional accounts as part of the multiple-counselor system.

When Capital began using the multiple-counselor system, total assets under management were only $400 million. Today, assets are over 1,500 *times* larger and over 150 investment decision makers are simultaneously running parts of various funds and portfolios, making decisions to buy and sell specific securities every day. Explains Rothenberg, "It's really a case of diversity promoting continuity."

CHAPTER 4

ORGANIZING
THE CORE

NOTES FOR READERS

Far from being a charismatic personality, Jonathan Bell Lovelace was modest, reserved, and unassuming. These personal traits continue to characterize Capital's organizational culture. Even more important, Lovelace was bright, rational, and self-disciplined. He sought talented people and backed individuals with ideas. His calm demeanor was ideally suited to both long-term investing and nurturing a professional organization through its formative years.

In addition to being nondirective as a *manager*—encouraging others to take responsibility for investment decisions and for entrepreneurial initiatives to build up Capital—Lovelace was often a bold *leader*. He backed large and decisive actions: innovating the mutual fund concept; taking over a troubled Investment Company of America; organizing American Mutual; agreeing to a novel arrangement for Washington Mutual; empowering Ward Bishop to build an independent mutual fund sales organization; launching venture capital; and backing the multiple-counselor system of investment management.

His son, Jon Lovelace, has had a continuing leadership role at Capital for more than 40 years, during which he has taken a series of strategic initiatives, beginning with designing and proposing the multiple-counselor system: orchestrating the transition to Capital Group as a holding company; supporting several important acquisitions; strongly supporting a sustained commitment to international investing; and leading the creation of a comprehensive compensation and ownership strategy that is magnificent in its lack of self-interest.

As vital to Capital's future ascent to professional and business leadership as the early "survival" years clearly were—particularly in embedding in the fledgling firm the values that Jonathan Bell Lovelace epitomized—the late fifties and the sixties were crucial years in building an organization that would be capable of continuing to strengthen and grow after JBL's era.

Over and over again, the thin threads of possibility were made into the strong fabric of an enduring and dynamic professional service organization. In investment management, this is the highest form of entrepreneurial leadership. While the accessibility of individual possibilities may be "fortunate," the creation of a great firm is *never* lucky: It is always the result of determined, imaginative persistence in the iterative realization of an inspired vision.

ANOTHER IMPORTANT MANAGERIAL thread became part of the fabric of Capital during this period: recruiting. After graduating from Stanford and Harvard Business School, Jim Fullerton went to Mexico—"where polo was fast and living was cheap"—to try his hand as a writer. After publishing several short stories, Fullerton gave up the writer's career and went into selling insurance. He soon did a comprehensive personal insurance review and analysis for . . . Coleman Morton. And Morton quickly recognized that Fullerton was just the man to fill the challenge Jonathan Bell Lovelace had given him: "Find us a man who's got a good head for numbers."

Fullerton was good with numbers and very good with words and, most particularly, with people.[1] Tall, slim, and good-looking, Fullerton has an engaging personality and a warm, baritone voice with which he cheerfully demonstrated his soon-to-be-legendary ability to tell original and entertaining stories—including an extended series of exploits by two apocryphal Japanese adventurers that he modestly acknowledges are "simply too good to tell."

Recruited to Capital in 1957,[2] Fullerton soon launched an extensive nationwide search for talent.[3] At the Wharton School of Business, the placement officer gave Fullerton a set of carefully selected candidates' résumés. All had good grades and six solid years of business studies, with both a bachelor's degree and an M.B.A. from Wharton.[4] Fullerton read the résumés with increasing dismay and then pleaded: "I can't use *any* of these fellows! They may sound good

---

[1] Fullerton's wife, Harriet, a striking beauty, dated John F. Kennedy while he was briefly a student at Stanford—until their relationship got so serious that Rose Kennedy decided to visit California to check her out. For both Harriet, who was not Catholic, and for Rose, who was remarkable in her lack of warmth, the interview was decisively not favorable and the young couple soon went separate ways. Still, Harriet kept on a side shelf a framed photo of herself seeing Jack off at the Pasadena railroad station. Even many years later, both figures were quite recognizable, and guests of the Fullertons instantly identified JFK. House painters, after several days' work for the Fullertons, couldn't resist asking about the part of the picture they'd recognized: "Mrs. Fullerton, may I ask you, ma'am, in that picture, is that . . . the . . . uh . . . *Glendale* railroad station?" Harriet Fullerton's laconic reply made the story all the better in future telling: "Yes. You have a very sharp eye."

[2] When Fullerton joined Capital, there were only 32 employees and the Investment Committee consisted of JBL, Coleman Morton, Hardy Hall, and Chuck Schimpff.

[3] The first recruiting at business schools began with Jon Lovelace going to Stanford, where he found only two candidates signed up for interviews. Fortunately, one of these was Ted Hinshaw, who served in a series of very different positions—a "nonpattern pattern" that Capital celebrates. Beginning as JBL's assistant, the prized position he was initially recruited for, he became the transportation industry analyst (in part because he'd once been a truck driver) and, in the early 1960s, was an all-star airline analyst. During the formation of Capital Group, he was director of planning and then managed the transfer agency. In 1976, his love of sailing took him to the Olympics and into retirement from Capital.

[4] Wharton offered both bachelor's and master's degree programs.

to some recruiters, but they're not for me! They'll know exactly how to do every *routine* thing correctly, but that's not at all what we're looking for. We need men who'll be great *investors*. That means they simply must be imaginative, creative, and independent thinkers. Do you have any men who might be the sort we need?"

The placement officer was perplexed. Then he brightened up: "We do have a fellow you might speak to. First in his class, but he's not sure what he wants to do. He'll be over in the library." Fullerton went to the library and met Bob Egelston, a graduate of West Point. They talked for half an hour and learned they had both served—in different eras—in the same field artillery unit.[5] They were getting along well, when Fullerton surprised Egelston by suggesting they stop talking. "All we can learn in an hour of talking is whether we don't or won't get along. I now know I don't *not* like you. If you feel the same about me and think you might be interested in investing, why don't you come to our New York office and meet some of our people?" Egelston agreed, and Fullerton handed him a self-administered psychological test, explaining that Capital had found it helpful in matching odd-shaped pegs and odd-shaped holes—the sort of individuals and the sort of firms found in investing.

Next day, as Egelston interviewed in New York with Hardy Hall and others, Fullerton looked over what Egelston had written on his psychological test. To complete the sentence, "I feel a lack of confidence when . . . ," Egelston had written, "jumping out of planes."

"Have you ever jumped out of an airplane?" Fullerton asked Egelston.

"Yes."

"How often?"

"Fourteen times."

Egelston was hired as an analyst. In 1964, he became research director with a staff of eight—including his earlier mentor, Jules

---

[5] The 76th Field Artillery Battalion. When Fullerton joined on April 7, 1942, the battalion still had horse-drawn French 75s, a model first produced in 1897.

Hoffman.[6] Other promising young professionals were being hired by Capital.

Fund management was what Howard Schow really wanted to do: "It was explained to me that fund management at Capital was done in Los Angeles not New York. Since I'd been in the Navy and knew how to say 'Aye, aye, sir!,' I moved from New York to L.A. in 1962." Increasingly recognized during the 1960s as an unusually imaginative and effective investor, Schow was one of Capital's leading investment managers through the 1960s and 1970s. He made a major impact on Capital's mutual fund product line by successfully advocating establishing a growth stock fund to extend the firm's offerings beyond the middle-of-the-road "growth and income" positioning of Investment Company of America.

In 1967, Capital's fourth fund, AMCAP Fund,[7] was launched at Schow's initiative to represent Capital in the growth sector of the mutual fund market. At the time, stockbrokers were agog over the apparent "performance" of such hot funds as Gerry Tsai's Manhattan Fund, Fred Carr's Enterprise Fund,[8] and Howard Stein's Dreyfus Fund. Americans were reading *The Money Game* by 'Adam Smith,' and everyone was talking about performance investing and go-go funds. But Capital's new growth fund did not, at first, experience much growth at all.

[6] In 1969, Egelston became the president of Capital Group and, for the next 23 years, was either president or chairman of this holding company.

[7] The name was chosen after the Securities and Exchange Commission resisted using the name proposed originally—American Capital Growth Fund.

[8] Under Fred Carr, Enterprise Fund mushroomed in assets as new sales poured in because of apparent "hot" performance, but much of the performance was self-generated because the fund bought more and more of the shares in small companies it already owned. The fund suffered large redemptions when letter stock holdings collapsed in market value, and performance seriously disappointed investors. Shareholder's Management Company is now out of business, but at its peak, it was managing more assets than Capital. Over its career, this apparently top-performing fund's real time-weighted results fell noticeably *below* the market average, and most investors lost money because they invested when the record of superior performance appeared to be proven. As is so often true, appearances were deceiving.

The best part of the strong demand for growth funds was missed due to delays due to internal uncertainties over the exact type of "growth" fund to launch. Also, Capital's mutual fund sales organization (see Chapter 5) was not enthusiastic about selling a growth fund and so did not really try. As the AMCAP fund manager, Schow feared that he had missed the market and would get whipsawed if he tried to reach for current performance, so he held back. Finally, with pressure from the directors, he got the fund fully invested. But by then, it was too late to catch the wave of the mid-1960s market, and sales came very slowly for several years. Later, as good investment results accumulated (particularly after the 1973–1974 bear market), AMCAP's assets increased substantially. And this success helped solidify Schow's leadership position within Capital.

Believing he should devote most of his time to investing, Schow was reluctant to devote extensive time—as others were prepared to do and as Jon Lovelace clearly preferred to do—to careful discussion of each and every aspect of each business question to be sure they explored and understood every alternative. While in investing at Capital, each portfolio counselor could operate in whatever way worked best for him—and such independence worked well for Schow—in managing Capital as an organization, everyone would have to work together. And increasingly, the way they would work together was being determined by Jon Lovelace.

Greatly admired as an investor, Schow was not always an easy person for others to work with and could be very confrontational—first intellectually, then personally, and finally politically. As a leading portfolio counselor with direct responsibility for substantial assets, and with both long tenure and sizable ownership, Schow expected to be a clear leader on both the professional and business sides of Capital. This was particularly true with major organizational decisions.

Another great investor came originally from Canada. Bill Newton graduated from the University of Southern California, and worked briefly at Transamerica, the insurance and financial services conglomerate, prior to entering the U.S. Army in 1951. After basic training, he was sent to Okinawa where, to relieve boredom, he read books in the Post Library. After completing almost all the books in the Post's motley collection, Newton began browsing through its *Wiesenberger Report on Investment Companies.*[9] This compendium was neither light nor entertaining reading, but to Newton it seemed better than the alternatives because it was about his real interest: investing. In *Wiesenberger,* Newton noticed that senior investment executives at IDS, a big mutual fund outfit, were paid the princely annual salary of $300,000. That was far better than anybody working in mortgages at Occidental Life (a subsidiary of Transamerica), where he had been employed. So when he got out of the service and returned to Occidental Life, Newton applied for a position in the investment management unit. (Just in case, he had also scouted out job offers from three other investment organizations.)

The head of investments at Occidental[10] decided he would interview Newton; liked him; and virtually concocted a new position for him on the spot. Newton would cover all companies whose names began with the letters from N to Z—which included U.S. Government securities. (Two other staffers would divide coverage of companies with names beginning A to M.) A strong mentor, Newton's new boss listened in on telephone conversations with broker analysts and then carefully critiqued them with Newton, who was a determined student and a fast learner. They worked well together and Newton expected to stay for a full career of investing at Transamerica. But in 1958, a phone call changed his plans.

A friendly stockbroker[11] called: "I think you ought to meet Jon Lovelace. He's one of the best young investment professionals in

---

[9] *Wiesenberger's* editor was Lucille Thompson, who was working at *Barron's,* where Capital's Al Drasdo wrote an article about the recapitalization of ICA that compared performance records of all the leading mutual funds. Thompson liked Drasdo's idea and used it as the basis for *Wiesenberger Reports.*

[10] George Bjurman.

[11] Henry Buell at McDonnel & Co.

Los Angeles." Less than a day later, Lovelace was on the phone to Newton, saying, "I'm told you're one of the best young investment professionals in this area and that we ought to get together. How about lunch?" They got together for lunch—and hit it off. Not long after, Bill Hurt of Dean Witter invited Newton to become a member of the Every-Other-Thursday group that met twice each month for luncheon. Members of the group also included Bob Kirby[12] and Jon Lovelace.

Lovelace approached Newton about joining Capital, but Newton demurred. He was learning a lot where he was and felt personally loyal to his mentor. Besides, in comparison to Transamerica's billions, Capital was small: It managed less than $300 million. Monthly calls from Lovelace asking Newton what questions he might want answered culminated a year later in one decisive call: "The position we've been talking about here at Capital needs to be filled. We really want you to join us. But if you're not ready to come now, we'll have to hire another person." Newton joined Capital[13] in 1959 to manage money market reserves and serve as JBL's assistant.

As key individuals joined and Capital grew as an organization, the firm's business was expanding. "Assets under management first crossed $1 billion in early 1966,"[14] recalls Morton. "Our offices were in the Statler Building, which could get room service from the adjoining Statler Hotel, so we ordered champagne to celebrate this major milestone. With only 40 people to serve, it didn't require very

---

[12] Additional members included Harold Tanner (later cohead of investment banking at Salomon Brothers and then head of his own firm), Doug Fletcher of Shareholders Management, and Bob Thuerkoff, who developed the Korea Fund at Scudder, Stevens & Clark, where he was chief investment officer. Noting how difficult it must have been for Capital to be second in Los Angeles to Shareholders Management, Bill Hurt says: "I was insensitive to it back then, but it must have been very uncomfortable for Jon to be at those luncheons with Doug Fletcher."

[13] A few years later, his mentor, George Bjurman, would leave Transamerica and start his own firm: George Bjurman Associates.

[14] 1960 was the first year Capital earned over $1 million.

many bottles. Later, when the market fell off and Capital's assets went *below* $1 billion, Chuck Schimpff suggested we should have another party to mark the event with comparable emphasis—as an affirmation of our professional integrity."

Coleman Morton was the heir apparent at Capital, and Jon Lovelace was neither expected nor expecting to succeed his father. While JBL and JL had mutual respect and regard for each other, theirs was more of a professional connection than a personal, father-son bond. Moreover, JBL had personal loyalties toward Morton's father, an early investor in Capital. Most important, Jonathan Bell Lovelace was conscientiously rational in all his decisions—particularly about people and organizations—and would have been quite cautious about the well-known dangers of soft thinking so often glossed over in nepotism.

"Through the 1950s, we had all assumed Coleman would succeed JBL," recalls Jon Lovelace, "but an unfortunate article in a business magazine appears to have been the turning point." With a photograph of Coleman Morton and Jim Fullerton, the article indicated that a young team might soon take the lead at Capital and "liven things up compared to the old fogies." The tone of the article understandably miffed Chuck Schimpff, Hardy Hall, and Jonathan Bell Lovelace as well as several of the mutual fund directors who also read it.

Then, in the late 1950s, two more things happened. First, Chuck Schimpff became opposed to Morton's succession. As JBL's right-hand man for administration—and the firm's dour, Germanic conscience—Schimpff was very protective of JBL and his company. At least as significantly, Morton virtually took himself out of consideration in the following way: Apparently doubting a small investment firm located in remote Los Angeles could ever amount to much, Morton proposed, more than once, selling out. This clearly dismayed JBL. Although Morton may have been objective in his appraisal of Capital's business prospects, it was irrational for him to be so rational. Simultaneously, some mutual fund directors were encouraging the idea of JL's becoming JBL's successor, even though Jon Lovelace was not personally interested in being CEO and did not consider himself particularly well qualified for the role.

Ironically, an unexpected problem with his own health made a significant impact on Jon Lovelace's thinking.[15] At home in Whittier in February 1961, acute pain struck him in the abdomen. Rushed to the local hospital, he was incorrectly diagnosed as having diverticulitis instead of appendicitis. Running a fever of 104 degrees, he very nearly died. For six weeks, Lovelace remained under doctors' care at home. The consulting physicians finally decided: "The only thing to do is cut him open and find out what's the problem here" and found that he had a ruptured appendix of an unusual kind: retrocecal or "tucked in back," where it had been hard to find. After a month of proper treatment, he was feeling fine, but knew he'd had a close call with death.

Later that year, Lovelace took his first business trip to Europe, in 1961 accompanied by Ken Mathysen-Gerst. They visited Denmark, the Netherlands, France, and Germany. (In Berlin, shortly after the wall went up and a week after JFK's visit, corporate officials they met were impressed to see Americans in their city.) Returning home two weeks later, he was put back in the hospital with an abscess from his first bout with appendicitis—and a second close call with death. During his convalescence, several ICA directors visited Lovelace, at least in part to say that his future role and responsibilities were on their minds. After all, JBL was 66 and still had not stated any plans to step down. Some directors felt pressure from Morton, who must have wondered about his own future, to get JBL to make plans for leadership succession. Then, in November 1963, Jon Lovelace was hit with severe pneumonia after another exhausting European trip. Lying in bed while recuperating from his third

---

[15] This was one of several times that serious health problems precipitated significant decisions at Capital.

brush with death, he came to a personal realization: "I'm surely living on borrowed time, so what the hell, let's do it"[16]—and accepted the inevitability of becoming president of Capital.

Shortly after Jon Lovelace's decision, JBL announced the selection of his son as his expected successor and named him executive vice president—but did not say exactly when he would become president. Significantly, particularly for the small firm that Capital then was, the succession decision was made without losing Morton.[17]

At about this time, Jon Lovelace made a seminal contribution to the long-term growth and development of Capital by preempting a potentially divisive internal debate about Capital's primary strategic objective. Two separate camps had been developing within Capital concerning the organization's primary purpose: Some emphasized service to *investors;* others emphasized return to Capital's *owners.* Before he would take on the presidency, Lovelace met with Morton, Hall, Schimpff, and JBL in 1963 to gain agreement on the overall corporate objective. Then in a short memorandum that crystallized the conclusions from the group's discussions (see Appendix I), Lovelace put forward the agreed central proposition: Capital would not be managed to achieve either one or another of those three

[16] Near encounters with death may well have contributed to Jon Lovelace's existentialist approach to management and organizational development. He believes in *carpe diem* (seize the day) but has almost infinite patience with continuous development, as is shown in the following chapters.

[17] After eight more years, Morton would leave Capital in 1971 for the Trust Company of the West and to invest in venture capital. Demonstrating affection and respect for Morton would be a characteristically persistent priority for seniors at Capital. For many years, until age-determined retirement, Morton would continue on the Advisory Board of Investment Company of America.

In 1972, Jon Lovelace initiated a program of sabbaticals—and promptly took one himself. (During his sabbatical, the idea for New Perspective Fund was developed.) At about the same time, Lovelace and his wife moved to Santa Barbara for four months. At Capital, some put these two "facts" together and assumed he might be planning to retire. During this period, Coleman Morton made a desultory attempt to gain control. (Only two Associates have ever taken sabbaticals.)

competing goals. Instead, it would be managed for the balanced achievement—as fully as possible and on a continuous basis—of reasonable objectives for *three* groups:

1. Clients
2. Associates
3. Owners

As the largest share-owner,[18] Jon Lovelace's explicit commitment to treating all three constituencies *equally* was and is recognized by many Capital Associates as very significant and unusual.[19] During the several decades since his original declaration of the three-way, balanced objective, Lovelace has demonstrated the strength of his commitment on several occasions by making major decisions to assure the three-way balance.

Capital's newly clarified troika of objectives was matched in importance by simultaneous changes in the nature of Capital's investment organization. Although individual responsibility for investment decisions and long-term results would always remain a given, a strong complementary commitment was also made to a remarkably open sharing of investment information and ideas. Some of Capital's independent-minded investment professionals did not easily accept the deliberate mixing of individual responsibility for action with collective development and sharing of information. It would, however, become accepted as essential to Lovelace's transformational organizational innovation: the multiple-counselor system of managing investments.

---

[18] In 1967, JBL was still a large share owner and JL owned 39 percent of the B shares, and back then only B shares had a vote. (JL's economic ownership, combining both A and B shares, peaked at 25 percent.) Today, both A and B shares vote (see Chapter 13).

[19] Since Capital Group's owners are its Associates, and the Associates have well over $1 billion of their own money invested in the American Funds—primarily through the organization's retirement plan for Associates—the three interest groups overlap like a three-dimensional Venn diagram.

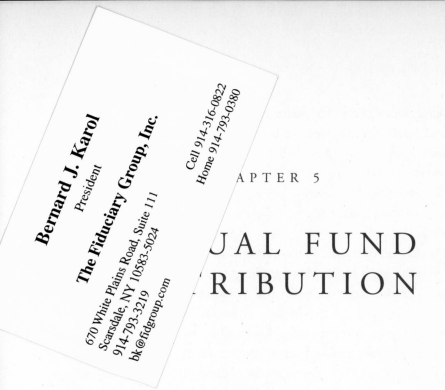

CHAPTER 5

MUTUAL FUND DISTRIBUTION

NOTES FOR READERS

Mutual fund organizations are almost always either sales-centered or investment-centered—and most are *sales*-centered (as are most institutional investment organizations).

Buyer beware or *caveat emptor* is the byword in an industry where headquarters decision makers have no direct contact with the ultimate consumer; where investors' average ownership lasts only a few years; where investors flock to short-term performance and flee short-run difficulties; and where competition is intense and profits are so driven by current sales that such cynical phrases as "If we don't do it, others will," and "Let's take it while we can," and "Everyone else does it" proliferate.

Capital is different—very different. It is neither sales-centered nor investment-centered. While its clear priority is investing, Capital also has great strength in its mutual fund sales organization: American Funds Distributors.

After more than 50 years of development from a tiny start-up and semi-independent mutual fund distributor—followed by a rescue buy-in[1] at the grim nadir of the mutual fund industry nearly 30 years ago—integration of American Funds Distributors has provided Capital with a strong, balanced combination of both investment *and* sales centering that may be unique in the mutual fund industry.

Openly paternalistic in its relationship to investors, in sharp contrast to most other mutual fund managers, Capital believes it should make those decisions it deems are in the long-term best interests of its present and prospective investors. Since Capital believes that the really right fund at a particular time will *never* be popular because investors understandably find it hard to recognize why it is often right to go against the dominant tide of general opinion, Capital frequently avoids sectors that have been doing very well in the market and emphasizes sectors that have been beaten down. Going against the crowd is what experienced investors like Capital's always look for in investments because it can be so rewarding in the long run. But it is understandably difficult for individual investors to think and act independently when "the crowd" seems most convinced—and convincing.

Capital conscientiously does what other organizations might find naïve or unrealistic: It concentrates on long-term value judgments and is persistently skeptical about short-term prices and popularity. One example: deciding not to join the parade of fund organizations introducing money market funds in the early 1970s out of concern that investors might be tempted by the convenience of switching to get out of their equity funds and into "cash" at those low stock market levels—an

---

[1] The capacity to acquire the money-losing distribution business and rebuild it was a signal example of Capital Group's corporate strategy of assuring its fiscal independence for strategic decisions by reserving substantial sums during good times and investing those funds boldly during bad times (see Chapter 11).

action that would have done grievous harm to investors' long-term results. Similarly, although the clear leader in emerging markets investing, Capital would not introduce a retail mutual fund specializing in emerging markets at the height of broker and investor interest. Its leaders believed—as was later shown to be the case—that individuals would not fully understand the price volatility inherent in emerging markets investments and would be all-too-tempted to sell low—*after* a market decline—what they had bought high at the peak of public interest or excitement.

Most mutual fund organizations concentrate on selling to individual investors, touting recent performance; developing public recognition for their star investors; and spending heavily on advertising. They openly describe themselves as "asset gatherers" and focus on "selling what sells." Capital goes the other way. Being very deliberate about introducing new investment funds is only part of Capital's deeply felt, constructive conservatism. It is equally conservative about innovation in methods of distribution, such as 12(b)-1 trailer commissions and 401(k) Defined Contribution employee benefit plans.

Conservative and often reserved in making strategic decisions—but consistent, sustained, and steadily assertive in execution—Capital enjoys the several advantages of having developed unusually strong mutual fund distribution. Broker-dealers and investors *know* Capital puts sound investing well ahead of sales or marketing in every business decision.

While most mutual fund organizations concentrate on advertising and selling to individual consumers, American Funds Distributors concentrates on the broker-dealers who sell mutual funds, striving to influence their thoughts and actions toward what will work best for individual investors over the long term. Capital believes that if broker-dealers are well served and correctly motivated, they can and will provide the steady guidance that individual investors need in difficult markets to stay focused on the long term and so be truly successful in investing.

The wholesalers who represent American Funds Distributors are working with brokers who are, of course, "economic animals." So the wholesalers' challenge is to find the right brokers and show them how they can make good money over the long run by "taking the high road" and helping investors to invest well. Particular attention is devoted to assuring dealers get first-rate service and providing an array of investment alternatives that are unusually reliable in fulfilling expectations.

It takes long years of patient, persistent work with both dealers and investors to gain their confidence, but Capital has already devoted those many years to developing that vital component of a great business and professional franchise: *trust.*

Most mutual fund organizations concentrate on building public recognition and consumer brand awareness through advertising. Ironically, even though it now serves over 20 million individual shareholder accounts, Capital Group Companies has never developed a strong consumer brand or franchise. Quite the opposite: Capital avoids publicity and does not advertise. Its family of mutual funds is even known by an entirely different name: The American Funds.

Like a modern illustration of Aesop's fable, *The Tortoise and the Hare,* Capital expects to lose market share in mutual fund sales during bull markets, but more than make up for this with both higher retention and higher market share of new business during bear markets.[2]

Among those particular broker-dealers that Capital is most interested in working with, AFD is well recognized as one of the very best—usually *the* best—at every aspect of investor service and mutual fund distribution. After many long years of building and nurturing its distribution system and its investor service capabilities, the American Funds are clearly gaining market share—from a high base.

---

[2] In 2002 and 2003, two fund groups—American Funds and Vanguard—jointly gained more than 100 percent of the mutual fund industry's total net sales because they gained assets while other funds collectively lost assets through redemptions.

A MERICAN FUNDS DISTRIBUTORS began[3] in earnest with Ward Bishop—the youngest person to earn a Ph.D. at the University of Illinois.[4] Bishop started at Capital as an analyst. Although research clearly fit with his academic background, he was much more interested in sales and put it to JBL in his characteristic blunt way: "You can't be a 'money manager' if you have no money to manage!"

Bishop first got acquainted with the mutual fund concept in the 1920s, while working as a securities analyst in Detroit under Jonathan Bell Lovelace at E.E. MacCrone & Co. Then, as an economist and teacher at Lehigh University in the 1930s, Bishop became more and more fascinated with the whole idea of mutual funds. He spoke and wrote about mutual funds with increasing enthusiasm. As World War II began, two former students persuaded Bishop to join with them in buying a screw-machine company they hoped would earn large profits in the war-induced buildup of demand. Bishop hated every minute of it. He was looking for an alternative when Lehigh's academic dean mentioned his name to Lovelace, who remembered Bishop as a hard worker and was soon recruiting him to join Capital. Leaving Garden City, Long Island, for distant Los Angeles and Lovelace's unknown little outfit, Bishop didn't even know what his pay would be, saying with typical candor: "I didn't give a damn."

In 1947, less than 10 years after ICA had been converted from closed-end to open-end status,[5] Bishop was working in accounting,

[3] Before Bishop took over AFD, ICA shares were distributed by Investment Company Distributors (which was originally formed by Hayward Thomas). He worked with two local dealers until 1943. Then an assistant, named Yarnsey ran the company from 1943 to 1945. Then Roy Georgeson & Company, the proxy solicitors, took over distribution for six months. Georgeson's interest was bought out for $20,000 when AFD was formed.

[4] His career in academe was aborted because he would not take the time to write a book.

[5] Closed-end mutual funds (or investment companies as they are formally known) have a fixed number of shares outstanding and are often listed for trading on the New York Stock

but complaining about Capital's anemic sales, saying "Jon, you're not getting anywhere and I can help!" Lovelace invited him to see what he could do to develop mutual fund sales and distribution for Investment Company of America, suggesting Bishop own the wholesaling organization. (A wholesaling organization will typically have 25 to 75 missionary salespeople who visit stockbrokers, seeking to convince them by services and persuasion to give preference to the particular "family" or group of mutual funds they represent.) Bishop jumped at the opportunity: "That's for me! I'll quit being an analyst; I'll pay my own expenses; and my daughter will keep the books!"

Dramatically different in personality and manner, Bishop and Lovelace somehow worked well together. Bishop was bold and outspoken, while Lovelace was modest and soft-spoken. Lovelace was calm and consistent, while Bishop could "shatter you with words and then melt your heart with his winning smile and another flow of warm words," says Graham Holloway. Bishop also played an unusual and decisive role in the long-term growth and development of Capital by making a special appeal to JBL: "All I have to sell is the Lovelace name—so please bring your son Jon over here!" His timing was good: The younger Lovelace happened to be considering a job change (see Chapter 2).

Stocky and only 5 feet 8 inches tall, Bishop was a compelling salesman with a commanding presence and a hardworking, forceful personality. But he had little else when he began as the single wholesaler promoting Capital to stockbrokers and representing only one mutual fund—Investment Company of America.

Bishop also had to overcome an interesting marketing handicap: Over JBL's objections (as explained in Chapter 1), Eddie MacCrone's firm had granted perpetual warrants to Investment Company of America's initial shareholders. Those warrants were a major sales

---

Exchange, where they typically sell at a discount of 10 to 15 percent to net asset value. Open-end mutual funds for investment companies offer to sell new shares or redeem outstanding shares at the net asset value of the fund's portfolio of investments.

problem for Bishop because competitors would darkly ask stock-brokers: "Do you *really* want to sell *your* customers a mutual fund with all that overhanging risk of dilution of the net asset value per share when those warrants are exercised?" (To get rid of this nuisance, JBL would personally buy—and retire—any warrants offered on the market.) Over the years, as the size of Investment Company of America expanded, it simply outgrew the steadily diminishing problem of potential dilution.

Bishop expansively named his tiny new firm American Funds Distributors[6]—in part out of patriotism and in part out of sheer bravado—and set off to build a sales organization, saying, "I'll sell enough mutual fund business so Capital's investment management fees will be large enough to pay me what I know I'm really worth!"[7] Bishop's stated ambition was to bring Investment Company of America's total assets up to $50 million. (Today, ICA's assets are now 1,000 times larger—nearly $50 billion—and Capital's total assets are well over $600 billion.)

Traveling three and four weeks at a time, Bishop recruited and trained an outstanding group of mutual fund wholesalers to do the all-important missionary selling work of persuading stockbrokers to sell more shares of the American Funds Group of mutual funds. (The 80-plus wholesalers who now represent the American Funds are typically on the road from early Monday to late Friday—week after week. They are proud of what they are doing, are recognized as the best in the business, and are one of Capital's outstanding business strengths.)

Graham Holloway, the "Billy Graham" of mutual fund sales and, for many years, the leading wholesaler for the American Funds,

---

[6] Organized in 1939 as Investment Company Distributors, Inc., its name was changed in 1944 to Investment Company of America Distributors, Inc. In 1947, Ward Bishop became president and sole owner. The name American Funds Distributors was adopted in 1951.

[7] A compelling speaker, Bishop once signed on as a speechwriter for Wendell Willkie's 1940 presidential campaign. Going aboard Willkie's campaign train at a whistle-stop, he was aghast to see Willkie having breakfast with Franklin D. Roosevelt's son, Jimmy. Decisive as always, Bishop quit on the spot.

explains the serendipitous way his career developed: "A friend who was a wholesaler for American Funds[8] recommended me to Ward Bishop and urged me to become an American wholesaler, too. I was already in mutual funds, but I was very reluctant to change from the small firm two of us were then running in Atlanta: North American Investors. (We'd inherited that small firm with its big name when the unpaid sales commissions owed to us got larger than the value of the whole firm—so the prior owners just gave us the keys as a settlement.) While I was saying 'No' to the idea of leaving Atlanta and joining American Funds, my friend urged me, 'Don't jump to any conclusions before you talk to Ward Bishop. At least *talk* to Ward.'"

Growing up as a poor boy in the South, Holloway became a dynamic and imaginative speaker with a fine sense of theater. (His father had run movie theaters, and Holloway says he learned dramatics while watching movies in the 1940s.) Holloway was particularly effective in the day-in, day-out hard work wholesalers do with stockbrokers. His selling skills combined effectively with his obviously sincere commitment to help individual stockbrokers achieve better sales results.

Bishop invited Holloway up to Washington, D.C., where he did a lot of business and visited often. They had lunch and Bishop, who could drink gin like a horse drinks water, ordered up a second round of martinis. "Serious drinking was not my custom," recalls Holloway, "so I could soon feel the effects. But we kept on talking right through the afternoon because we both appreciated, even loved, mutual funds. Every so often, I'd say, 'Ward, I'm happy where I *am*. I really don't want to move and travel a lot.' And Ward would say, 'Now, you're gonna take this job!'—and continue right on."

Late that afternoon, as he had said he would, Holloway turned Bishop down.

A week later, Bishop had Holloway on the telephone and was charging straight ahead: "Get off the dime! I'm *tired* of talking to you. You are *going* to take this job!" Holloway turned him down

[8] Claude Thomas.

again, but Bishop was persistent, and pretty soon, Holloway was the American Funds wholesaler for the territory that stretched from the Mississippi River to the Rockies.

While Capital focused on serving the long-term interests of investors, Bishop defined his target market at AFD as the broker-dealers who would sell Capital's funds to investors. So while Dreyfus[9] was creating a public image through consumer advertisements featuring their growling Dreyfus lion coming up out of the New York City subway, Bishop accepted public anonymity for American Funds. He focused directly on showing brokers how to be more effective and successful in selling, particularly repeat selling. Meeting the broker's everyday needs was and is AFD's most important priority.

Bishop's objective was to sell the overall idea of mutual funds, particularly their benefits to investors and to stockbrokers. He was widely recognized as a great salesman of mutual funds in general and of Capital's American Funds in particular. Over and over again, when visiting a brokerage firm, he would tell the American Funds story to a small group of stockbrokers and then he would say, "Give me the names and phone numbers of a few people you'd really like to prospect," and cheerfully dial away on the telephone to give a live demonstration of how to use the American Funds story in real-life selling.

A compelling personality and speaker, Bishop never had any interest in addressing large groups of stockbrokers and no patience with the "desk-hopping" approach taken by most mutual fund wholesalers—selling to individual stockbrokers, one at a time in short visits. "Busy stockbrokers stop what they're usually doing for only one reason: because they are *enthralled.* The challenge is to develop a meeting that all the stockbrokers want to go to and that the office manager *wants* his people to go to. Time is money for

---

[9] Jack Dreyfus, founder of the Dreyfus Fund, had been one of Ward Bishop's students at Lehigh University.

everybody, so the key is to help brokers succeed at their work by being very well organized, interesting, and *useful*."

Bishop was an entrepreneur and wanted each of his wholesalers to do very well as entrepreneurs within their marketing territories: "The more they make, the better!"[10] Still, Bishop never got over the cost-consciousness he had learned during the Depression. (In the early years, it helped when Bishop got elected to the board of directors of the Chicago and North Shore Railroad: The railroad paid his way to Chicago for directors' meetings—after which he would sell mutual funds in that region of the country.) Bishop's wholesalers paid all their own expenses: If the wholesaler thought it productive to host 150 stockbrokers for a dinner, fine. But he paid for that dinner himself. Bishop had a clear-cut policy: "No overhead—and no other business!"[11]

Bishop also knew the importance of his wholesalers enjoying each other personally—so they would want to help each other and feed each other ideas and encouragement in the good times—and emotional support in the tough times. "Capital is very family oriented, seeking always to have *families* feel happy," observes Holloway. "They encouraged us wholesalers and our wives to get together as couples and to support each other, sharing ways to handle the problems of our being on the road so much. That original group of wholesalers grew very close to one another—and we still are!"[12]

---

[10] Following JBL's lead, Bishop shared ownership in American Funds Distributors with his best wholesalers. Graham Holloway still remembers with pleasure receiving a $1,000 bonus Bishop paid out at Christmas in Holloway's first year with AFD.

[11] Bishop believed in giving the maximum possible allowance to the stockbrokers who would sell the American Funds. So out of an 8¾ percent "load" or sales charge, he kept just ¾ of 1 percent for American Funds Distributors and paid out the other 8 percent to the stockbrokers. And most of AFD's ¾ percent went to the wholesalers who paid all their own expenses.

[12] Claude Thomas, who introduced Holloway to American Funds, left many years ago to join Massachusetts Financial Services (at least in part out of disappointment in seeing Holloway promoted to National Sales Manager ahead of him). Thomas continues to be Holloway's great "fishing buddy," and the two men visit and stay in each other's homes regularly.

Bishop always looked for ways to gain the vital competitive advantage of having enough time to sell the American Funds in depth and detail. A man who loved to drink and talk, Bishop believed in taking small groups of interested stockbrokers out for drinks—and then on to dinner and then back to his hotel for more drinks—so he would really get to know them as individuals while continually selling the concept of mutual funds and the American Funds.

Bishop looked for connections that mattered personally to stockbrokers and bonded his wholesalers with individual stockbrokers. He particularly wanted to find those special interests that gave his wholesalers the opportunity every salesperson prizes: extended time in a favorable setting where he can engage the customer's attention and develop real interest in his particular product or service. Bernie Nees lived in Washington, D.C., and liked to fish. So Bishop would say to the stockbroker, "If you like to fish and you ever get to Washington, the man to see to find the best fishing in the whole Mid-Atlantic region is your friend Bernie Nees." Or, on a different tack, "If you ever get to Washington, Bernie Nees would just love to take you and your kids to see places in our nation's Capitol that you just won't find on any of those standardized bus tours. So, if you want to get off the beaten track and see something really special, just get in touch with Bernie Nees, and he'll take good care of you."

With Bishop's support, Graham Holloway organized a series of two-day "total immersion" programs, where stockbrokers would learn all the advantages of mutual funds and how to sell the mutual fund concept better—*and* learn why their best choice would be the American Funds managed by Capital. Holloway believed that any stockbrokers who had spent two full days in Los Angeles meeting with Capital's investment professionals, in a format the investment professionals found effective and convenient—followed by meetings with the managers and staff of American Funds Distributors—would naturally want to sell to his individual clients the funds managed by Capital. Even brokers not yet committed to selling Capital's funds were welcome to come to Los Angeles and learn about selling mutual funds *and* about Capital's investment capabilities, its shareholder services, and its services to brokers. He believed these brokers would inevitably become convinced they should be selling the American Funds.

Bishop was much more interested in building his business with small stockbrokerage firms than with the major retail wire houses. He understood that a small mutual fund firm—as Capital certainly was in the 1940s—could not hope to be considered important by a major wire house that would always be served intensively by all the biggest fund groups. Bishop wanted to develop relationships where American Funds would clearly be important to particular brokerage firms and to each stockbroker at those chosen firms. For example, building business with a stockbrokerage firm like Edward D. Jones & Co.[13] was attractive to Bishop because it would be recognized as very challenging by *all* wholesalers. "Tough for our competitors makes it better for us!"

Edward Jones's strategy is to have a large number of very small offices in small communities all across the country, with many offices having only one broker. And this is where the difficulty centers: As a matter of policy, Edward Jones insists that any mutual fund group that wants to do business with the firm must do business with each and every branch office. "Cover 'em *all!*" Bishop realized that this daunting requirement, difficult as it clearly was for every other mutual fund organization, meant American Funds could create a strongly advantaged position by playing by the Edward Jones house rules. As long as other mutual fund organizations shied away from making the necessary commitment, American Funds Distributors could be each Jones office's most important mutual fund distributor. Bishop and AFD made the requisite commitment while other mutual fund groups did not. As he demonstrated the sincerity and persistence of his commitment over the years, Bishop's strategy worked better and better. And it worked well *both* ways: Capital's American Funds are Edward Jones's most

---

[13] Now Edward Jones & Co.

important mutual funds, and Edward Jones is consistently among American Funds' largest selling dealer firms.[14]

In the early days, Edward D. Jones, the founder of the firm, was only interested in trading individual stocks. He really didn't much care about mutual funds, so his firm only offered the Fidelity funds. But his son, Teddy Jones, believed he could build an important business in mutual funds with "investor savers," a separate market from "traders." So he concentrated on mutual funds.

"In the late 1960s, I called on Teddy Jones," recalls Holloway. "He knew and liked farmers, and he loved small towns, where folks will take time to visit—and will listen. So Teddy waved me off, 'Don't want you selling any big city ideas to our small town brokers!' To this, my simple reply was, 'How about if I could help them sell small town ideas that are right for them and right for their customers?' Now, *that* caught his interest."

Teddy Jones told Holloway he should come for lunch. When he arrived at Jones's office, fully expecting to take him to the best restaurant in town, Jones announced, "I've already paid for lunch," and pointed to the bag in his hand. Walking over to a bench looking out over the Mississippi River, they sat together and enjoyed hot dogs and Cokes. "Teddy said, 'Tell me the Capital Story'—which I did. Then he probed, 'Can you tell this story without pushing our brokers to trade?'"

That was easy for Holloway, because American Funds was looking for brokers who would stay with them and would encourage their customers to stay with the American Funds for the long term. "All I wanted to do, as I told Teddy, was just to show brokers how to sell mutual funds effectively."

"Will you travel?" asked Jones.

"Yes!" said Holloway with obvious conviction.

"Okay, you try Kansas—and we'll see."

[14] In some years, Merrill Lynch sells even more shares of the American Funds.

"And that was the start of it. I must have eaten more than one hundred hot dogs with Teddy Jones!"

Holloway remembers stopping his car in the middle of the Kansas prairie and making his wife and friends get out and look. As they were all standing beside the car thinking there truly was nothing to see except the unending flat land stretching forever in all directions, Holloway proudly announced, with a sweep of his arms, "Stop! Look! Listen! This is *my* territory!" They all laughed—and piled back in the car. For Holloway, that territory, which looked so barren, would actually prove very fruitful because nobody else would go there!

An important advantage of doing business with Edward Jones is their customers' very low rate of redemptions. In an industry that averages over 20 percent annual redemptions, Edward Jones' customers are never above 6 percent. Since mortality runs over 4 percent—because the prime age group for buying mutual funds is people in their late 50s and 60s—Edward Jones' low redemptions are indeed remarkably low. And many Edward Jones investors never redeem: They simply pass their mutual fund shares directly to their children. With such strong shareholder persistence, Edward Jones has been something of a bonanza for American Funds.

On the other end of the spectrum from Edward Jones is Merrill Lynch.[15] In 1966, Merrill Lynch, having previously focused on selling only individual stocks, decided to sell mutual funds actively. The head of mutual fund sales at Merrill Lynch was on the phone to American Funds Distributors every month, asking the same question: "Are we your Number One seller yet?" Patiently explaining that other firms had lots of experience and sales momentum, the answer for several months was: "No. Not yet!" But after just seven

---

[15] Over the long term, an important change has forced its way through the mutual fund market. Most of the big "wire house" stockbrokerage firms are gone. All the firms that were major mutual fund distributors in the 1960s—Bache, Harris Upham, Hayden Stone, W.E. Hutton, E.F. Hutton, Blythe, and so on—are gone. They could not adapt to the institutionalization of the stock market.

months, the answer was "Yes! This month, Merrill Lynch is Number One." Since then, Merrill Lynch has been a consistently important dealer for American Funds.

Ward Bishop met Bill Bagnard, his successor as head of AFD, while Bagnard was still in college: "I was at USC and courting my future wife, who was at UCLA. As a student, my special project was financing a new fraternity house for Lambda Nu Alpha, of which I was President. We developed the idea of selling construction bonds to the alumni and had several different kinds of bonds to offer. When I called on my girlfriend one evening, it was one of those rare occasions when her father, Ward Bishop, was at home. This was an opportunity! Pretty soon, I was trying to sell Ward some of our fraternity bonds." Instead, Bishop sold Bagnard on a new career: selling mutual funds—at least part-time.[16]

Later, when Bagnard was heading Harris, Upham's Los Angeles office, Bishop recruited him to join AFD. In making his case, Bishop got help from JBL, who took Bagnard to lunch. With a series of probing questions, he soon had Bagnard selling himself on making a switch from the pressure cooker work of managing a retail stockbrokerage office over to the calmer world of Capital and the American Funds. Says Bagnard with a smile, "I thought I'd live a lot longer. Ward Bishop was a truly great salesman, but he was no businessman. So we made a good pair." Bagnard helped develop the home office operation and congenial relationships with senior people at the major stockbrokerage firms that sold American Funds.

Bishop wanted each of his wholesalers to have the freedom to develop his own personal style. "I drove a white Cadillac," reminisces Graham Holloway. "It helped me get the attention of the

[16] But not right away: First Bagnard had to join the Army, land on Omaha Beach in the Normandy invasion, and serve under General George S. Patton. "After the war, I worked for Republic Supply, selling oil field tools, and began selling mutual funds part-time at night. I made more money selling mutual funds for an hour each evening than I made in a full day's work selling tools, so after ten years with Republic, I went to Harris Upham and got into the securities business."

stockbrokers. They noticed. At the end of a week of selling, I'd park my Caddy[17] in a garage and fly home to Dallas for the weekend—and then fly back to my territory and drive from town to town. With so much territory to cover, I had to have a schedule all worked out—and stick to that schedule—to make the most productive use of my time."

Brokers can be demanding, making it clear that they expect extra services and extra favors. But Holloway was always so well organized, with his every hour committed to a carefully structured day's schedule, that when a broker would ask him to change that preset schedule, Holloway could show the broker how tightly organized he was and graciously explain that it was impossible to change his plan. The brokers' respect for Holloway and his self-discipline grew and grew over the years as he always stayed "on plan."

Stockbrokers *wanted* to go to Holloway's meetings. He would establish rapport at the start by first telling some of his warm, engaging jokes. Then, with his audience in a receptive mood, he would launch into the American Funds Story.[18] In the early 1970s, when mutual fund sales were very low and stockbrokers were badly discouraged about mutual funds, Holloway's favorite speech had a surprising title for a mutual fund missionary: "Why Mutual Funds Are No Damned Good!" Catchy enough to stimulate attention, the speech was, of course, a strongly developed *positive* case for mutual funds. It was an appeal to stockbrokers to take the bull by the horns and sell mutual funds—*now* and with extra vigor—even though the times looked dangerous, they would surely prove to be a major opportunity.

"Everybody needs a story," says Holloway, "a story that makes sense to them; one they can relate to and remember. Stories are the best way—maybe the only way—people will remember. So I always told stories. Everybody likes to laugh. They listen better and they remember more when they're enjoying themselves. Brokers

---

[17] Holloway covered so much territory that many people assumed he must have several white Cadillacs—each parked in a garage in a different city.

[18] Holloway was always sharing interesting and useful sales stories with the other AFD wholesalers, so it was natural to make him National Sales Manager.

want to learn useful things that will help them sell funds even better, so I made certain they would all learn new ways to sell funds that they could use." Brokers went to Holloway's meetings, some driving 40 or even 60 miles, because his meetings were so useful. They also knew that after the meeting, which always ran from 6:00 to 7:30, Holloway would have a case of whiskey in the trunk of his white Cadillac. Then, after a drink together, the brokers would drive the 40 or 60 miles back to their homes, while Holloway drove to his next town.

Some stockbrokers don't want to give up their hopes of success as stock pickers managing other people's money. So, Holloway explains, "I'd just pass them by. Nothing personal; we were just in different movies. I wanted to find those brokers who would really sell mutual funds and then convince them to concentrate on the American Funds. I'd tell them the Capital Story. And then I'd work closely with them, year after year."

Capital wants long-term investors for its American Funds. So Capital and AFD want stockbrokers who will discourage redemptions, particularly in those difficult market environments when individual investors are under the most emotional pressure to sell—which is usually the *worst* time to sell. So AFD wholesalers seek out and build long-term relationships with conservative stockbrokers who will find and work with conservative, long-term *investors,* not short-term *traders.* That's why redemptions for the American funds are less than half the industry average.

Even with its low rate of annual redemptions, Capital now needs $40 billion in sales each year just to replace redemptions. Less than one third of this huge sum will come from the reinvestment of dividends by current and continuing investors: The other two thirds—over $25 billion every year—must come from new sales or new investors, creating a large and recurring need for substantial new business.

Using history, Capital gives a compelling illustration of just how large a role can be played by an unusually patient, stabilizing stockbroker who convinces mutual fund investors to stay invested during difficult market periods. In the 1968 to 1974 market slump, the unweighted index of New York Stock Exchange shares dropped 78 percent *before* the further hurt of adjusting those nominal results for the negative impact of serious inflation. During the same period, the average stock on the American Stock Exchange fell 83 percent. And, many investors got hurt even worse than those market averages indicate. Many of the investors who got burned by "hot" fund products back in the early 1970s left the stock market and mutual fund investing forever. They never came back. So they missed the great bull market of the next 25 years.

Capital understands the secret to having a stable group of shareholders is to offer investors only those funds that will work well for them through many different market environments over many years. The right way to build its business is to develop products and their channels of distribution so the appropriate customer can and will find the appropriate product to buy and own with the satisfaction[19] that leads to consumer loyalty and to repeat purchases. Specifically, Capital's intention is to have mutual funds bought and held indefinitely, with additional purchases made through the reinvestment of dividends and future savings.

American Funds' wholesalers focus on long-term results for the investor and always try to work with those stockbrokers who sell what people need, not what people currently think they want. The right fund to buy at any particular time in the market is usually currently unpopular and appears unattractive to most people. And it will appear most unattractive exactly when it is the best value and

---

[19] Under Fullerton, Pete Langer, with suggestions from both Graham Holloway and Bill Bagnard, organized the *Investment Company of America Investors' Guide* to put several disparate pieces of sales literature into a single brochure. Langer also undertook the main responsibility for writing the annual reports for Capital's several mutual funds. He found it frustrating to have the printing of his mutual fund annual reports held up as Jon Lovelace typically "worried" over the wording. However, Langer came to understand that JL was working his way through each page to assure himself that it would also read well to a reader returning to it 10 years later.

set to deliver the best results over the long term. So, to be helpful to investors, Capital believes the broker who is in direct contact with the individual investor at the time of decision must be well compensated for doing the right thing: convincing investors *not* to do the currently popular thing. This is difficult work.

So the individual investor will do the right thing in turbulent markets when feelings and anxieties are particularly strong, the broker-dealer needs to have and hold the investor's trust and confidence when discussing investments that go against the tide and against the crowd. The most helpful broker-dealer understands and always takes the long-term view. But that means he will often say things that are contrary to the way most people usually think. He will convincingly say such things as "Stocks are *down,* so it's time to buy more" or "Stocks are *up,* so let's be cautious." While such advice is sound and based on a long-term perspective, it is not easy work to get investors to understand and use such advice—and go against the crowd that is heading for trouble by doing what looks like the obvious way to go.

Investors and broker-dealers have learned they can rely on Capital to protect their long-term interests by only offering new funds when investment prospects *appear* all wrong, but are really attractive for long-term investment. This is unusual. Most mutual fund organizations are sales driven and so will launch new mutual funds when comparable funds are "performing" well and are getting good sales.[20]

Capital has carefully avoided "hot" investment ideas,[21] much to the benefit of the long-term investors it seeks to serve *and* the frustration of brokers looking for something "hot" to sell. That's why Capital

[20] During a recent five-year period, Capital introduced only *one* new fund, while T. Rowe Price introduced 14 new funds, American Century introduced 45, and Fidelity unveiled an incredible 138 new funds.

[21] "Some of the more bizarre ideas of the past few years: The mutual fund industry has given investors the Stock Car Stocks fund and the Pauze Tombstone fund, which invests in mortuaries and cemeteries." "Capital Appreciation," Christopher Oster, *SmartMoney,* March 1999.

has been slow and careful about introducing new mutual funds, recognizing that good timing on introducing new mutual funds almost always looks like quite poor timing at the actual time of introduction, acknowledging, "We launch new funds into a sea of doubt." As a result, Capital expects to lose market share—and does lose some—when investors and stockbrokers have a market outlook that is euphoric or speculative, and Capital expects to gain market share—and does gain a lot—when the outlook is uncomfortable or even negative.

The American High-Income Municipal Bond Fund was introduced in 1994—at the very *bottom* of the municipal bond market. Riding the recovery in fixed income, this fund later ranked in the top 3 percent of its fund category. The New World Fund was introduced in 1999—*after* five years of generally disappointing emerging market returns and *after* the Southeast Asia capital crisis[22] had substantially reduced investors' expectations for the emerging markets and most competitors' emerging market mutual funds were experiencing net redemptions due to investors' disappointment.

At Capital, any idea for a new fund has to start—and can stop abruptly—with the judgment of the investment professionals. If they don't say, "Over the *long term,* investing in this fund *now* will prove to be a good idea for shareholders," it simply can't and won't happen.

Recalling one of his early contributions to Capital's successful concentration on long-term marketing as differentiated from selling, Jim Fullerton says: "Since I liked to play with numbers, it was more than interesting to me that Investment Company of America had beaten both the Dow Jones and S&P averages over the prior 10 years. Soon enough, I'd played around with the results enough to make a startling and marvelous discovery: Investment Company of America had beaten those market averages in *every* 10-year period." Fullerton became the first person to show investment results with rolling 10-year periods that enable investors to see for themselves

---

[22] Also contributing to investors' caution were the severe crises in Russia and the collapse of Long-Term Capital Management in 1998.

the importance of cumulative long-term results. "One year is much too short a measurement period to provide meaningful information. Even ten years may be too short, but it certainly is a move in the right direction and long enough for most people. Pretty soon, we had enough calculations to show that *all* our funds at that time had outpaced the market indices for *all* 10-year periods."

True enough for the 33 years covered by the study when it was completed in the late 1980s and for the next few years, but as the bull market roared into the 1990s, Capital's "safety first" defensive orientation kept the funds it manages too conservative to keep up with the S&P averages. With the turn of the century stock market "correction," all of Capital's funds are again well ahead.[23]

Capital cares that its two largest stock funds, Investment Company of America and Washington Mutual Investors, are the only two equity mutual funds to have outperformed the S&P 500 in over 90 percent of the many different 10-year periods over the last 40 years. Knowing there are always going to be fund groups with temporarily better 1-, 2-, and even 5-year numbers, Capital emphasizes the consistency of those 10-year records over the very long term.[24]

"Our job is to create wealth for shareholders," says Holloway, "with the least risk and the most opportunity. Most mutual fund investors are over 50 years old, so 10 years matters a lot to them. They just don't have 30 or 40 more years to accumulate savings for their retirement.

"There's *always* a reason to save. And if you somehow save too much, the worst that can happen is that you'll have more to give to your kids or charity. So start with your goal. What do you want to do in life? What do you want to accomplish? In particular, how do you

---

[23] In the bull market of the 1950s, Capital's funds also lagged the market.
[24] Later on, consistently superior long-term investment records would be particularly significant for investment organizations such as Capital Guardian Trust that wanted to develop institutional business managing pensions and endowments. Ten-year rolling records were the keys that opened many doors.

visualize the kind of life you'll want to lead when you retire? And how will you get there?"

With its knowledge of investing and investments, Capital feels a deep responsibility to investors to tell them a lot about what it *cannot* do and *won't* do. It has often presented itself consciously as "the firm that can't do," explaining that to have the very best performing mutual fund, the manager must be very smart, do lots of things right, take big investment risks in the portfolio, and have . . . *lots* of luck!

If an investor could pick a series of stocks that would each go up 50 percent—from $10 to $15—in every six months and started with $10,000 at age 30, he would have over $1 million at age 36. He would have nearly $1 billion at age 44; the value equivalent of the whole American Stock Exchange at age 48; the equal of the New York Stock Exchange by age 56—and all the wealth in the whole world by age 60. The obvious implication: It can't happen and it won't happen—all the way back to that first six-month move from $10 to $15 in a single stock.

Of course, if an investor does get lucky, he'll think he's a lot better than he really is and will be tempted to try again—even harder. This can put him in real danger. Understanding the limits—and all the risks and negatives—*before* looking for opportunities and possibilities is characteristic of decision making at Capital and is exemplified by Mike Shanahan,[25] who has been a leading investor and a leading executive in Capital nearly four decades. "I've never known anyone who could so quickly and consistently understand

---

[25] After graduating from Stanford, where he played "scratch" on the golf team, and then from the Stanford Business School, Shanahan joined Capital, where he quickly acknowledged to friends that he intended to become CEO. He had already demonstrated two life-long characteristics: brilliance and an acute case of stubborn persistence—the former through his stellar academic record; the latter in the various ways he saved money. Shanahan put himself through college with a Naval ROTC scholarship and money he'd earned during summer vacations until his free-spending ways left him flat broke. Determined to make his own way, he cut costs sharply by sleeping for several months in the backseat of his car. A stubborn chain-smoker, he has almost given up flying rather than abstain from smoking, even for a few hours. An intense and competitive personality, he has thrown golf clubs in frustration, practices almost every day, and continues to play to a 3 handicap in his 60s.

the essential realities of virtually any business situation and see the common sense answer to a problem so clearly," says Holloway. "If something was ever to go wrong, Mike could figure it out. And he could straighten it out, too!"

While American Funds Distributors distributes only mutual funds managed by Capital, it does not handle every aspect of all the funds managed by Capital.[26] In a unique and long-standing arrangement, one of the nation's largest mutual funds, Washington Mutual, has its portfolio managed by Capital and its shares distributed by American Funds Distributors, but the business manager for Washington Mutual is a subsidiary of the Washington, D.C., brokerage firm[27] that organized Washington Mutual back in 1952.

Washington Mutual's story[28] began with the 1929 Crash. Personal trust investments suffered badly, so laws and regulations were promulgated to prevent a recurrence. Many were quite strict, particularly in the District of Columbia, where Rule 23 limited personal trust investments to bonds that were on Standard & Poor's Blue List. No stocks were allowed. And only about 200 individual bond issues, mostly issued by public utilities with a few from small railroads, were admitted to S&P's select list.

As a lawyer,[29] Bernie Nees became fascinated with Rule 23 and was determined to learn all about it. Believing there are always

[26] Capital Research and Management Company.

[27] Johnston & Lemon.

[28] Washington Mutual was originally distributed separately, but since 1953, American Funds Distributors has distributed it. In addition to an equity stake in Capital Research and Management Company, Bishop owned all of American Funds Distributors.

[29] After graduation from high school, Nees's first job—as a runner—was with the Commercial Bank of Washington at 14th and E Streets NW. After six months, he was advanced—to Head Runner. The bank was prepared to pay the tuition if employees went to banking school, so Nees signed up. As a runner, he had plenty of time for schoolwork during lulls in a day's routine. Taking a draft from downtown Washington over to Georgetown took at least an hour on the trolley, and a runner could easily read all the way.

In 1928, an officer of the bank told Nees about a local savings & loan (where he was a director) that had an opening, at far better pay, for a bookkeeper. The president of the S&L, whose son had decided to go to law school at night, asked Nees if he would be interested in doing the same course of study, with the bank paying the bills. "Why not go together?"

exceptions to any rule, Nees found 10 bonds on the Legal List that were selling for just 50¢ on the dollar—even though they had always paid interest. In time, this insight would lead to the creation of what has become one of the nation's largest mutual funds: Washington Mutual.

During World War II, Nees sold mutual funds part-time[30] and studied a chart book of 300 mutual funds. The best chart was Investment Company of America's, so Nees said to himself, "I've gotta find out who in hell is running *that* baby!" In 1946, he went to Los Angeles to meet Jonathan Bell Lovelace, whose firm had less than 20 people. He also met Chuck Schimpff, who invited Nees to his home that evening, beginning a close personal and business friendship.[31]

After the war, with stocks yielding more than bonds and the whole stock market starting to move up and up, bank trustees argued that they simply must be allowed at least *some* investments in common stocks. Eventually, the courts modified Rule 23 and allowed up

---

[30] "I'd always been impressed by the dress and appearance of bankers, but was even more impressed by the fellows working in the stockbrokerage business. So in September 1929, I became the first male employee—as both a runner and a bookkeeper—for Jim Johnston at Johnston, Lemon, the stockbrokers. But 30 days later, I was asking myself, 'What the hell am I doing?'" Nees had a personal challenge too. He was in love. "My gal told me, 'I don't want to get married until you pass the Bar exams.' That took four years of study."

In January 1931, Nees knew he had to decide between a career in law or a career with Jim Johnston, who then had 10 salespeople and two partners. Times were tough in the securities business. Salespeople were giving up and leaving the business. "I made a few extra dollars selling bonds to the customers of salesmen who'd left the business." In 1932, he passed the Bar exam. He then went to a law professor he'd gotten to know better while selling him receivership bonds, and asked his advice on what career to choose. "'Bernie, you did pretty well in law school, but do you like Jim Johnston?' That's all he said—and all I needed to hear."

Married in 1939, Nees got increasingly active in civic work, particularly the Junior Chamber of Commerce in Washington, rising from serving on committees, to the board of directors, and ultimately, president of the 2,000-member organization. "Jim Johnston allowed me the time to do it. He was that kind of guy."

[31] Visiting back and forth, the Lovelace, Nees, and Schimpff families got to know each other well. "Chuck Schimpff was then an officer in the National Association of Investment Companies, which became the Investment Company Institute, and was interested in moving the headquarters from New York to Washington, and I helped him in his search for new offices in the Capitol," recalls Nees.

to 40 percent of a personal trust to be invested in common stocks—or mutual funds.

Nees originated Washington Mutual by carefully matching it to the modified mandate of Rule 23 so the fund would be attractive to bank trust departments and to the many Taft-Hartley pension funds that were then being organized in and around Washington.[32] When a banker asked Nees, "You may have something here, but how do we know you won't get anxious about the market and put one third of the 40 percent that's supposed to be in stocks into cash?" Nees's answer: "We'll put it right in the prospectus that we'll *always* have 40 percent in stocks, even when it looks the worst for stocks!" So a core policy of Washington Mutual became never having more than 5 percent in cash and governments.[33] Another core policy requires each stock owned to have a consistent record of paying dividends.[34]

Nees thought he had such a great idea that it would sell itself and believed he wouldn't need middleman wholesalers to represent Washington Mutual to the retail brokers. To sweeten the proposition, Nees reduced the sales charge from 7½ percent to 5 percent, thinking the banks wouldn't stand for 7½ percent. "But you just try to sell a new

---

[32] Washington Mutual never attracted much from the unions, according to Bill Bagnard.

[33] Conformance to this policy is now reported to the directors of Washington Mutual every month.

[34] Nees's record in effective selling goes back many years. His high school principal was impressed with Bernie and asked if he would help sell some advertisements for the school yearbook. So before going to his job at the store where he worked, Nees would be out early, seeking to renew ads that had been taken in prior years. Having had some success, Nees soon got up the confidence to try selling new ads. He started with the proprietor of the ice cream store who had never taken an ad in the yearbook. Since it was then winter, and student demand for ice cream was naturally at a seasonal low, the challenge was considerable. Even more disconcerting was the flat rejection Nees got from his prospect: "I have never advertised! And there's no need to start now!" And then came the clincher: "The world will come to an end in June—before your graduation and before your yearbook will ever come out!" Nees was up to the challenge: Knowing how religious his prospect was, he quoted from the Bible about the great importance of being kind to young people. He then locked in on a powerful closer: "You will only pay when you see your ad in print, so if your fears of the world coming to an end are realized, you'll pay *nothing*!" Today, some 75 years later, Bernie Nees chuckles, "I sure got that s.o.b.—*and* the sale!"

mutual fund that pays only 3½ percent to the stockbroker on the firing line!" warns Nees. "Man, we struggled for the next five years.[35] Struggled!"[36]

Nees planned to ask Standard & Poor's to be the investment manager for Washington Mutual, thinking that since they rated all the stocks and bonds, this arrangement would be a natural. But after several discussions, S&P said "No!" They were a rating agency, not investment managers. "No problem," said Jim Johnston. "We'll manage it ourselves!"

"No way!" retorted Nees. He knew that Johnston & Lemon, as one of the most active new issue underwriters in the Washington area in the 1930s, had already shown the trouble inherent in *that* conflict. Instead, Nees went back to Los Angeles to talk with Schimpff and Lovelace about Capital's managing Washington Mutual. JBL took a positive approach right away.

Then Lovelace and Jim Johnston, Nees's boss, hit it off well at their very first meeting. Both were Southerners: Johnston was from South Carolina and had been a professor of statistics at the University of North Carolina, while JBL loved numbers and was from Alabama. Johnston had been a pilot in World War I; Lovelace had served in antiaircraft. Both were gentlemanly and soft-spoken. Their personalities and manner coincided naturally. In just one meeting, they had a deal: Johnston's firm would handle the administrative and legal aspects of Washington Mutual and get 50 percent of the sales charge or "load."

---

[35] At least part of the sales problem was that in its first half dozen years—from 1953 to 1958—the fund had a substantial position in bonds and underperformed relative to the S&P 500 Average stock price.

[36] Ward Bishop cold-called on Nees because Nees had been selling shares of Investment Company of America. The next time he visited, Bishop wanted to meet Jim Johnston, hoping to convince him to sell Investment Company of America.

Johnston told Bishop that his firm should get 4½ percent instead of the usual 3½ percent *if* they could sell $1 million of ICA's shares. Since ICA then had only $10 million in assets under management, Bishop agreed—and Johnston & Lemon promptly sold over $1 million.

Then, after just 10 years, Washington Mutual's special niche nearly disappeared: In 1952, the District of Columbia courts relieved all trusts of the Rule 23 restriction. Since avoiding this restriction was the key criterion on which Washington Mutual's unique selling proposition was based, the initial reaction was near panic. Nees soon calmed the fears: "No big deal! Our Board of Directors will simply fill the same role as Rule 23: We'll create our own set of criteria for our own special list, and use *that* in lieu of Standard & Poor's!"[37]

While they were at it, the directors of Washington Mutual considered other possibilities. One in particular was put forward by a Director who was also the treasurer of the Seventh-Day Adventists: "Alcohol and tobacco are *out* for my people. Why not rule them out for the fund?" So Nees went back to Los Angeles to check with JBL, saying apologetically, "I hate to do this because it might interfere with your responsibility for making all investment decisions, but could you possibly make an exception and agree never to invest in a company that gets 50 percent or more of its earnings from liquor and tobacco?"

Nees was happily surprised by Lovelace's positive response. "That might be a very good idea. It could be useful for us to have such a fund in our family." JBL explained his reasoning: Only a few stockbrokers would be particularly interested in this sort of "ethical" fund, but for those few brokers, that one difference could be decisive. And for committed conservative Christians among the nation's stockbrokers, Washington Mutual could immediately become their first-choice mutual fund. Having a clear and compelling reason always to prefer Washington Mutual—a reason that would not be affected by short-term factors such as recent investment results—could make a decisive difference in mutual fund sales.

[37] With 50 stocks that met both the S&P criteria and the criteria of Washington Mutual's board of directors, Nees created sales literature that simply showed the long-term history of those corporations' earnings and dividends. "The case made with these data was so strong, we used the very same list of companies for 40 years!"

A few years later, Washington Mutual became one of three mutual funds used by the Federal Reserve System's employee benefit funds. Such acceptance was, of course, more than encouraging to stockbrokers who could say to uncertain investors, "If it's good enough for the Board of Governors of the Federal Reserve . . ."

Washington Mutual now ranks as the world's second largest growth-and-income mutual fund and serves more than 1.5 million shareholder accounts. In total return over its lifetime, Washington Mutual ranks in the top decile—4th out of 54—among growth-and-income mutual funds.[38]

In recent years, a major sea change in the mutual fund business has come with the increasing popularity of 401(k) employee benefit plans. Investing for these plans is dominated by mutual fund managers, and the conventional wisdom is that all major mutual fund managers should get on board. This is particularly the view of mutual fund organizations that define themselves as "asset gatherers." Capital, of course, has never considered itself a mere "asset gatherer": It focuses instead on investment management. In the early days of 401(k) plans, competitors treated administration as a loss leader to win the investment business. Then, "open architecture" resulted in a proliferation of different fund families being offered to the participants in each plan with the result that the early "winners" were doing all the costly administration for everybody's funds—a classic Pyrrhic "victory."

As an investment management organization, Capital took a "go slow" approach to this business and still views the 401(k) business

---

[38] Washington Mutual became extraordinarily important to Johnston & Lemon and eventually produced more than 100 percent of the firm's profits because their brokerage business was not profitable. Johnston & Lemon manages the business side of Washington Mutual—meeting with directors, preparing annual and quarterly reports to shareholders, and so on—while Capital provides all investment management and distribution and transfer agency services. Bernard J. Nees continued to serve as chairman emeritus into his 90s. Capital's Jim Dunton has played a key role for more than 20 years, working well with the leaders of Washington Mutual's Johnston & Lemon, at least partly because he is a true Virginian who went to the Episcopal School in Alexandria and then to the University of Virginia.

with care.[39] The U.S. mutual fund business generally experiences annual redemptions or turnover of about 20 percent. Turnover in the 401(k) business will surely be higher because 10 percent of the U.S. labor force changes jobs each year, and when workers change jobs, they usually move their 401(k) assets out of their current employer's plan over to their new employer's plan. This results in a redemption for the mutual funds used in the prior employer's plan. In addition, with more and more investment options available to plan participants, they will make changes more frequently. Since Capital's investor turnover rates—buying and selling—are much lower than the industry average, the notion of spending heavily to compete in the 401(k) business of very large companies that offer a wide variety of funds managed by several different managers has a lot less appeal for Capital. These large 401(k) plans unintentionally encourage switching from one fund to another among the many options they offer, which for the mutual funds in the plan can result in 25 percent or greater turnover.

Now, with a focus on smaller company plans, which have less switching between mutual funds, Capital has become the third largest investor for 401(k) plans. As Rothenberg summarizes: "The 401(k) business is intriguing, but it is not the Yellow Brick Road."

---

[39] Capital Group helped develop the legislation and regulations for Individual Retirement Accounts and the retirement accounts for the self-employed known as Keogh Plans, which established the legislative basis for the increasingly important 401(k) retirement programs. However, Ward Bishop was not interested in Keogh Plans, which took many years to become profitable because they involved frequent, small transactions as each individual gradually accumulated his or her retirement fund. So, until Bishop reversed his decision, Washington Mutual was the only fund within the Capital Group funds that offered Keogh Plans.

Later, as 401(k) plans became increasingly popular for funding retirement benefits, Capital was slow to participate because competitive success in the early years required a commitment to providing record-keeping services as a loss leader, so the business was driven more by skills in administration than by skills in investing.

CHAPTER 6

CROSSING THE RUBICON: CAPITAL GROUP

NOTES FOR READERS

In his seminal study on *Strategy and Structure*,[1] business historian Alfred Chandler found a perverse repetitive pattern. Chandler's careful research showed, surprisingly, that instead of strategy determining structure, in the long run, it's the other way around: Structure eventually dominates strategy.

Chandler took a historian's approach to examining several highly successful American corporations, going all the way back to their earliest roots. Although the great corporations were in very different industries, the similarities in their histories were stunning. Each of the corporations examined—Sears Roebuck, Du Pont, Standard Oil, and so on—had once been successful because that company's strategy had

---

[1] *Strategy and Structure: Chapters in the History of American Industrial Enterprise* by Alfred Chandler, Beard Books (January, 1992).

been so well suited to the particular business opportunities in the particular market it intended to serve at that particular time in history.

But then, each company had gotten out of touch with its particular market—because the market changed, but the corporation did not change enough to keep up. Despite its past success, each corporation got into worse and worse trouble and very nearly failed. Why? asked Chandler. Why would corporation after corporation allow itself to move from success to grave disappointment? Why would they get so seriously out of touch with their markets?

As Chandler demonstrated, success with a specific strategy all too often leads to the buildup of a corporate structure that gets more and more consistent and efficient—and eventually rigid. This appears to enhance efficiency, as reported results get better and better for awhile. But over time, "the way we do things here" gets celebrated and codified, and the organization gets staffed more and more with "our kind of people" who increasingly have the same values, the same points of view, and the same blind spots. Because they care primarily about protecting and sustaining the organizational structure, with its familiar practices and comfortable practitioners, they reinforce rising rigidity.

Increasingly, the organization is managed by those who are *internally* focused and care less and less about developing vibrant new strategies that are imaginatively adapted *externally* to the free market's ever-changing priorities and the future. Meanwhile, the world and the corporation's particular market keep changing. So whereas the organization may appear to be doing better and better through efficiency, it is actually getting more and more out of touch with its own market and less and less effective.

As a historian, Chandler showed, in example after example, that as the organizational structure of corporations grows more precisely developed, efficient, and familiar, those structures (and the way the organizational managers think) become more and more rigid and confining. The structure's increasing preference for stability and efficiency eventually dominates. In advanced stages of this organizational disease, the corporation is confined to squeezing out smaller and smaller increments of efficiency—usually accomplished by cutting costs instead of by increasing the value of products and services it delivers to customers. Through this process, the corporation dooms itself to steady decline, and the inevitable trap silently closes.

Chandler's study concluded with this irony: The more successfully a corporation perfects the efficiency of its structure, the more surely that structure will eventually strangulate the effectiveness of its strategy.[2]

Over and over again (see Chapter 13), Capital has deliberately changed its organizational structure in a persistently adaptive search for *effectiveness* by dissolving rigidity and developing the capacities for innovation in many individuals. Of course, it's not very *efficient,* but that's okay with Capital because those involved know it is *effective.*

One of Capital's major changes may, at first, have appeared to outsiders as virtually no change at all. Capital became a one-firm holding company. The explicit reason was to liberate organizational strategy and effectiveness from the constraints of organizational structure and efficiency. While almost nothing strategic happened at the time of converting to a holding company structure, Capital freed itself to take a series of strategic initiatives in the next few years, and these initiatives became engines that drove strategic change.

Circumstances at the time certainly did not appear favorable for any investment organization to launch strategic initiatives. Both inside Capital and in the outside markets, circumstances were moving from "poor" to "dreadful." Mutual fund sales dried up; the stock market fell off badly, collapsing the assets managed by Capital and shrinking the management fees earned; clients terminated their accounts; and inflation, the Vietnam War, and President Lyndon B. Johnson's credibility gap combined to cause many Americans to lose confidence in the economy, their nation, and themselves. American Funds Distributors was failing, too. And Capital itself, briefly, went into the red.

---

[2] The dominance of the future by the past is what lawyers so appropriately call *mort main* or the "dead hand."

———— ◫ ————

S OME DROVE. MOST flew. In early 1967, more than two dozen key people of Capital—the largest such gathering it had ever held—gathered for a long weekend of meetings in the beautiful Arizona desert at Phoenix. Executives at Capital had chosen the place deliberately for its combination of two characteristics: reasonable proximity and lack of familiarity. The group came together to consider the several strategic possibilities that could follow the expected creation of Capital Group as a one-firm holding company. Organizing The Capital Group Inc. was a deliberately revolutionary proposition.

The unfamiliar locale might encourage new ways of thinking and open-mindedness. If so, it would be well worth the trip. In addition, Chuck Schimpff and lawyers at O'Melveny & Myers, worried about the "loose cannon" nature of California's regulators and state legislature, so they urged Capital to move its legal domicile to a more conservative state and suggested Arizona. Recurrent populism might lead to unexpected changes in the law, particularly in a state that was "BofA-centric" and likely to pass laws that were helpful to the state's largest bank, the Bank of America.

More than a year earlier, Jon Lovelace and Chuck Schimpff had—separately, but almost simultaneously—recognized the risk that Capital could be developing a real problem, a problem of rigidity in its organizational design or structure. Without modification, Capital's *structure* would inevitably dominate and might already be limiting—its future *strategy.* To prevent structure's dominating strategy, they wanted to take preemptive action to change the structure and liberate the organization's strategy.

Capital was already sufficiently successful in its mutual fund business to be showing signs of structure prevailing over strategy. One example: The possibility of pursuing the separate account business of managing investments for wealthy individuals and institutions was getting no serious attention. "Not me!" was the response of Capital's senior investment managers: "Why should I give up the prestige and the compensation of being a leading investor in our large and existing business—managing mutual funds—to go off into a risky little start-up business unit? Besides, if the institutional business *does* succeed, I'd have to be out on the road away from the office and away from home, traveling from city to city to meet with clients whenever and wherever they might require. That's not for me!"

Given Capital's former organizational structure, they were being realistic—and correct—as individuals thinking about their own careers. Staying in the center of the well-established business of managing mutual funds was clearly in each individual's own self-interest. That was Capital's main business; all the internal status and prestige were there; and that's where compensation was both largest and most assured.

Meanwhile, the mutual funds' independent directors worried about Capital's doing anything other than managing the mutual funds. Several directors opposed any diversion of resources—particularly investment research, but also trading and portfolio management—away from Capital's primary mission of managing mutual funds. Others questioned how Capital would allocate major costs like investment research.

Pricing was another concern. Institutional investment managers were charging considerably higher fees for investment management than Capital was charging the mutual funds. So, directors of the mutual funds (see Chapter 7) asked, if the new institutional business paid higher fees, how could the directors be sure the mutual funds would still get the best people and the best ideas?

Some worried that while Capital was doing well in the mutual fund business where it had so much experience and knowledge, it might not do so well in new businesses where it had little experience. And any difficulties in the new businesses could be distracting for Capital's mutual fund managers.

Searching for an organizational structure that would enable Capital to develop good answers for these and other questions, Schimpff and JL had come up with the idea of a one-company holding company. It was the era of creating one-bank holding companies, so that format was familiar. A similar organizational structure for Capital stimulated considerable discussion about the pros and cons of the idea and engaged many people in asking questions and considering possible alternatives over several months. "So it was not just one meeting, but lots of in-house discussions over many months," says Shanahan, "including lengthy discussions with legal counsel at O'Melveny & Myers and Ben Long, our lawyer in Detroit."

As was typical of JL's management style, many meetings and discussions had already been devoted to carefully collecting and sharing each person's views and preconditioning the group toward consensus. That consensus became clear: Capital should change its structure and create a holding company, initially with just one subsidiary—the mutual fund management company,[3] then the only business Capital had. (The process of Capital's creating its own parent organization was, with some humor, dubbed "Project Mutation" by Schimpff.)

"The long-term consequences and results of creating the holding company have certainly been impressive," says Shanahan. "But at the 'creation,' we were not focused on ends, just on providing appropriate means." The reorganization program resulted, on paper, in the formation of Capital Group. Over the ensuing years, this paper organization would become substantive as one after another of the spaces on that paper got filled in with real business developments.

The meetings in Phoenix were set up to consider several possible strategic initiatives: a trust company to pursue the separate account business, a transfer agency for the mutual fund business, a data processing unit, and a commitment to exploring an international business. Discussions of these initiatives, each led by different individuals, continued for two days—and back in California over the next two months.

The filling-in process proceeded irregularly. The group strongly supported forming Capital Guardian Trust Company.

---

[3] Capital Research and Management Company.

While it was expected to serve well-to-do individuals, it became the way to enter the fast-growing institutional business of managing pension funds and endowments (see Chapter 9). In addition to *de novo* start-ups, the holding company structure facilitated several important acquisitions.

Later, one of the first business units brought into Capital Group would be American Funds Distributors, Ward Bishop's mutual fund wholesaling organization (see Chapter 3). At the bottom of a long bear market for mutual funds, the real meaning of AFD's independence—which had always been an unusual arrangement in the mutual fund industry[4]—switched from "freedom" to "fearsome."

American Funds Distributors suffered three major changes: one internal and two external. The internal change was the loss of its forceful, driving leader when Ward Bishop retired. Bill Bagnard succeeded his father-in-law as head of AFD, while Bishop continued to be the owner. "Bill was good on overall administration and developing favorable relationships with the top guys at major stockbrokerage firms," says Shanahan, "but he was not very interested in the day-in-day-out, one-on-one, sales management work down in the trenches with the individual wholesalers and branch managers." That essential work devolved increasingly to Graham Holloway.

Up until the early 1970s, with Bagnard and Holloway as the young "Mr. Inside/Mr. Outside" management team, American Funds Distributors had worked pretty well. But in the gruesome bear market of the early 1970s, sales of mutual funds plunged year after year. In those difficult times, AFD's wholesalers sorely missed Bishop and wanted AFD's leader to be someone with direct experience working in the field as a wholesaler.

The first external change was all too obvious. In the early 1970s, the mutual fund industry was imploding. As investors lost interest in

[4] Vance Sanders, the independent wholesaler for Massachusetts Investors Trust, was also independent for many years. During the past quarter century, Vance Sanders combined with Eaton & Howard to become Eaton-Vance and set up its own investment organization, while MIT was acquired by Sun Life of Canada and developed its own sales and distribution organization.

buying mutual funds and the number of stockbrokers selling mutual funds fell even faster, wholesalers saw their incomes fall off again and again—and expectations for a future recovery in mutual fund sales fell even farther. The media were full of articles that said, "If you think *this* is bad, brother, just you wait!" The outlook for the whole mutual fund industry was depressing, particularly for wholesalers. "The mutual fund business in the mid-1970s was obviously terrible," recalls Shanahan. Mutual fund sales were down a chilling 90 percent. The number of stockbrokers in the nation had fallen all the way from 120,000 to just 50,000. Most mutual fund organizations had seen most of their wholesalers give up and leave the business. Some mutual fund groups had virtually no wholesalers left.

The American Funds had specific problems, too: Capital was clearly positioned as an *equity* manager that downplayed—even avoided—the bond funds and the money market funds that most other fund groups were now selling. This meant AFD's wholesalers had nothing to talk about and nothing to offer to the retail stockbrokers, who were unwilling to listen to the no-longer believable case for steady, long-term investing in equities. Even worse for AFD and its wholesalers, the value stocks favored by Capital's investment professionals were particularly hard hit by the dreadfully high interest rates of those unusual times. Capital's concentration on assuring brokers and investors of the long-term superiority of investing in equities— no matter how beneficial it eventually might prove to be—was hard to accept in the worst of a major bear market.

A third change was particularly painful: AFD was losing money and its annual losses were getting worse—with no real hope of a near-term turnaround. As the earnings and the prospects for wholesalers had fallen, one wholesaler after another gave up and quit. AFD had shrunk to just six active wholesalers. Protecting this small core group of loyal wholesalers was essential to AFD—and to Capital—because these wholesalers sustained the organization's relationships with the most important brokers at the most important brokerage firms and "being there" would be important if and when mutual fund sales ever improved. So to keep them alive, senior wholesalers were being paid more than they could earn in such a poor market.[5] In this acute crisis, some concluded that Capital could not and should not try to help AFD—and that AFD would probably have to be jettisoned and cast adrift. But wiser heads would go the other way.

American Funds Distributors was clearly facing grim challenges far beyond its capacities to develop effective solutions. AFD needed a rescue—and Capital Group's own strategic need for a strong mutual fund wholesaling organization had to be met. "Bill Bagnard couldn't be expected, as an individual, to take on the major refinancing and rebuilding job needed at AFD," recalls Graham Holloway. "And we wholesalers couldn't afford to buy the company and take all that business risk. So we had to work out a way for Capital to do it."

Bob Cody (see Chapter 7) and Jim Fullerton set in motion the process—which Mike Shanahan developed in detail and carried through to successful completion in 1974—to end the isolation of AFD, bring it into the Capital organization, and into alignment with the Capital culture. This would need to be done without either breaking the investment-oriented culture at Capital or losing the sales effectiveness of AFD.

Capital had numerous challenges to overcome; for example, AFD wholesalers were sure that in normal times, they made more money than the investment professionals at Capital. So wholesalers worried that if Capital took over AFD, particularly at a cyclical low for the industry, their compensation would get squeezed down—probably permanently. In addition, the investment professionals at Capital looked quite skeptically at merging with AFD, where the key people were salespeople and any new ideas would be sales ideas. Only one thing was common to both groups: skepticism verging sometimes on outright antagonism.

---

[5] "The stockbrokers recognized this, and they remembered this demonstration of Capital Group's commitment to the mutual fund business—and to them," says Wally Stern. "As in any other selling situation, turnover hurts because it always disrupts working relationships."

Although the combination would eventually prove remarkably rewarding, at the time of the acquisition, Capital's takeover was universally considered a much-needed rescue—and an obligation, not an opportunity. Bishop was 70 years old and, naturally, tired. As the owner, he wanted to be taken out. He was paid a good price on the simple theory that somehow, someday, there would be a recovery and the company would again sell mutual funds.

Saving AFD and bringing it into Capital was a major undertaking. Holloway was effective as Shanahan's agent in persuading each of the individual AFD wholesalers to come into Capital. Shanahan gave Holloway a real voice and trusted him—and Holloway delivered. As noted, mutual fund organizations are either sales-driven or investment-driven: In combining AFD into Capital, Shanahan's great achievement was to develop an organization that would have real strengths in both sales *and* investments.

Soon after AFD was brought into the Capital organization, the stock market began what became its longest-ever bull market, and the market for mutual funds gradually turned strongly positive. With substantial growth in the mutual fund industry and Capital's strong, steady gains in market share, AFD was rebuilt to over 60 wholesalers by 1995, and to over 70 by 2000. Now there are 86 wholesalers: 65 of them concentrate on traditional mutual fund sales; 18 focus on the retirement business, primarily 401(k) plans; and 5 work with personal investment advisors. In California alone, there are 11 AFD wholesalers.

AFD wholesalers are usually on the road five days a week and know they work very hard, but they also believe deeply that they are treated well; are the best paid in the industry; represent the best investment product; and, as they say, "get to wear the Yankee pinstripes."

CHAPTER 7

SHAREHOLDER SERVICES

NOTES FOR READERS

Investment managers understandably agree that, while necessary, the detailed information and data processing work required to provide good service to each mutual fund shareholder and each institutional client is not nearly so valuable or remarkable as is good investing.

This prioritization can easily be taken too far—and usually is. It causes most investment organizations to underestimate the great importance of service-based trustworthiness in their client relationships. They fail to recognize that trust is, for most clients, based at least as much on reliable service as it is on investment results because investment results are hard to understand and appreciate whereas service seems so obvious. Most investment organizations consider service a cost, not a sound investment in building investor loyalty. As a result, most do only what they consider necessary.

Managers who do not recognize how much clients value service leave their business franchises exposed to serious harm when—as from time to time will inevitably happen—investment results falter.[1] The long-term history of the investment management business documents the great and enduring power of any organization that is superior in both investor services and investment results.[2]

In investment management, service starts with communication. Relatively sophisticated, often using arcane terms, professional knowledge and advice must be expressed in ways a layperson can understand and will use with confidence. Part of service is quite routine—particularly as viewed by investment professionals immersed in the complex and demanding work of investment management—but accurate reports produced on schedule, correct payments made on time, and reports that are clear and easy to use are always important to clients. The truly outstanding professional organizations—in management consulting, investment banking, law, and investment management—repeatedly confirm their commitment to superior professional work by insisting on excellence in routine customer service.

As an investment organization, Capital made a major commitment to excel in mutual fund shareholder service—and, with its institutional accounts, in client service. Making this commitment depended on Capital's having the right person in the right place at the right time with the skills and personality to be effective as an "intrapreneur." It also meant having an environment hospitable to major organizational change and the leadership that would confirm the decision to change with a sustained, follow-through commitment.

---

[1] Partly because two thirds of investment managers underperform the market averages in a typical year and partly because the magnitude of underperformance exceeds the magnitude of outperformance.

[2] Airlines run by great pilots lose out competitively to those run by managers focused on customer service for the same reason: Customers develop preferences based on what they can understand and the pleasures of good service are easily understood.

———————————⊡———————————

A PLAIN, ORDINARY shoebox had a decisive impact on strategic thinking at Capital because it signaled real trouble.

The simple shoebox was not even at Capital; it was in the Bank of America's[3] main securities processing facility, which handled stocks, bonds, and cash worth hundreds of millions of dollars every day. Some of this money was Bank of America's, but most of it belonged to others. And much of it belonged to shareholders in mutual funds, including the American Funds.

The shoebox was stuffed with papers that were essential for the bank to maintain accurate records. A shoebox was no place to store essential records. The Bank of America was clearly in crisis, literally drowning in a sea of paperwork. And like a drowning person, the bank threatened to take others—in this case, shareholder services for the American Funds—down with it.

The problems at Bank of America were no great concern for Capital's investment professionals who, like investment professionals everywhere, had no particular interest in such mundane "green eyeshade" tasks as shareholder accounting, securities custody, or transfer agency services. That work was not even marginally profitable and involved large numbers of clerical workers doing dull, routine tasks. The conventional wisdom at Capital was clear: "We are *investment* professionals. Leave all that routine stuff over at the Bank of America—where it belongs!"

Bob Cody took an entirely different view. He recognized the importance of accurate, reliable, and convenient service to mutual fund shareholders—many of whom would be unfamiliar, and therefore

---

[3] An expert in computer systems who did much of the administrative work in Geneva, made the discovery and, recognizing how serious the bank's problems must be, knew that prompt action was necessary. Further study uncovered extensive problems.

uncomfortable, with investments and investing. "Administration and service are the keys to earning an investor's trust," says Bob Egelston. "You can be forgiven if your investing goes through a choppy patch, but if you blunder on service to investors . . . that's *it.*"

The American Funds were investing real money for real people, and Cody knew that accurate, timely information was essential to earning and building shareholder loyalty and broker confidence through superior shareholder service. To meet Capital's stated standard of "always striving for the best in everything we do," Cody and the key executives he had recruited[4] to Capital believed it would be necessary to bring all back-office operations in-house.[5]

After 25 years at Commonwealth Funds, Cody[6] knew the transfer agency business. "I'd lived it. I knew the problems. We explored every alternative because I was the *least* enthusiastic person at Capital about organizing to do transfer agency work ourselves—because if we did, we would want to be innovators and deliver a very high-quality service. Ultimately, we accepted reality: To get the service we wanted for our shareholders and broker-dealers, we had to do it ourselves."

---

[4] Exemplary among Cody's recruits was Jim Ratzlaff, who had joined the National Association of Securities Dealers (NASD) as an examiner in Washington, D.C., after mustering out of the Marine Corps in 1961; he also studied law at night at George Washington University. "My supervisor at the NASD made a point of having my wife and me go to National Airport to greet Bob Cody, who was arriving for yet another NASD meeting. A few years later, as our friendship developed, Bob said, 'If you ever decide to leave the NASD, let me know. The place for you may be at Capital.' And in a few years, I went to Los Angeles to join Bob Cody."

[5] The facilities in which cash transactions were handled required extra security. The conventional way to assure security against theft was to construct facilities with heavy-gauge wire mesh walls and doors. Naturally, such rooms are aptly and disdainfully known in most organizations that handle cash and securities as "the cage."

[6] Cody was a certified investment man (see Chapter 8) and could easily have used those credentials to gain personal acceptance by Capital's investment professionals. However, he was alert to the we-they separation so often found in investment organizations between investors and administrators who handled cash and securities and send reports to shareholders and wanted to identify with the administrators. *Note:* Bob Cody died in 1998, but his comments are presented as though they were being said currently because he is such a continuing presence at Capital that using the past tense would seem somehow artificial.

Cody was confident that Capital had the requisite capabilities to set up its own transfer agency as a new unit: American Funds Service Company.[7] More important, he recognized that only under its own management could shareholder services meet Capital's high standards. To do this, Cody recommended establishing comparability in pay and career potential for comparable responsibilities in administration. As Cody says, "The words 'striving for excellence in everything we do' are, of course, important, but the *feeling* behind the words is far more important. We've tried to apply this thinking consistently to all aspects of our business." In 1968, American Funds Service Company was organized so Capital could control product quality and transform AFS from just a transfer agency into a full-service organization.

Cody made it clear to all that Capital was going to be the industry leader in shareholder services, saying: "This cut the fuel line to the fires of paranoia within AFS." To assure accomplishing a quality job, Cody knew that Capital would need to attract, recognize, and reward first-quality people and recognize the quality job they would do. Capital would need to inculcate this new and different kind of thinking about the shareholder services unit throughout the whole Capital organization, so one of Cody's priorities was to make the importance of superior administration recognizable to everyone at Capital.[8]

This would increase expenses—and significantly increase the operating losses Capital was then experiencing—but both JBL and JL took the long-term view and endorsed Cody's costly recommendations.

Cody's timing was perfect. As the shoebox stuffed with records indisputably signaled, Bank of America's transfer agency operations

---

[7] Coleman Morton had been an early proponent.

[8] Bob Cody established and managed an effective Management by Objectives (MBO) program. As a colleague observed, "Only after Bob retired did we realize what was required to do what Bob always did: carefully review each individual's actual results relative to his or her objectives. When we realized how much work was involved, we had to suspend the commitment for a few years—and give everyone the same percentage bonus—until we had the managerial capacity to get back to where Bob had always been: carefully reviewing each person's real accomplishments and matching compensation to results."

were in real trouble. Part of the problem was the Enterprise Fund,[9] managed by one of Bank of America's other customers. (The Enterprise Fund had rapidly grown very large with numerous small investors investing through long-term contracts that called for regular monthly additions as small as $10 or $15. These small monthly additions generated lots of unprofitable transaction activity. In addition, each shareholder's account had to be accurately priced twice each day. All this activity flooded the Bank of America's data-processing systems at a time when Wall Street was still paper-based and so-called fails to deliver[10] were severely clogging the whole industry's plumbing.)

Making matters worse, Bank of America's centralized data-processing department was headed by classic computer technicians who were unable to anticipate—and therefore were surprised again and again by—the exploding bankwide demand for data-processing capacity. This exploding demand caused data-processing priorities and schedules to change often and without warning. The bank's California retail banking system, with over a thousand branch offices, was the Bank of America's real moneymaker, so its data-processing needs always received top priority and were allowed to jump the queue. And many other profitable units easily took priority over such low-margin units as the one serving mutual funds—including the American Funds.[11]

---

[9] Sponsored by Shareholders Management.

[10] In the paper-based system used in the 1960s, the broker representing the buyer and the broker representing the seller had four business days to deliver money or the securities to complete the previously agreed-on transaction. If the seller's broker was unable to deliver the securities, that broker had a "fail" or a "fail to deliver" and would not be given the cash payment—but would have to pay the cash proceeds expected by his customer. Occasional fails were a small matter—until volume mushroomed and fails increased geometrically. Several brokers could not make up the difference with their own funds and were bankrupted. For others, it was a painful, costly mess that took many months to clean up.

[11] Mutual fund shareholder processing was not the only casualty area. The bank's large master trust and custody business of serving corporate and public pension funds was starved for computer power and, in a few years, was obliged to drop out of the business.

If Capital's switch to in-house shareholder services had not been made when it was, the mushrooming service shortcomings at Bank of America would have severely damaged Capital's franchise with investors and with stockbrokers. Cody's timely initiative enabled Capital to dodge what soon would have become a fusillade of serious service problems.

Cody's persistent efforts made the operations group—now comprising the majority of Capital's employees—equal in accountability for excellence with those in marketing and investing. So the operations people would be physically on their own and in equal facilities with "Capital standards," they moved in 1983 from downtown Los Angeles to suburban Brea[12] in Orange County.

In the past 26 years, AFS has increased from 160 to over 2,000 Associates and now serves over 20 million shareholder accounts from four interconnected call centers in different locations around the country. The four call centers handle a daily average of 25,000 incoming calls—with peak load capacity of 35,000—and a standard of answering every call within three rings. Calls come in from 180,000 financial advisors and shareholders—usually in a 60:40 mix. The staff at AFS service centers differ from the investment organization in education and pay, but are well above the level of other fund companies' service center staffs and are treated with equal personal respect. In a field where 60 to 70 percent turnover is common, the turnover at AFS is only 12 percent, and if transfers of Associates to other Capital units are excluded, it is only 9 percent.[13] AFS strives to

---

[12] The move to Brea continues to serve as a model for opening new offices—for investors or shareholder services or both—around the world. In the 1990s, branch offices were set up in San Antonio, Texas; Norfolk, Virginia; and Indianapolis, Indiana.

[13] The lowest employee turnover is in California. The highest is in Hampton Roads, Virginia, which at 13 percent, is driven by the frequent transfers of Navy families from the major U.S. Navy base at Norfolk. "Ironically," says Weiss, "while AFS pays good bonuses for good introductions, Associates are often reluctant to recommend their personal pals because they know that Capital has very high hiring standards, and they recognize that many of their chums would not be accepted at AFS." Low turnover has been achieved through deliberate effort: Before the move to suburban Brea 15 years ago, it was close to "industry normal."

increase service capabilities *and* lower costs every year.[14] In recent years, its powerful information technology capabilities enabled AFS to serve five million additional shareholder accounts with only 100 additions to staff. Put another way, the number of accounts served per Associate has increased from 5,000 to over 9,000. And this greater productivity enables the American Funds to keep expenses charged to the American Funds well below industry norms.

People feeling good about who they are, where they are, and what they do is central to people wanting to stay with an organization. And their direct supervisor is key to how people feel on the all-important "soft" dimensions, so Capital devotes extra time to helping supervisors understand and appreciate the great importance of their roles. Being truly respectful of people—always the key to effective middle management or line supervision—takes direct, person-to-person involvement over years and years and is helped by Capital's flat organizational structure. One of AFS's most popular employee benefits is an indicator of the personal warmth and informality underlying the strongly productivity-conscious work unit. "If you ask our Associates, it's clearly the 6 to 8 days each year we declare Denim Days—usually to celebrate something pretty lighthearted— like a big win by the Lakers."[15]

One reason for American Funds' low shareholder redemptions or turnover while still gaining market share is very visible: the written materials produced for shareholders. "The American Funds' written materials are tops," says Cody. This traces right back to Jim Fullerton and his determination to convert all American Funds reports from

---

[14] In 1976, Tim Weiss came out of Cal State at Northridge as an English major. "I'd never heard of Capital or AFS, but I needed a job and was lucky enough to join AFS's IT operation—Capital Data Systems—I was assigned as an ombudsman to help facilitate communications and cooperation between the end-users and the producers—two groups that for understandable reasons in company after company just do not get along. It was, for me, love at first sight: This was family—and an opportunity to show what I could do." Weiss became President of American Funds Service Company in 1987.
[15] Kevin Clifford.

simply meeting the legal requirements into being truly interesting reading that informs shareholders and gives them useful understanding about their investments.

After joining Capital and reading the pedantic, legalistic text of the annual and quarterly reports that all fund managers were then sending shareholders, Fullerton decided to make American Funds' written materials the very best.[16] Searching for Best Practices, he gathered in every example he could find of what competitors were doing, and then committed to provide attractive graphics and to write the most informative and accessible text in the industry.

"Capital has never advertised and we like it that way," says Fullerton, "but we decided to make our reports to shareholders truly readable, interesting and *useful*. We don't want to have our reports sitting on the coffee table, just looking pretty. We want our investors to read them and learn what they really ought to know about their funds. Since investing is not an easy subject—but is so *very* important—we work hard to make them reader-friendly and rewarding for the time readers invest in them. We really want to educate our readers and have our reports understood."

As a writer, Fullerton knew he had to hook readers with the first sentence and then develop a story throughout the report. He also realized that layout devices like sidebars would make the reports more readable; that highlights in large type enable hurried readers to get the main messages; and that pictures of people are important to readers. One report took its main idea from a talk Bob Kirby had given, using his experience as a leading amateur race-car driver. "In investing, as in auto racing," explained Kirby, "you don't have to win every lap to win the race, but you absolutely do have to finish the race. While a driver must be prepared to take some risks, if he takes

[16] Fullerton also served as Chairman of the mutual fund trade association, The Investment Company Institute, in 1973 to 1974, the last two years of the severe bear market. *U.S. News & World Report* wrote that Fullerton was well suited to the job because he had—and would surely need—a good sense of humor. Chuck Schimpff and Bob Cody had both served at earlier times and Paul Haaga would in the early twenty-first century.

too many risks, he'll wind up against the fence. There are sensible risks—and there are risks that make no sense at all."

In 1974, after a long, severe bear market, another report to investors spoke about the possibility of there being a great buying opportunity, asking the embattled investor's natural question, "What should I do with my money *now*?" For most investors, it had been one of the harshest market experiences in memory, so Fullerton compared that market's difficulties with those of the prior worst market: 1937 to 1942. "Back then, we were in a major war—and we were *losing*. Excess profits taxes were being imposed; price controls and rationing were on; and our former international business markets were largely closed to American companies. That comparison really put things in perspective. Luckily, my timing was right too!" Within days of that report coming out, the stock market started going up—eventually, of course, way up.

Governance, a very different kind of service to investors in mutual funds, involves selecting mutual fund directors and providing them with the information they need to carry out their responsibilities effectively. Mutual funds are required to have independent directors, but at many organizations, the degree of independence is not all that obvious. Although a director is notionally chosen by the other independent directors, the investment manager that sponsors the fund often has considerable influence over who receives consideration. (Fund management companies easily recognize the advantages of having "cooperative" directors, and at some fund organizations, the aggregate annual compensation for a director is over a half-million dollars. Given these realities, the risks of cronyism are obvious.)

In clear contrast, Capital's approach to fund directors has long set the highest standard in the industry, a tradition that dates back to JBL's early days in the mutual fund business. Lovelace knew prominent people, so following his lead, directors of funds managed by Capital have always included the Los Angeles business elite. JBL believed in having strong and truly independent directors and in keeping them very well informed on all matters of potential importance so they will know they are fully informed and will ask the right questions and insist on getting good answers on matters of governance. Capital looks for experienced people who understand the difference between *governance* and *management* and does not want directors discussing individual stocks or decisions[17] because that's management. Later on, it was JL's idea to have the funds' directors chosen not by the management company, as was the practice at most mutual funds, but by the independent directors already serving on each fund's board. (A compliment to Capital, the SEC now requires this procedure.)[18]

Capital's commitment to watch out for the long-term interests of long-term investors shows in many ways: creative conservatism on new product introductions; consistent "steady as she goes" perspective on investing; informative reporting, always with a long-term perspective; consistently superior service to investors; and the determination to keep costs down, minimize capital gains taxes, and charge low management fees. Long before others got interested, Capital was conscientiously concerned for its shareholders about taxes, particularly in seeking to avoid taking short-term capital gains.

Capital will wait to launch a new fund until the market goes down so that investors who invest at the launch date will achieve good results. Some brokers, wanting product to sell when demand for a particular type of investment is strong, complain about what they call Capital's "holier-than-thou" attitude. For example, Capital

---

[17] Stanford Business School professor Jack McDonald remembers, "When I joined the board of the Investment Company of America, as the youngest Director, in the mid-1970s, JBL, then an emeritus Director, always took the time to talk with me about director conduct—how directors could best contribute to the fund and its shareholders. I remember vividly a board meeting in 1976 when one independent director was critical of a specific investment in a semi-conductor company, which he regarded at the time as too cyclical. JBL, sitting at my right side, whispered to me, 'That speech may be heartfelt, but it is not helpful to the portfolio counselor who has to make the decisions.' It made an enduring impression on me, and I wish that every new director of a mutual fund had a tutor with the wisdom and experience of JBL."

[18] Bob Cody, Jon Lovelace, and Jim Ratzlaff, for many years, were the key people who assured the strength of and worked with the directors of the mutual funds.

has run an emerging markets portfolio for institutional investors with strong returns[19] since 1986, but brokers buttonholed Capital executives and asked when such a fund would be available to individual investors, they always got the response that the public couldn't be expected to understand fully the serious downside risk of investing in less developed countries. So, although Capital International is, by far, the largest manager of emerging market investments for institutions, Capital decided not to launch an emerging markets mutual fund for individual investors in early 1997. The fear was that it would sell too well and later on result in investor disappointment, because investing in emerging markets involves exposure to the risk of major changes in valuation.[20]

Then in 1999, after the average emerging-markets mutual fund had lost 10 percent a year since the end of 1993—and well over 50 percent in aggregate—Capital[21] was ready to roll out a retail fund that would invest in emerging markets. At the very bottom of the market, it launched New World Fund,[22] carefully composed of emerging market debt and the stocks of international companies headquartered in developed countries and doing substantial business in the emerging markets.

Not doing what works for other fund management organizations is a familiar policy at Capital. Back in 1974, JL decided not to follow or compete with Fidelity and Dreyfus in offering money market funds, partly because he didn't want to encourage Capital's investors to switch out of stocks at what could and did prove to be a market low, but primarily because he felt Capital had no special competence at that time in the money fund management business.[23] (Nor did

---

[19] *SmartMoney*, March 1999.
[20] Even in the institutional Emerging Markets Growth Fund offered by Capital International, the new shares made available to investors each year are carefully limited.
[21] Capital Research and Management Company.
[22] With implementation leadership by Rob Lovelace and Mark Denning.
[23] Abner Goldstein, California's Deputy Savings & Loan Commissioner under Governor Pat Brown, joined Capital in 1966 and helped set up Capital Data Systems and then advocated and took the lead on developing fixed income investment management.

any other manager have demonstrable superiority, but others went ahead with their offerings anyway.) After the stock market began recovering, Capital developed the specific skills and did offer a money market fund.

Capital's caution is clearly constructive. "A real strength of Capital's franchise with stockbrokers," says Wally Stern (see Chapter 10), "comes from our never having to apologize to brokers and, even more important, from their never having to apologize to their investors."

Capital, like all investment managers, is a combination of two very different disciplines: a business discipline and a professional discipline. "We strive always to put the professional investment discipline ahead of the business discipline," explains Bill Hurt. "Speaking broadly, there are four widely recognized professions: law, to keep you out of trouble or get you out of trouble; the ministry, to help you find and stay with your religion; teaching, to show you how to learn and understand; and medicine, to keep you alive and protect your health. We think there is a fifth profession: helping individual investors manage their money and their relationship to money."

In 1995, Dave Short[24] and Kevin Clifford[25] were identified as two young men who could provide the leadership that would build the business and develop the necessary alternatives to AFD's longtime stubborn commitment to having only one share class of mutual funds. As Ward Bishop often said: "We'll explore *any* alternative to

[24] Dave Short grew up in Pittsburgh, studied communications at John Caroll University where he serves as a trustee, and joined AFD as a wholesaler in 1985 after a few years at Federated Securities.

[25] "In 1981, I was working for a contractor in Chicago," says Kevin Clifford, who graduated from Wabash College (where he now serves as a trustee). "Graham Holloway was looking to hire younger people to offset the steady aging of the wholesaling group, and Jim Skinner wanted to give up part of his 9-state territory—so Gary Reamey of Edward Jones gave them my name. At the time, AFD wanted to hire five people for a three-week training program. (The formal training program for wholesalers now takes four months.) I knew I was really interested, but there was one big problem. I was getting married and the training program was to start on the very same day our honeymoon was to start. So, I said to Graham: 'Let me see how good a salesman I *really* am,' and called my fiancé and proposed: 'How about postponing our trip for a few weeks—and going to Hawaii instead of Cancun?' "

*any*thing—with one exception: There will never, ever be more than one class of shares!" For many years, that policy had been right for American Funds and right for the long-term investor.

From the 1940s through the 1970s, both brokers and investors were generally better served with one class of shares—the "A" shares—with one sales charge, or load, schedule. All investors had to do to be better off with A shares than with any alternative was simply to hold the shares long term because Capital's low fees would save enough in a decade to offset the sales charge. This understanding was central to Capital's decision not to go "no-load" and has been the solid foundation from which Capital fought off a series of unwise innovations in mutual fund pricing. But major changes in the market significantly altered reality and made it important for Capital to change.

Rothenberg took Short and Clifford out for dinner in Los Angeles to give them the good news: Even though they were just 38 and 42, they were being made chairman and president and co-CEOs of AFD. Clifford was delighted. Short was aghast.

Clifford liked Los Angeles, but Short's family was deeply rooted in Pittsburgh: Being forced to move to southern California would be a bone-breaker. Rothenberg let the tension build in Short's mind for a few long moments before dropping in the clincher: Given modern technology and communications, Short could operate as sales manager from *any* location—including Pittsburgh. He would not need to move to L.A.

As the new leaders of AFD, Short and Clifford had important work to do. Communications technology was not the only way things were changing. Distribution of mutual funds had also been changing—and AFD needed to change, too. Stockbrokers were moving, at an increasing rate, to a different business model.[26] Instead of

---

[26] Capital knows from experience that the sales charge, or load, is seen as substantial, so some brokerage firms try, at the senior management level, to deemphasize the American Funds. (When Bill Hurt was in senior management at Dean Witter, he acknowledges, "I know that's what we felt—incorrectly—and tried to do at Dean Witter.") In the 1970s, Capital considered switching from load funds (with a sales charge that gets paid largely to

being paid for *transactions* with advice provided free of charge, the new model had brokers being paid for *advice,* with transactions provided free of charge. As the industry was transforming, AFD's consistent commitment to one single class of shares had gone from "wise" to "wasteful." AFD appeared to be working hard to achieve a Pyrrhic victory (a victory not worth winning) because AFD had the dominant share of the most rapidly shrinking channel of distribution in the mutual fund business.

"A too-standardized marketing strategy is simply not okay in a free and competitive market," acknowledges Rothenberg, pointing out that brokers were shunting sales over to other fund groups that offered several different share classes with different sales charges. All three men knew that major change was needed, and Rothenberg, who had switched back from the institutional business to help manage the mutual fund business, asked his two new lieutenants: "What will you fellows need to achieve real success?" and set down a key decision rule: The new pricing arrangement would have to be fair to the funds' current shareholders.

Privately, Rothenberg advised Short and Clifford that since there were no simple answers that would also be really right for existing shareholders *and* the brokers *and* new investors, they'd be smart to get Shanahan engaged in working out the solution early in the process. Rothenberg knew Shanahan's indirect, Socratic approach of asking question after question would take time.[27]

---

the stockbroker who makes the sale) over to no-load status. The case for not changing was made by Jim Fullerton, who feels a deep obligation to do the really right thing all the time and is highly regarded within Capital Group for asking just the right questions during business discussions or organization retreats. His case for keeping the sales charge was based partly on the investor's need for a steadying advisor during turbulent markets. This meant having someone paid well to do that difficult work; over 10 years, however, the total cost to the investor in the American Funds—when the initial sales charge is amortized and combined with the organization's low annual management fees and expenses—is less than the annual fees and expenses of most no-load funds.

[27] Rothenberg also advised his colleagues to schedule time with Jim Ratzlaff and Paul Haaga early in the process—and well before any questions would be raised by the fund directors.

After many months of analysis and running computer simulation after simulation to look at all the options from every angle, they agreed on a series of alternatives. It took American Funds from *one* pricing structure to *fourteen* to cover each significant segment of the complex mutual fund market—four plans for college tuition savings plans, five for retirement funds, four for retail sales, and one for the financial planners.[28] "I never realized that being fair was so very difficult," Clifford confessed to JL, who replied laconically: "Yes, it usually is."

The combination of strong investment results and the several variations on pricing to match different investor groups' preferences is working very well. "During the past decade, it's reported to us, we've been one of the fastest growing mutual fund management organizations in the industry," says Rothenberg with understated pride. "In 1987, we ranked fourteenth and today we rank third.[29] And we have done this the plain vanilla way. Our funds grew beyond all expectation because we deliver good value in service and investment results and because we've developed very strong support among the brokers who sell mutual funds." Capital currently has the leading market share in mutual fund sales.

To attract and keep the right stockbrokers doing the right work with investors in the right way—year after year and particularly during bear markets—Capital believes the broker simply must earn appropriately high rewards.[30] When overall mutual fund sales slow down, as they always do when the stock market declines, AFD's regular, steady sales momentum gains increasing market share.

"The 1987 market break was important to AFD's mutual fund sales, because the American Funds really delivered on their promise,"

---

[28] B shares convert to A shares after 7 years, and the amount that can be invested in B shares is limited to $100,000. There is no sales charge for 401(k) purchases or for sales over $1 million.

[29] In 1974, gross sales by AFD were only $75 million. In 2002, $75 million in sales were made every 2 to 3 *days,* and total sales exceeded $70 billion for the year.

[30] Selling $400 to $500 million of fund shares a year is considered very good for a dealer, and a few (nine in 2001) will sell as much as $1 billion of mutual fund shares in a year.

says Clifford. "Competitors had hurt themselves by pushing a bunch of short-term products, like closed-end bond funds and short-term multimarket trusts that maybe looked great for awhile, but in the long run, really didn't work at all.

"We just will not even begin to offer to get 12 ounces of juice out of an 8-ounce orange. The investment guys at Capital had said they just couldn't figure out a way to deliver superior long-term results with those products. Here's the acid test: Can we really do for the investor something he cannot do for himself?"

An important aspect of Capital's contract with investors and stockbrokers is that it works consistently to earn their trust and confidence. As Graham Holloway says, "We're the only guys who never bagged 'em! And that means a lot, even more than the financial incentives of being well paid for today's work—particularly for our kind of investor and our kind of stockbroker, the ones who're in it for long-term results. In the long, long run, the good guys *do* win."[31] American Funds' redemption rate, or loss of mutual fund shareholders, is typically less than half the industry average. The industry averages 25 percent; American averages about 12 percent.[32]

Capital's mutual funds have grown by producing steady, long-term investment results; by developing a powerful sales and service

---

[31] "When Shareholders Management went public, JL must have been concerned," recalls Bill Hurt. "Doug Fletcher bought the management company (despite Jon Lovelace's cautions about getting into the mutual fund business, when Fletcher asked his opinion after services at the church they both attended) for $50,000 when the fund it managed had only $2 million in assets. Some years later, Fletcher briefly enjoyed seeing a market valuation of over $40 million for his part of the business. He was in the newspapers all the time.

"It must have been hard for JL because the vast bulk of investors in the Enterprise Fund did *not* do well as investors. In fact, the fund's investors did quite badly. To JL, that just wasn't right."

Enterprise Fund was the principal mutual fund sponsored by Shareholders Management. Although it was advertised as a "high performance" fund, the average dollar invested in the Enterprise Fund received far lower returns than the market averages.

[32] The average investor in the American Funds has over $20,000 in a fund and owns two of the American Funds with a total of $40,000 invested. Since they typically have an equal amount with other mutual fund families, their total mutual fund investments are usually over $75,000.

TABLE 7.1 DIFFERENCES FROM INDUSTRY NORMS

	American Funds* (%)	Industry Average (%)	Difference
American Mutual	0.58	1.43	.85
Income Fund of America	0.61	1.34	.73
Investment Company of America	0.56	1.43	.87
Washington Mutual	0.64	1.43	.79
Growth Fund of America	0.72	1.51	.79
New Perspective	0.79	1.83	1.04
AMCAP Fund	0.69	1.51	.82
EuroPacific Growth	0.90	1.92	1.02
Fundamental Investors	0.63	1.43	.80

*Includes 25 basis points for 12(b)-1 fees.

organization aimed at servicing brokers[33] and financial planners; and by keeping annual mutual fund operating expenses low. Capital's mutual fund annual expense ratios are typically only half the industry average.[34] Rothenberg explains, "Our mutual fund fees were set originally in the 1930s, and we keep them internally consistent across our whole family of funds. So the marginal fee on marginal assets is *very* low—less than ¼ of 1 percent for the Investment Company of America."

Capital quietly emphasizes its low expense ratios,[35] citing the differences from industry norms on A shares for several of its funds, as shown in Table 7.1. Such differences can and will add up—for the long-term buy-and-hold investor.

A difficult question of appropriate practice came to a head for Capital and the independent directors of the American Funds in

[33] Not far from the old 80:20 Rule, 71 percent of AFD's sales come through 17 percent of the brokers who sell American Funds.
[34] For example, Fidelity's Magellan Fund, which is less than 25 percent larger than Investment Company of America, generates three *times* as much in management fees.
[35] Part of the low expense ratios of the American Funds is due to their large size, because the ratio is, of course, total expenses divided by total assets.

1988 with the introduction of 12(b)-1 programs.[36] (The 12(b)-1 programs are named for an SEC regulation that allows mutual funds to pay a continuing annual service fee to broker dealers who provide ongoing services that encourage investors to maintain their mutual fund investments.)[37] Before 12(b)-1, the brokers received all their compensation in one lump payment through the up-front sales charge or "load"—and had no incentive to continue servicing the investor nor to encourage him to staying the course with his fund. In fact, a broker was rewarded for persuading the investor to switch from one fund to another. For cynical brokers, the goal was to encourage switching as frequently as possible so they could pick up another sales charge on the purchase of the next new fund, and then the next. Most switching hurts investors, who leave a fund that *appears* to be underperforming, usually because its particular type of stock has been lagging relative to the overall market; and then buy into a fund that *appears* to be doing well because its type of stock has been leading the market. Unfortunately, this often results in a double whammy with the investor selling low and buying high. Industry data indicates such switching results in investors losing more than one third of all the investment returns they would have earned if they had simply remained with the mutual funds they already owned.

The movement to 12(b)-1 fees—where the stockbroker gets a ¼ percent annual service fee commission[38] for as long as the investor stays in the same fund—has changed the whole concept of the

---

[36] Graham Holloway is recognized as the father of 12(b)-1 programs.

[37] While studying for a joint M.B.A.-J.D. degree at the University of Pennsylvania, Paul Haaga worked part time at Wellington for Jack Bogle—for $6.00 an hour—writing prospectuses and shareholder reports. After graduation, he went to the SEC in Washington from 1974 to 1977, and then joined Dechert, Price & Rhoades, where he became a partner. In 1985, when Jim Ratzlaff heard that Haaga might leave, he called and said, 'If you ever decide to leave private practice, come talk with us at Capital.' With two brothers already living in Los Angeles, the idea of living on the West Coast was "not out of the question," and Haaga joined Capital in 1985.

[38] When introducing 12(b)-1 fees, Capital charged 25 basis points on new shareholders and 15 basis points on existing shareholders.

mutual fund industry. With 12(b)-1, the stockbroker receives a service fee each year as long as the investor remains invested. The stockbroker now has a major incentive to sell the fund that is right for the particular investor long term and then to provide service so that the investor stays invested.

In the beginning, the largest stockbrokerage firms campaigned hard to bring 12(b)-1 plans into being. They started with the smaller fund groups with the weakest investment records and said something like this: "You know, we'll probably have to stop selling your funds completely. But there is one last hope we just might be able to offer to you. If you would set up a 12(b)-1 program, we just might be able to continue selling your fund shares." Given this proposition, the weaker mutual fund organizations had no choice but to go along. Then, 12(b)-1 programs spread to stronger and stronger fund organizations. Now, they are the industry standard.

The annual 12(b)-1 payment to the broker[39] is paid by the fund—which increases the expense ratio, and this cost is borne by all the fund's shareholders. Over the long term, the 12(b)-1 trailer fee encourages a closer, longer-term relationship between the investor and the stockbroker. This should bring greater stability to investors' behavior, particularly at major stock market stress points, and this stability is expected to be good for everyone invested in the funds.

Capital studied 12(b)-1 programs thoroughly and concluded it could and should provide industry leadership on this major pricing issue. Capital decided that the upper limit on service fees would be held to 0.25 percent[40] and that above this level, any 12(b)-1 program expenses would be borne by the management company, *not* by the

---

[39] Depending on the firm and its type of business, the broker will keep somewhere between 35 percent and 90 percent of the 25 basis points as long as he or she is the listed "broker of record" for a particular investor's account.

[40] As a "transitional bridge," the funds paid only 0.15 percent or less on established shareholders, whereas new assets paid 0.25 percent. American Funds put forward the pattern. It has held and now the same pattern has been confirmed by the NASD in the maximum sales charge rules.

mutual fund investors. Second, the 12(b)-1 service fee would be offset by a lower sales charge on new purchases (and add-on investments by current shareholders). Capital reduced the initial sales charge from 8½ percent[41] to 5¾ percent and completely eliminated the sales charge for investments over $1 million—and for most 401(k) retirement plans.

"The 12(b)-1 fee the fund pays out for investor service and retention can be greater than our incremental management fee for continuously managing these same assets," observes Rothenberg. "These service fees can really add up for a strong mutual fund salesman—as much as $200,000 to $250,000 a year—and they'll keep right on coming, year-after-year, if the broker has sold good, persistent business. And that's what we and our wholesalers always emphasize with the stockbroker."

[41] The 8½ percent load was an artifact of the 1950s, when brokers were diverting small accounts into mutual funds and the individual broker pocketed $400 on a $10,000 investment.

CHAPTER 8

ACQUISITIONS
AND START-UPS

NOTES FOR READERS

The record of corporate mergers and acquisitions is not good. Too often, the price paid is, in retrospect, too high. All too often, the presumed strategic synergies are never found because so many acquisitions are really *sales*. They are driven by the knowing seller who wants out—not purchases by an astute, informed buyer. Acquisitions that fail, as a majority do, are driven more by emotion than rational judgment. The record of acquisitions in the investment management field has been particularly poor.

Capital, however, has made several highly successful acquisitions by being rigorously rational; being prepared to look for and see long-term value when others were concentrating on the acute distress of short-term cyclical adversity; and by having ample resources available so it could buy on favorable terms.

In addition, Capital has made itself the preferred buyer by being the kind of organization that inspires trust and confidence that combining into the Capital organization will work out well. Being trusted to serve mutual fund shareholders faithfully, even in the worst of times, has proven decisive. Even acquisitions not consummated have brought key people to Capital.

Capital's successes with acquisitions have several attributes: favorable financial terms and modest use of capital; clear strategic business complementarity; and thorough organizational integration.

Not everything Capital tried in corporate development worked. Some moves failed, but some moves succeeded beyond all expectation.

CAPITAL GROUP'S LARGEST acquisition began with a failure, while its largest start-up failure began with dazzling success; and a highly successful venture capital investment program very nearly failed to get started at all.

In 1963, when it was likely that San Francisco's Commonwealth group of mutual funds would be sold,[1] Commonwealth's Bob Cody invited Capital's Chuck Schimpff up to San Francisco for a luncheon. As they talked together over the next few weeks, both saw a real combination of strengths: Capital's abilities in investing could combine with Commonwealth's abilities in custody and shareholder services.

Cody and Schimpff were sure the combination would have been a good one, but classic northern California parochialism precluded it. As a senior pillar of the San Francisco Establishment, Waldo Coleman, the controlling stockholder in Commonwealth, couldn't bear to merge his fine San Francisco firm into an organization based in—ugh—Los Angeles. And that ruled out Capital.

[1] Ultimately, 34 potential acquirers got involved.

This came as a great surprise to Cody,[2] the president of the Commonwealth Funds, who thought he had been authorized to complete final negotiations with JBL.

Fireman's Fund Insurance, an accepted member of the San Francisco business establishment, swooped in. The president of Fireman's Fund was determined to acquire Commonwealth and get into the investment management business.[3] The goal was to replicate with Stanford's endowment the kind of investment firm others had set up with Yale, Harvard, and MIT to manage their endowments and then build a profit-making business managing corporate pensions and mutual funds.[4] Fireman's Fund bid a zero fee to win the Stanford account.

"When Commonwealth was sold to Fireman's Fund," says Cody. "I immediately resigned as CEO—without a new job to go to and without even a mention of my plans to Capital. I called Jonathan Bell Lovelace on the phone, and he asked right away, 'When can you come to Los Angeles?'" Cody would play a key

---

[2] Cody had joined North American Securities, the investment manager and custodian for the Commonwealth Fund, as an analyst after graduating from Stanford and Stanford Business School in the late 1930s. Later, he got deeply involved in every aspect of conforming to the rules and regulations under the Investment Company Act of 1940. The 1940 act was the foundation for the modern mutual funds industry, so he knew all the ins and outs of the mutual fund business. Years before, when offered a starting job at Commonwealth, Cody had jumped at the chance to get into what was considered to be the higher class work of administration. After all, in the 1930s, investment people were looked down on as guys who all wore green eyeshades. At Capital, Cody would find indicators of status reversed. The administrative staff were the ones wearing green eyeshades and laboriously calculating by hand the net asset value of mutual funds twice a day so shareholders could invest new money or redeem shares at accurate prices. Administrative workers sat in the center of the small office area, while the analysts sat on the outside perimeter, where they could look out the windows.

[3] Explains Vic Parachini: "Fireman's Fund bid to take on the Stanford endowment at zero fee, hoping it would serve as a prestigious flagship account. The account was assigned to me, and I managed all of it, and then at Capital, part of it, for the next 30 years."

[4] Yale linked with Endowment Management & Research; Harvard with State Street Research & Management; and MIT with Colonial Management.

role at Capital, developing its leading shareholder services organization (as explained in Chapter 7). And he would have another turn at combining Commonwealth and Capital Group 11 years later[5]— during another round in the convoluted restructuring of the mutual fund industry.

Two years after Fireman's Fund acquired Commonwealth, American Express acquired all of Fireman's Fund, and renamed its mutual funds the American Express Funds. Then, as part of a product line extension strategy, American Express launched the American Express Special Fund, an "aggressive growth" fund that invested heavily in illiquid private placements and special situations.

Responding naively to the trusted American Express name, many conservative investors, who didn't realize the risky sort of investing they were getting into, bought into the go-go AmEx Special Fund just as a severe bear market was settling in. Investment performance of the AmEx Special Fund was not just bad: It was awful. By 1974, after several years of poor investment performance in a difficult market, the American Express funds were in heavy redemption as investors angrily cashed out.

Even more serious for image-conscious American Express, the bad publicity caused by the funds' poor investment performance threatened to hurt the vaunted reputation of the American Express Green Card. (To protest poor investment performance, some shareholders cut up their AmEx credit cards and sent the pieces back to American Express with their mutual fund proxy statements.) Another worry was the flurry of aggressive class action lawsuits[6] being filed against mutual fund managers. If AmEx or the AmEx Funds were sued, the bad publicity could really hurt.

American Express decided it had to act decisively to protect its all-important image and credibility. The fastest way out was to sell the fund unit to another mutual fund manager. AmEx was the classic

[5] 1975.
[6] Often filed by Abe Pomerantz, a high-profile, self-promotional litigator.

"highly motivated" seller, and Capital, with Cody in a key position, was an obvious potential acquirer.

AmEx needed to get the word to Capital very quietly and in just the right way. Luckily, it had a convenient and discreet channel because, as part of its overall financial services diversification strategy, AmEx had also taken a major ownership position in Donaldson, Lufkin & Jenrette. This securities firm did stockbrokerage business with Capital, so the president of American Express asked the president of DLJ,[7] to call Bob Egelston, the president of Capital Group, to ask if Capital would be interested in acquiring the American Express mutual funds.[8]

It was not an easy question to answer. At least not in late 1974 when Capital—and every other mutual fund outfit—was struggling financially. New sales of mutual funds were virtually nil. With the stock market in a harsh bear market, fund assets—and investment management fees—were down substantially. With mostly fixed costs, Capital operated at just breakeven—and then, for several months, at a loss. Moreover, the serious slump in business caused the formulaic valuation of Capital stock to drop, precipitating margin calls from the Bank of America to some of the new, young owners who had been borrowing[9] from the bank to finance purchases of Capital stock and had little or no reserves to answer the call. A decision to pass on the

---

[7] Howard Clark was CEO of AmEx and William Donaldson was CEO of DLJ.

[8] Legally, of course, Capital was being asked about acquiring the management company, not the mutual funds. Only the independent directors of a mutual fund can approve the governing advisory agreement. John G. McDonald, a professor at Stanford Business School, was then serving as one of the "outside" or independent directors of the several American Express mutual funds and recalls: "As an independent director, I determined that Capital had great people and planned to hire some of the best people from American Express Investment Management Company. The resulting capability to manage our funds would be that of an enhanced investment organization, a 'Capital Plus.' So, I voted positively for hiring Capital as our new investment advisor of all the American Express funds which I served as director."

[9] Borrowing from banks to buy equity in privately-owned investment firms at book value was the established industry norm.

American Express offer would have been easy to justify, even for an organization with a long-term focus such as Capital.

Fortunately for American Express, Cody was in a senior executive position, and from his long experience at Commonwealth, knew a great deal about the renamed American Express Funds. Within Capital, he was well liked and respected, and Capital had accumulated ample reserves and was ready to weather a storm—and recognized an extraordinary opportunity to add assets quickly and at low cost.

For just $1, Capital acquired the American Express mutual fund management company and took responsibility for managing $700 million—including the Stanford University endowment. Equally important, Capital gained a core group of strong investment professionals[10] and an investment operation in San Francisco. Timing was, in retrospect, nearly perfect. The purchase agreement was finalized at the end of what had been a long bear market and so became a classic illustration of the advantages of Capital's history of investing: buying into price weakness with a long-term focus on unrecognized value.

The Anchor Group of mutual funds was acquired in 1978 on even better terms: The assets were absorbed without assuming any responsibilities for the costs of their people or the organization. The CEO[11] of the Anchor Group called Jim Fullerton at home one Thursday night (the two men had known each other through their work at the Investment Company Institute, the mutual fund industry trade association) and explained: "Our parent company, National Life Insurance, wants to get out of the mutual fund business." Saying he felt a great responsibility for assuring the welfare of their mutual fund shareholders, the caller concluded: "Capital would do a good job for our shareholders. Will you take over?"

"We would—and we did!" recalls Fullerton.

---

[10] Including George Miller, Victor Parachini, Bob O'Donnell, and Claudia Huntington.
[11] John Haire.

Capital bought Anchor Group for $1 plus 1.2 times book value—when the Anchor management company's book value was almost all in cash—minus an adjustment depending on future redemptions, which eventually proved large enough to eliminate almost all of the original premium over book value. Only one fund, Fundamental Investors, continued as a separate fund; the others were merged into Capital's existing funds.

Two other possible acquisitions never happened. One could have been a major winner. Alliance Capital was nearly acquired from Donaldson, Lufkin & Jenrette for $5.5 million, but Alliance's then chief investment officer[12] managed to block it. (Later, Alliance would go public and have a market value more than 100 times greater.)

Investor Overseer Services (IOS) was also considered, but only very briefly. Ken Mathysen-Gerst was a neighbor of IOS's Bernie Cornfeld in Geneva, Switzerland, so Cornfeld easily made the initial contact. However, takeover talks were quickly aborted when serious study of the IOS books revealed that the firm owed large contingent payments to mutual fund salespeople.[13] (Of course, Confeld's flashy, unsavory personal reputation meant there was little chance of making a corporate arrangement with a conservative outfit like Capital.)[14]

Another acquisition by Capital was "within the family." Back in 1969, Greenwich Management Company had been launched in

[12] Peter Vermilye.

[13] The adverse publicity of IOS and its contractual sales programs would hurt sales across the whole mutual fund industry for several years.

[14] Ironically, IOS management failed to recognize the real strength of the IOS business: Very low redemptions would characterize the IOS funds for many years. IOS management, fixated on their cash-basis business economics and their large front-end sales charges, worried that investors would terminate their investments early. If so, the sales compensation already paid out to the IOS salesmen would never be recovered through investment management fees. They were wrong. IOS redemptions proved to be unusually low by industry standards for a simple reason: The IOS funds were among the few safe-haven alternatives then available anywhere to "flight capital" investors from the Arab world or Latin America as well as some communist countries. These flight capital buyers put their IOS fund certificates in safe-deposit boxes in safe countries and left them there indefinitely. Redemptions were, therefore, very low, so managing IOS funds had surprisingly large economic value as a continuing business.

Connecticut by two Associates,[15] who wanted to develop their own business unit within Capital. They intended to manage more differentiated mutual funds, believing that Capital's other portfolio managers were too conservative and were missing the market. In addition to backing their new venture,[16] Capital agreed that the unit would be operated under a separate name; would be independently managed; and would be located on the East Coast—geographically far away from Los Angeles. The initiative would help diversify Capital business. It also gave the advocates a chance to earn significant equity and make a distinctive contribution to the organization.

In 1969, Greenwich Management took over an aggressive growth fund, whose principal attraction was its name: Growth Fund of America. (The seller was paid with a 5-year non-interest-bearing note for a mere $30,000. The fund assets were only $300,000.) With its way-too-small asset size, the fund was in a hopeless situation because operating expenses—always deducted from investment returns in calculating performance—were a daunting annual 8 percent of assets! With this huge handicap, the fund could never achieve good performance at its small size. But, with substantial growth in assets, those same operating expenses would, as a percentage of net assets, decline steadily toward insignificance. And American Funds Distributors could produce the needed growth in assets.

Eighteen months later, Greenwich Management offered its second mutual fund, the Income Fund of America. It, too, was deliberately aimed away from Capital's traditional "down the middle" approach.

In addition to a great name and a low purchase price, Growth Fund of America had another attraction: a supercharged incentive

---

[15] Ed Hajim and Steve Reynolds: Ed Hajim joined Capital after graduating from Harvard Business School in 1964. Steve Reynolds joined Capital from the University of Virginia's Darden Business School in 1967 and switched to Greenwich Management in 1969. From 1969 to 1973, the management of Greenwich Management owned 30 percent and Capital Group owned 70 percent.

[16] Jim Fullerton and Bob Egelston served, respectively, as Chairman and President.

fee arrangement with 20 percent of all investment gains paid to the manager![17] Greenwich Management's deliberately aggressive style of investing, encouraged by the incentive management fee, produced spectacular results: Growth Fund of America was one of the top 10 growth funds in the country in 1970 and again in 1971.

But 1973 was different—very different. If Greenwich Management was an attempt to encourage entrepreneurial initiative by giving committed young people room to pursue their dreams, the eventual result was no dream: It was a nightmare. The stock market slumped, and investment results were suddenly very disappointing as "small cap" growth stocks plummeted. Greenwich Management was merged back into the parent company in late 1974.

"Going in, we knew it would be risky," remembers Shanahan, "particularly in a market that was already high, but Capital did not have an aggressive growth fund then and the key people were very keen to try." Capital has a history of allowing capable and committed individuals with an idea and conviction the chance to run with their ideas. This goes back to JBL and his approach to enterprise and entrepreneurs. Shanahan continues, "I really don't think JL expected a great success, but he may have been more willing to go along with the decision made by others because Greenwich Management was set up as a separate unit with its own name—on the opposite coast, too far away to contaminate or harm Capital in Los Angeles."

"Afterwards, we felt that the problem at Greenwich Management was really *our* problem," explains Jim Rothenberg. "We felt we owned it, because we gave the people the chance they wanted. The Southern gentleman's protective and paternalistic views of JBL still live on here. Later, we recognized that timing and environment had conspired against the more aggressive approach Greenwich Management adopted. Besides, it must seem inappropriate to hold onto hard feelings: The Growth Fund of America was only $15 *million* in assets

---

[17] Until Congress outlawed such pricing arrangements for mutual funds. Hedge funds still charge 20 percent of profits.

when it was absorbed into Capital;[18] it was over $30 *billion* at the end of the century and is one of America's 10 largest equity mutual funds."[19]

Buying-in Greenwich Management was one of a cluster of actions that included buying-in American Funds Distributors (see Chapter 6) and buying-out the minority interests of those Associates involved in starting Capital Guardian Trust (see Chapter 9).

Greenwich Management was not the only unit that risked imploding. In Europe, the Capital International Fund got down to just $5 million[20]—but, thanks to Jon Lovelace's persistence, it was kept going. While absorbing losses in the international operation in Geneva for many years, Capital decided to sell 50 percent of Capital International S.A. (see Chapter 8) to a unit of Chase Manhattan Bank[21] in 1972.

Another major investment vehicle, while not actually within the Capital organization, produced remarkable returns on the investments made by Capital Associates: venture capital.

Mike Shanahan, as the analyst covering Steel and Technology stocks, recruited Jim Martin to be a technology analyst at Capital.[22] Shanahan and Martin came up with the idea of investing in venture capital as a way to keep up-to-date on important new developments in technology. Acquiring "knowledge capital" by working inside small high-tech companies might help analysts to evaluate large public companies from the outside.

Venture capital investing began when Don Valentine[23] joined JBL's Capital Management Services unit in 1971. Bill Newton got

[18] Ed Hajim has since had a rewarding career in stockbrokerage and investment management at EF Hutton, Lehman Brothers, and ING.

[19] In the mid-1970s, when Bill Newton and Jim Rothenberg each took over half of the fund, its accumulated capital losses exceeded the remaining net assets—so capital gains were tax sheltered for several years.

[20] Capital had other international assets under its management at this time.

[21] Chase Manhattan Overseas Banking Corporation.

[22] Martin had been a salesperson at Fairchild, the semiconductor pioneer, with Don Valentine. At the same time, Bill Griswold, an industry expert with great experience, was recruited from Kern County Land as a geologist and oil analyst.

[23] And Gordon Russell.

acquainted with Valentine's expertise, his thought process, and his vision for venture investing during a long dinner in Palo Alto. Newton recalls being very impressed and before the evening was over, reaching a clear conclusion: "If we're ever going to engage in venture investing, he's our guy." Then, smiling, he confesses he really can't remember any details from that whole evening's discussion, because when leaving the restaurant, they saw a man who was beating his wife. "He slugged her—hard. As she fell to the ground, we immediately focused on just one thing: stopping the assault and helping that woman. All else simply disappeared from memory!"[24]

Through an extended—almost endless—series of meetings, Shanahan, Valentine, and Martin[25] worked out what they hoped would be an acceptable business proposition, which Newton took to the board of directors. "Of course," recalls Newton, "I prepared very carefully and put together what I was confident was a very strong, well-documented case for venture capital investing at Capital."

The presentation was going well, until Chuck Schimpff announced his absolute opposition to venture capital investing within Capital with a terse pronouncement, clearly intended to be decisive: "Over my dead body!"[26]

With Schimpff's boycott, the meeting was, for all practical purposes, over—even before Jon Lovelace had expressed his own concern about the risk of Capital's portfolio counselors and analysts getting diverted from their primary responsibility: managing mutual funds for investors, many of moderate means. Venture investing in exciting new technologies and new markets via new and untested companies that were not yet public was a very different discipline,

---

[24] Thirty years later, Newton has taken a leading role in establishing a "safe house" for battered women in Jackson Hole, Wyoming, where he and his wife, Gloria, now live.

[25] Jim Martin had space in Capital's offices, but was seldom there. Upbeat and gregarious, he was remarkably well connected throughout the technology community. Although he was not necessarily a great securities analyst, he truly *understood* technology and, in Don Valentine's estimate, made "hundreds of millions of gains for clients" and was often very helpful to Capital analysts. Martin is quoted as saying: "It's a *jungle* out there—and those guys in Silicon Valley are *animals!*"

[26] Don Valentine describes Schimpff sarcastically as "a true nineteenth-century 'visionary'!"

far removed from Capital's focus on deeply researched value investing in major, publicly-owned companies.[27] It was also recognized that the compensation for venture capitalists would be very different in structure, magnitude, and method of determination from the compensation at Capital.

Newton left the Board meeting sadly sure it was all over for venture investing at or through Capital. But when he got to his office, the telephone was ringing. The caller was JBL. "Don't get down about that discussion. Chuck can get way too conservative sometimes. He didn't really mean what he seemed to be saying. I think we're on the right track." Lovelace counseled Newton that it would be important to understand Schimpff and the problem with venture capital investing, as Schimpff saw it, so they could prepare a stronger case for going ahead.

The subject of venture capital investing came before the board again in a few months. That interim was used by JBL to achieve the two process objectives he cared deeply about: The subject would be well and thoroughly discussed—and the decision would be democratic. At about the same time, JBL, always a venturesome investor at heart, did two deals with his own money.[28]

When venture capital investing was again on the agenda, the vote was divided. Schimpff again voted "No!" and Jon Lovelace abstained, saying he was still concerned about venture investing distracting Capital's analysts and portfolio counselors from their main mission of investing for the mutual funds and for clients of Capital Guardian Trust.[29] The directors agreed that Capital should not use clients'

[27] At approximately that same time, examination of the public record of American Research & Development (AR&D)—the celebrated venture investing company started by Harvard Business School Professor General Georges Doriot—would have shown that venture capital investing was no Golconda. Except for the fluke of investing almost accidentally in Digital Equipment, AR&D's long-term portfolio return—without any adjustment for the obviously large risk of investing in illiquid investments in new, untested companies—was no better than the S&P 500.

[28] One, simply because he liked Jerry Sanders, had him paying Advanced Micro Devices' first payroll out of his own pocket.

[29] Jon Lovelace never did invest with Sequoia.

money to build its knowledge of venture investing. If Capital wanted to go ahead, it should invest its own dollars in Sequoia,[30] the name chosen for the venture fund. But would Capital make the necessary financial commitment? Maybe.

Before raising any money from outsiders, the inside advocates, such as Shanahan and Newton, must first provide a significant starter pool of capital themselves. This was not easy when Capital's investment professionals were not particularly well paid and it was the worst part of a major bear market. JBL took the lead as an investor; Shanahan, Martin, and Newton together put up $15,000; and JBL arranged to add corporate funds from Capital to reach the $1 million minimum.[31]

The first investments were not all winners: One failed and on a second, Sequoia only got its money back. But the third became Advanced Micro Devices—a spectacular success. After the first three investments, Don Valentine became the principal investment manager; Valentine took up Capital's role as general partner in venture management; and the name was changed to Sequoia Capital.[32]

The initial fund-raising strategy for Sequoia included raising money from pension clients of Capital Guardian Trust. But in

---

[30] Don Valentine and Gordon Russell were, until fairly recently, employed by Capital Management Services—the consulting unit through which JBL advised such companies. JBL wanted to keep this subsidiary alive and busy—and saw the link with Sequoia as a way to do this. This arrangement also allowed Valentine and Russell to participate in Capital's employee benefit package.

[31] At the closing, Shanahan ruefully recalled years later, "One 'investor' was reported to us to be in an airplane over Texas. After waiting for two hours for him to land and still hearing nothing, we decided to go ahead. We never heard of his landing—and never heard from him again."

[32] The arrangements with Valentine were worked out by Ned Bailey, on points set out by Newton and Shanahan. Bailey, who was a lawyer and for several years an understudy for Schimpff, spent several years in Personnel, which he then headed. Later, he served as chairman of Capital Guardian Trust. He also produced (see Chapter 9) one of the most effective new business sales presentations ever: a series of slides of Capital's investment professionals with his voice-over describing their academic and professional achievements. Because there were many professionals at Capital and each had impressive credentials, the slide show seemed capable of going on forever. Prospective clients got the message: Capital had lots of talented investment professionals and a remarkable commitment to proprietary research.

1970, venture capital investing was not considered an appropriate investment by most pension funds. The initial reaction to venture capital investing was clear: "No way!"[33]

And true to his word, Schimpff was actively opposed. As chairman of Capital Guardian Trust, he would not allow the concept to be marketed to "his" institutional clients. Newton's and Shanahan's solid support was moot as far as marketing was concerned because they had none of the personal contacts needed to get a hearing to make a case that would overcome the cautious reluctance of large institutional investors. The first and—for very nearly too long a time—only institutional investor was the Ford Foundation. It invested $3 million, expecting other institutional investors to follow.[34] None did.

Then, Bob Kirby of Capital Guardian Trust jumped in. He introduced Valentine to a series of large institutions and coached him on how to make the venture capital proposition credible and persuasive to institutional investors. Their joint efforts were successful—but not for an excruciatingly long time. As the months went by without other institutions joining in, the Ford Foundation, feeling that its outsized 60 percent participation was per se imprudent, very nearly withdrew. Fortunately, General Electric Pension invested $3 million and then Alcoa, Armco, and Yale University all joined in—so Ford remained.[35]

---

[33] As Valentine recalls, Schimpff was actively opposed and Ned Bailey gave passive resistance.

[34] Two other investors—for $1 million apiece—were Capital Management Services and Teijin Ltd. But these were not considered "institutions."

[35] For many years, the relationship between Capital and Sequoia has been special and close—and has produced investment gains of several hundred million dollars. Sequoia Capital has sponsored numerous partnerships—and for many years, each had a cloned side fund open to key Capital Associates without the customary carried interest charged to other investors for Sequoia's services. Both Capital and Sequoia have been careful to avoid any conflicts of interest with their respective firms. Capital does not allow individuals to invest in IPOs or in the pre-IPO final rounds of private market funding, or in early-stage private equity (such as venture capital), if any of the Capital Group Companies' mutual funds might want to invest. Relations were not always easy. (After over 20 years of remarkable professional cooperation, personal friendships, and great wealth creation, Capital management winced over a 1995 Sequoia brochure that made an unexpected reference to

As Valentine put it 30 years later: "Without Bob's introductions and guidance on pitching institutional investors, there would be no Sequoia Capital—and no Cisco or Yahoo! or five hundred other companies." Sequoia has become one of America's largest and most successful venture capital organizations, and investors wanting to participate in Sequoia's funds are "on allocation" because so many past and potential investors want to participate in any new Sequoia venture capital fund.

Capital Associates interested in venture investing have enjoyed very substantial successes. But the expected insights into how to invest in mature companies have not materialized. "We enthusiasts were terribly naive," Shanahan observes 30 years later, "to believe that what might be learned in venture investing would have *any* real transferability to our work in investing in mature public companies. The two kinds of investing are very, very different! At Capital, our business is based on fees and continuing *relationships* with investors: Venture capital is all about deals and *transactions*. The differences are large and absolute."

Sequoia's linkage with Capital and asked for a retraction. Valentine, who had not requested permission in advance and can be "tough on task," was not quick to make a correction. Later on, the compromise proposed and accepted was to rewrite and reprint the brochure; Valentine personally absorbed half of the cost.)

CHAPTER 9

CAPITAL GUARDIAN TRUST COMPANY

NOTES FOR READERS

Few developments are more favorable to the success of an enterprise than being the active and effective beneficiary of a profound restructuring of an important industry. Such a restructuring occurred in institutional investing in the 1960s and 1970s when a flood of pension and endowment assets were pulled out of the traditional banks and insurance companies where they had been accumulating.

Corporations, states, and universities went looking for organizations they believed could deliver superior investment results. These large institutional funds were looking for close working relationships with small groups of highly talented investors and felt no need for the safety of dealing with large, long-established, and well-capitalized organizations that had dominated institutional investing. They were dismissed as "too bureaucratic."

Institutions were looking for the best of a new breed: dynamic new firms of young, hungry, and exciting professionals from the best business schools who were organized to achieve beat-the-market investment performance and worked hard to achieve superior results. And these clients were prepared to pay high fees to get what they wanted.

Serendipitously, the unit Capital had just established to provide traditional investment counseling services to wealthy *individuals*—Capital Guardian Trust Company—became the vehicle by which Capital participated in the extraordinary surge of *institutional* assets suddenly searching for winning investment managers.

Proving once again that it's great to be lucky—particularly by being in the right place at the right time—Capital Guardian Trust went on to prove that it's not enough just to be lucky.

Like most of the investment firms that surged forward on the flood tide of assets leaving the banks and insurance companies, Capital Guardian woefully underestimated the importance of having the right organizational design, staffing, and investment procedures. It was not nearly prepared for the loss of control and coherence that would come with exponential growth, followed by the disruptive damage that the serious bear market of 1973 to 1974 inflicted on clients' portfolios and client relationships.

Capital Guardian not only missed the Nifty Fifty stock market; it was allowed to float free from its parent organization in structure, strategy, staffing, and process. As was virtually certain to happen, it stumbled badly.

Capital Guardian was asking for trouble—and got lots of it. The wonder is that the damage was not even worse or longer lasting. Surely, a principal reason for its survival was a combination of the personal confidence clients somehow continued to place in a few key people at Capital Guardian—and the staying power of the parent organization.

While Capital Guardian was certainly not alone, "others did it, too" explanations are no excuse for what happened. Senior management at Capital was focused on the mutual fund business and paid far too little attention to what was—and was not—going on at Capital Guardian Trust. Most of the senior investment managers brought into the Trust Company were new to Capital and to each other. They didn't work together: They took off in different and often contradictory ways. Instead of working closely with Capital's own in-house research analysts, they relied on calls from their pals on Wall Street. Instead of making independent investment decisions based on solid research of long-term fundamentals, they got caught up in that go-go era's trite misbehaviors: chasing popular stocks and reaching for short-term investment performance. The quality of investment decision-making deteriorated badly.

Fortunately, Capital had the executive leadership required to put the management of Capital Guardian into strong hands, but only after real harm had been done. It also had the organizational resources to integrate the Trust Company into the parent organization and the good luck to have the stock market turn favorably at just the right time.

Rising like a Phoenix from its near self-destruction—and eventually moving from strength to greater strength—Capital Guardian has more than rebuilt its franchise in the United States where it is now a strong leader in institutional investing. Affiliated institutional investment companies within the Capital organization have established important businesses in the United Kingdom and Japan—and are gaining strong businesses in continental Europe, Australia, Singapore, and Canada.

The institutional investment business differs most from the mutual fund business in the role of client relationship management. Individual investors expect—and get—very little contact with the portfolio managers who manage their mutual funds. Institutional investing is completely different: Clients expect and get an extensive and intensive service from both portfolio managers and professional relationship managers.

The most successful institutional investment managers have made large investments in dedicated, senior-level relationship managers. For years, Capital did not come anywhere near keeping pace with the competition. After years of dismissing the importance of superior relationship management with clients and doubting the effectiveness of ever working closely and cooperatively with investment consultants, Capital Guardian has become a leader in the complementary disciplines of client service and relationship development.

Still, like all institutional investors, Capital Guardian (and its Capital counterparts in other countries) is profoundly challenged by the increasing competition in institutional investing. In the United States, the proportion of public stock market transactions represented by the decisions of professional investors has gone from just 10 percent to a staggering 90 percent—in a single generation. And the 50 largest and most active institutions now do 50 percent of all transactions on the New York Stock Exchange. This is tough competition to beat and very tough to beat by much. As a result, the alternative of passive investing (in its many variations) is an increasingly pervasive challenge to all active investment managers—including Capital.

Capital will also be challenged by the difficulties—as well as the opportunities—in developing an institutional business that consistently serves multiple national markets with a multiproduct capability. Conceptually, that multiproduct capability includes large-cap and small-cap equity in all the major markets and in the emerging markets plus high-grade and high-yield corporate and government debt in every market around the world plus private equity in both developed and developing countries—worldwide. This broad array of capabilities will be delivered into a series of geographic and economic domains—each with differences in competition, regulation, and culture. The resulting complexity will present important challenges for effective management of investments and even more important challenges for organizational management and leadership at Capital and at any of its global competitors.

Capital continues to define its professional mission as achieving superior investment results in each asset class. Curiously, this definition leaves out the most important part of achieving superior long-term results for clients: wise investment counseling on appropriate objectives

Jonathan Bell Lovelace, founder of Capital. (*Photo credit:* Elson-Alexandre.)

Dinner meeting with Dr. Lionel D. Edie, 1950s. Clockwise from upper left: Jules Hoffman, Chuck Schimpff, Coleman Morton, Jonathan Bell Lovelace (JBL), Lionel D. Edie. (*Photo credit:* Drucker-Hilbert Co., Inc.)

CRMC meeting, 1950s. Left to right: Harleston (Hardy) Hall, Jules Hoffman, Jon Lovelace (JL), Al Drasdo, Sr., JBL, Chuck Schimpff, Marjorie Fisher, Reno Renfrew. (*Photo credit:* Weaver Photo Service.)

Ward Bishop, founder
of American Funds
Distributors, 1969.
(*Photo credit:*
Curtis Studios.)

American Funds meeting with JBL, 1973. Front row: Bob Lindstrom, Bill Bagnard, Sr.,
JBL, Graham Holloway, Jack Turner. (*Photo credit:* H. Lee Hooper, Photographer.)

Key people in the Capital investment group, mid-1970s.

Clem Tiampo and Bob Egelston, around 1964.

Wally Stern, JL, and David Fisher, 1979. (*Photo credit:* Roger Marshutz Photo.)

Left to right: Bill Newton, Marjorie Fisher, David Fisher, JL, Cathy Ward, Howard Schow, Inge Andenow, Bob Cody, Dan McMeekin, 1981. (*Photo credit:* Bill Varie.)

Left to right: Jim Zukor, Walter Fairfax, Ned Bailey, 1967. (*Photo credit:* Leigh Wiener.)

Jim Zukor and Jim Ratzlaff, 1975.

Jim Fullerton, 1971.
(*Photo credit:*
H. Lee Hooper,
Photographer.)

Left to right: Gordon Crawford, Paul Haaga, Cathy Ward, 1996.
(*Photo credit:* Peter Darley Miller.)

Ken Mathysen-Gerst. (*Photo credit:* © Ken Rogers, 1981.)

Joe Beles.

Nilly Sikorsky, Robert Ronus, Thierry Vandeventer, 1979. (*Photo credit*: Ives Debraine.)

Ray D'Elia,
Jim Rothenberg,
Bob Kirby,
Gordon Crawford,
1981.

Gregg Ireland, Karin Larson, Ken Griswold, Jim Dunton, Don Conlan, mid-1970s.

Facing, around table from left: Bill Grimsley, Karin Larson, JL, Bill Hurt, David Richards. (*Photo credit:* Bill Varie.)

Edus H. Warren, Jr.,
1984.

Jim Martin (center)
and Dick Barker
(right) on a company
visit in the 1980s.
(*Photo credit:*
Jon Brenneis.)

David Fisher, Karin Larson, and Andy Barth, 1994.
(*Photo credit:* Peter Darley Miller.)

Alan Wilson,
Gene Stein,
Donnalisa Barnum,
1994. (*Photo credit:*
Peter Darley Miller.)

John Seiter (standing) with CGTC marketing associates. (*Photo credit:* Bill Varie.)

Jim Rothenberg, 2002.
(*Photo credit:* © David Zaitz
Photography.)

Mike Shanahan and JL, 2002. (*Photo credit:* © David Zaitz Photography.)

and the asset mix most capable of achieving each investor's realistic objective. Developing demonstrable skill in this important work is a challenge to the investment management profession in general and to Capital in particular.

Finally, the Personal Investment Management unit, which serves the needs of wealthy families, has not, until recently, achieved much growth and is still less than $10 billion in total assets. Greater success should now be achievable with a reorganized approach—particularly in the United States, but also in every region or nation around the world where great wealth accumulates.

THE CRASH OF a speeding sports car played a key role in the start-up of Capital Guardian Trust. The driver was badly injured, but not killed.

Bob Kirby explains: "After Harvard Business School, I got into the investment business with Willis and Christy,[1] which became Scudder, Stevens & Clark's office, in Los Angeles. Pretty soon, we found we had an unusual question among us. I loved sports car racing, but others at the firm were *not* enthusiastic.

"This came to a head one day in 1965, when I called in to ask if someone could cover my account responsibilities for 30 days or so—because I'd broken eight ribs and would be in the hospital for

---

[1] Investment counselors organized by Paul Willis and Dean Christy as a correspondent of Scudder, Stevens & Clark—which meant receiving copies of Scudder's research reports and being welcome to visit them in Boston and New York City. Bob Kirby went to Long Beach High School, Stanford, and Harvard Business School, and then worked at Willis and Christy, after it acquired the business of Charles White where young Kirby had been working. (Willis and Christy was later combined into Scudder, Stevens & Clark.) Kirby resigned and joined Capital. Having experience in the traditional investment counseling business, Kirby expected—and was expected—to develop Capital's *individual* investment management business. He never got a chance to do that because the *institutional* investment management business soon became the real opportunity and Kirby's good-humored "aw, shucks" style was a natural hit.

awhile. That's when it was explained to me that I should decide: give up either my vocation or my avocation. I chose to give up my job—at least in part because I was offered a position at Occidental Life."

Kirby called Bill Newton to ask his advice because Newton had worked at Occidental Life: "Are you leaving Scudder? Hold on! We may have something for you here at Capital." At just this time, Capital was taking a serious look[2] at organizing a trust company as a vehicle to use in the long, slow process of building up a private investment counsel business with wealthy individuals.[3] Soon, Kirby joined Capital, specifically to help set up this new investment counseling arm—mostly for high-net-worth individuals and, perhaps, a few hospitals and colleges in southern California.

"'Money management' didn't really exist before 1960," explains Kirby. "There was no such thing. The big banks had all the money and focused on custodianship—not on beating the S&P 500 or anything else." Trust companies were traditionally expected to protect the funds entrusted to their care, produce a reasonable income, and watch out for the individual beneficiaries. But they were not expected to be great investors. With their personal trust experience, managing pension trusts didn't look all that different or difficult for the banks to do. In fact, pension trusts looked much easier to manage because they were tax-free and very long term—and did not involve the unusual

[2] Dick Staver, a popular insurance man, first came up with the idea of starting a trust company and pitched his idea to Coleman Morton, who passed it along to Chuck Schimpff. Schimpff asked a friend at the law firm of O'Melveny & Myers, who said he was quite sure the proposition would never get the necessary regulatory approvals from the state of California.

[3] Stuart MacLaren had left Scudder a few years before to join Capital. He began by successfully cleaning up the back-office operations, and had just completed a study of the merits of an independent trust company. He clearly identified the main business problem: In the individual counseling business, the largest clients were usually also the oldest. And when those clients died, their estates went into probate for delivery to a bank trustee suggested by the client's attorney (who usually got reciprocal business from the bank). The heirs might know little or nothing about all the great investment work the investment counselor had done, over many years, for the deceased and would feel no particular loyalty to the investment counselor. So it was not very hard for the bank to stimulate anxieties and get the heirs to switch over to the bank.

personalities found among personal trust beneficiaries. The actuarial rate of return assumptions[4] were low and all that a manager had to do was buy long maturity bonds that would meet or beat the actuarial assumption and it was "mission accomplished."

Investment performance was being discussed for the first time.[5] When these discussions included the records of the major banks and insurance companies, their performance records were more than disappointing. The typical pension fund was 75 percent in long-term bonds, and with postwar interest rates repetitively rising, bonds had been going down for years.[6] In addition, bank trustees bought the conservative, blue-chip stocks with large dividends—not growth stocks. Consequently, the investment results of the banks were seriously below average, whereas mutual funds, like Investment Company of America, had quite favorable investment records.[7]

Corporate directors began asking how large their company's pension fund was—and were stunned by the answer. The pension funds, originally organized to provide some fringe benefits, had accumulated vast amounts of money: Pension fund assets were often equal to the net worth of the whole company! Pension funds were not only large, they were underperforming, and this was hurting the sponsoring company because larger annual contributions had to be made to the pension fund to make up for the poor results. To reduce these costs, pension fund executives wanted much better investment performance.

---

[4] In determining the requisite contribution to be made each year to a pension fund, the consulting actuary will make reasoned assumptions about such variables as the rate of return on investments and the inflation in the wage base, estimate the prospective pension liability, and estimate the amount of contribution required each year to accumulate the requisite assets. An increase in the rate of return assumption would reduce the annual contribution required to fund future pension payments.

[5] A.G. Becker and Merrill Lynch were just organizing performance evaluation services.

[6] Interest rates had been rising—so bond prices were falling—since the 1952 accord between the Treasury and the Federal Reserve to stop holding rates at artificially low rates to help the government finance World War II.

[7] Capital took on two accounts with performance fees, but most fees were aligned with the mutual fund fees—to avoid any questions about comparative equity.

"I blame the creation of this whole 'performance' business on Jack Dreyfus," says Kirby. "Because in the late 1960s, Jack was the first guy—with the Dreyfus Lion coming up out of the Lexington Avenue Subway to look around and growl—telling everybody what great returns Dreyfus had gotten." As pension funds began looking for investment organizations with good performance, it was inevitable that they would notice the outstanding long-term record of Investment Company of America.

"In 1965," recalls Kirby, "opportunity was literally thrust upon us: It came from General Mills." General Mills decided to conceptualize the pension fund not as a *cost* center, but as a *profit* center, arguing that if more were earned on the assets already in the pension fund, the expense of annual contributions to the pension fund could be reduced, producing a direct increase in reported earnings. So Polk went to the General Mills board of directors and made a well-documented presentation with the conclusion that the pension fund should be managed in a more imaginative way. He won the day, and sent a team out to study the records of investment managers to find the very best. They were impressed by the long-term record of results achieved by Capital's mutual funds.[8] In late 1965, a few years before Capital

[8] Henry Porter, who led the team, explains, "Bo Polk, General Mills' Chief Financial Officer's father, was a local industrialist and had gotten to know General Ed Rawlings when he was in Dayton at Wright-Patterson Airbase developing logistics for the Army Air Corps during WW II, and Rawlings was CEO of General Mills when Bo Polk was hired. When he came to General Mills, the company needed major changes in all aspects of management to convert from an amalgamation of local and regional flour millers into a consumer products company with professional management. He was expected and authorized to be creative and *different*—what we now call a 'change agent.' He hired me—over the telephone—from Harvard Business School to come and join in making changes. We used financial analysis as our discipline and language. I started off to build an investor relations program for a company that had never before talked to analysts—at least in part because it had had no need to raise any capital in the market—so I got acquainted with Wall Street just as institutional investing and institutional research were coming into prominence.

"At General Mills, we came up with the idea that pension funds were a set of fixed benefits or liabilities, with pools of assets being accumulated to pay those benefits; so if we could increase the investment performance, we could cut back the annual costs of funding these pension obligations. We would simply convert the way we defined our pension problem

Guardian Trust was established, they found Kirby heading up the new separate account group at Capital and said, "We've studied your record and we'd like you to be one of our pension fund's investment managers!"

Kirby knew the language of investment counseling, was an experienced portfolio manager at an organization with superior long-term results, and wanted to build his business. He also recognized the profound difference between an elderly mortal's $5 million account, which would have such complexities as taxes, beneficiaries, and low-cost "favored holdings," compared with a perpetual corporate pension fund that was tax-free and could be managed for results alone. Kirby also understood the difference between a $5 million account that would be depleted by spending and eventually terminate versus a $50 million fund that could be expected to grow and might continue forever. Kirby also knew that a significant piece of a major corporate pension fund would be great for his new business.

As Capital made plans to organize Capital Guardian, the external opportunities looked inviting, but internal constraints were serious and several. To protect the American Funds from internal competition, Capital Guardian would be confined to very large accounts. The independent mutual fund directors insisted on assurances that Capital would not raid the managers and analysts of the mutual funds to staff Capital Guardian. Such assurances were hardly needed.

With individual compensation linked to assets managed and profits contributed—as was then the investment industry norm—

---

from 'asset accumulation' over to 'operating effectiveness'—or more conventionally, from 'stocks' to 'flows.' So our focus as financial managers would be on increasing the rate of return on pension assets, aiming to increase corporate profits by reducing the size of the annual contributions.

"Hard data on investment performance was just coming available. We could see that our pension fund's investment manager, Bankers Trust, was simply not organized or staffed to be among the best performers. So we went all over the country looking for the very best. Our search led us to State Street Research and Management; S&P/InterCapital; Brokaw, Schanen & Clancy; Thorndike, Doran, Paine & Lewis; and Donaldson, Lufkin & Jenrette—and to Capital."

Capital's leading investment professionals were reluctant to leave the prestige and high incomes that came to them as managers of large mutual funds for an uncertain new venture in a field that was considered stodgy and slow-growing. They were also understandably reluctant to shift over to a business that if successful would require traveling all over the country to compete for business and then traveling even more to service clients with quarterly meetings that would all be scheduled at the client's convenience. The new institutional business would require many long trips away from Los Angeles and away from the engaging, ever-challenging work of investing. Capital Guardian would have to look elsewhere within—and outside Capital—for many of its key people.[9]

---

[9] Bob Kirby was working with Howard Schow, so moving him over was easy. Ned Bailey was in Personnel, so he could move over. Bill Grimsley was hired from Title Insurance and Trust in Los Angeles and, later, Dick Barker came from S&P/InterCapital (where he'd gone from Connecticut General). Bill Grimsley grew up in Southern Georgia, graduated in 1962 from Harvard Business School, and joined a small firm headed by Eugene Black's son-in-law and Stanley Nabi. Later, he joined Doug Johnston at Title Insurance, where they hoped to acquire a group of property and casualty insurance companies, but the market for P&C companies ran up and away from them so Grimsley was looking for a place to work. Later, another addition was W. Emer Yeager.

Jim Dunton was the youngest portfolio manager at Washington Mutual, so he could transfer. Dunton got to Capital on a thin thread of connectedness. Ned Bailey, who was then leading Capital's recruiting, was back at Harvard Business School and asked, "Where's Charlie?" He was asking after Charles Abbott, one of HBS's great teachers, who specialized in banking and taught a lively, entertaining, and compelling course that was very popular among students. Abbott not only had large numbers of students taking the course, he was also a shrewd judge of talent and was more than willing to help the best employers find the best graduates. He respected Capital Group and had helped them identify M.B.A.s with superior brains and character. More important to Bailey, Abbott was gone. No longer at HBS, he had gone to Virginia, where he was Founding Dean of the Darden Graduate School of Business at the University of Virginia. So, Bailey left for Charlottesville and called on Dean Abbott at the Darden School, where Dunton would soon be graduating. Since Dunton knew he was not interested in commercial banking, he'd decided not to "waste" time taking Abbott's course. Fortunately, Abbott knew him anyway and urged Bailey to interview Dunton.

Dick Barker illustrates the improvisational informality with which the Trust Company was put together: "I met Bob Kirby at a dinner put on for a company's management in New York City." This chance encounter was followed by a coast-to-coast airplane ride—and time for a talk. Barker was then with a newly organized firm, S&P/InterCapital, that was going through serious difficulties that later led to its demise. He was exploring the possibility of

"The speed with which Capital Guardian's assets grew vis-à-vis our mutual funds took us all by surprise," says Rothenberg. "Pension money came pouring into the Trust Company. The once dull business was suddenly exciting and prestigious." As pension assets piled up, so did the formulaic asset-based compensation payout to the new boys in Capital Guardian—much to the surprise and increasing concern of the senior investors managing the mutual funds. So financial compensation would be independent of the scale of assets each portfolio manager was managing, changes were made. But for several years, Capital's institutional business was larger than its mutual fund business and this clearly influenced such factors as prestige, visibility, and recognized contribution to overall firm profits.

A few worried that Capital was becoming too big to manage all its new assets really well and began discussing a corporate spin-off to separate the institutional business from the mutual funds. Understandably, several of the split-up advocates were in the faster-growing institutional side of the business. However, the larger shareholders in Capital managed the mutual funds and they protested: "You can't expect us to give up owning the growth side of the business and accept getting stuck with the stodgy mutual fund stuff. That would be crazy!" So the split-up idea never got anywhere.[10] Ironically, even with strong growth in Capital Guardian over the past 25 years, Capital's "stodgy" mutual fund business has grown even faster and is currently 50 percent larger than Capital Guardian.

Because the team at Capital Guardian wanted to develop a substantial business, it launched a major campaign for new accounts.

---

relocating to California to set up an individual investor counseling business and asked Kirby his views. "Too many seeking business from too few," was Kirby's way of explaining that there were already too many managers looking for the available business. Then he asked: "Why not join *us*?" And Barker soon signed on.

[10] The advances made in the architecture or organizational design of Capital—including the holding company structure now known as The Capital Group Companies, the multiple counselor system of managing investments, and the development of several research groups within Capital—have accomplished the main operational objectives of a split-up, particularly expanding the organizational decision-making and asset management capacities of Capital Group without a structural division of the organization.

Jim Fullerton took the lead and spoke persuasively about banks being primarily in the *custody* business, whereas Capital was entirely in the *investment* business. He would emphasize Capital's commitment to investment research—and then point with pride to the long-term record of ICA. While acknowledging graciously that the past record was no guarantee of future results, he also pointed out that ICA's record was the only objective measure available and was produced over many years through three factors: a consistent philosophy of investing, in-house research, and the people to implement both. Pension and endowment funds saw in Capital Guardian just the kind of can-do manager they most wanted.

As the corporate pension market opened up, many public pension funds also became major prospects. For years, most public pension funds had invested entirely in bonds—and paid very low fees. But change was in the offing. In the mid-sixties, the state of California changed its laws to allow public pension funds within the state to invest up to 25 percent in equities, and Los Angeles County promptly advertised in the newspapers for proposals to manage equities in its pension fund. Bob Kirby knew the County Treasurer,[11] who asked, "What's wrong with you guys? Everybody's submitting proposals except you!"

"Sure," explained Kirby, "they'll offer to do the work for *nothing* because they want the prestige of having a giant account like yours, and your selection process will surely focus on competitive fees. The other guys will all cut their fees, but we won't cut our fees. Since we know how the world works, we know we simply can't compete against those other guys' very low fees."

A month later, the two men met at a Merrill Lynch seminar. Los Angeles County still had no submission from Capital, and the Treasurer wouldn't let it drop, so he asked Kirby, "Can you come to my office around 10:00 or 11:00 tomorrow? I've got something to show you."

[11] Harold Ostley.

The next morning, Fullerton, Kirby, and Jon Lovelace were ushered into a huge office. At one end, were three flags standing in stanchions: Los Angeles County, State of California—and the American flag. "How do you like our American flag?" asked the country treasurer. Kirby blurted right out, "It's *awful.* Red, white . . . and . . . *purple!*"

"Competitive bidding," said the treasurer, with a big grin. "Now will you guys please submit your bid?"

So Capital did submit a bid, with a fee of ¼ of 1 percent, which was far higher than any of the others. Most trustees of a public pension fund are teachers, firefighters, and police officers, and although they are very cost conscious, they do not know the arcane ins and outs of investing, including the way fees are set. So when the question of fees came up during the final discussions about which managers to choose, the county treasurer leaned back in his chair and laconically advised the fund trustees: "I've made a very careful examination of the fees of all the different bidders and have determined that all the fees are within just ¼ of 1 percent of one another. So I think, in making their decision on managers, the Trustees can safely ignore any differences in fees!"

That statement instantly neutralized what Kirby had assumed would be the decisive factor against Capital—and it won the enormous account. Actually, the account started at only $10 million, but that was $10 million of cash flow per month. And in no time, it grew to be more than $100 million. Then Oregon came in with $40 million—again at full fee[12]—and Capital was off to a strong start with the public pension funds.

Since Capital had *no* institutional accounts with long-term records, Ned Bailey[13] and Jim Fullerton developed the "20-man slide

[12] Five *times* the fee that had been paid to Scudder, Stevens & Clark, Kirby's prior employer.
[13] Ned Bailey—combining a warm, dignified demeanor "on stage" with self-disciplined organization—was a highly effective salesperson for Capital Guardian Trust. As a dutiful son, Bailey flew to Cleveland each month to visit his widowed mother, and made a practice of adding two or three days of sales calls onto the weekends so the trips would be "productive."

show" for new business presentations. All they had were people—the investment professionals of Capital—so that's what they put in the slides: one slide for each person, one person on each slide. Slide after slide, they told about each of the remarkable professionals who had achieved those superior long-term results. It was an impressive story.

Fullerton and Kirby took their slide show out on the road, calling on the major pension funds around the country. They were at Monsanto when Kirby told what became known ruefully as "the $40 million joke." Meeting with a very serious senior financial officer, who dressed quite conservatively, they should have known what to expect. The slide showing Kirby came up and, after extolling his virtues as a professional investor, Fullerton gave some color about Kirby's personal life, including his years as a race car driver.[14] The man from Monsanto observed that "race cars sound pretty dangerous" and wondered aloud what might happen if Kirby were their manager and had an accident. Knowing the sequence of slides, Kirby decided to play his joke and asked for the next slide—which he knew was of Bill Newton—casually commenting, "Bill Newton would take over if I smashed up." And then, as though he simply could not resist, came the $40 million joke: "Bill drives race cars, too!" Needless to say, they never got that $40 million account.

Ever since General Mills decided to hire Capital Guardian as one of their major managers, other companies came looking. As Kirby recalls, "This was the very beginning of a massive tidal wave of pension fund money. The dough was rising so fast, some of us thought we should rename our company The Betty Crocker Trust!

As a result, Capital Guardian, a southern California manager, soon became a dominant investment manager for the conservative corporate establishment of Cleveland, Ohio. Trained as a lawyer, he was recommended to Capital by the personnel manager at Pacific Finance and held a series of important administrative positions, including heading up Personnel and facilitating the establishment of The Capital Group, Inc. Because he was not an investor, even as president of Capital Guardian, he could not rein in the disparate portfolio managers at the Trust Company—only an investment professional could discipline another investment professional.

[14] Kirby drove Porsches, owned two Porsche dealerships in Los Angeles and Phoenix, and had an arrangement wherein Porsche paid part of his expenses as a competitive driver.

We got a *ton* of business from the pension funds—particularly after *Institutional Investor* ran a big article on how brilliant General Mills was to pick us. All of a sudden—Whammo! In no time at all, every big company said, 'If they're good enough for General Mills, they're sure good enough for us.' We went like a rocketship from nothin' to a billion-and-a-half dollars under management."

Capital Guardian even got approached by people who had never been given a sales presentation. One day, a call came into Bailey's office from a prestigious boarding school, Phillips Academy, at Andover, Massachusetts. The caller announced: "Our finance committee met today, and we'd like to talk to you about possibly managing a third of our endowment." Bailey replied: "Gee, that's wonderful. What are the circumstances?" After describing the size of Andover's endowment, the caller concluded, "And your assignment will be twelve *million* dollars."

"Well, gosh, I'm sorry," replied Bailey. "We can't accept your account. Our minimum account size is $20 million."

After a long pause, the clearly surprised caller asked archly, "Do you realize that this is Phillips . . . Academy . . . at . . . Andover, and I'm telling you, as Chairman of the Finance Committee of Phillips . . . Academy . . . at . . . Andover, that we're thinking of hiring you?" To this, Bailey replied, "Well, this is Ned M. Bailey of the Cleveland Union High School, and I'm telling you that you don't meet our $20 million minimum."

"You know, we really thought we were magic," recalls Kirby. "We all felt like World War I fighter pilots—daring young men pushing out the frontiers. We spun in from nowhere and were eating the big banks' lunch. It was the thrill of victory more than anything else." And the victories came rapidly: Capital Guardian kept adding more and more new accounts as one of the great success stories of an exciting new era.[15] "We felt that we were doing things that mortal men would never dare to do—and *succeeding.*"

---

[15] Memorialized in 'Adam Smith's' *The Money Game,* Random House (June 1976).

Clients also thought they were succeeding by being less conventional and more daring. At General Mills, there was understandable euphoria. From 1968 to 1972, investment results were truly wonderful: The funds were up over 50 percent! General Mills' board of directors decided to take advantage of this good news. First, they eliminated the annual corporate contribution to the pension fund and that cost-saving—accomplished with just a stroke of a pen—increased earnings per share nicely. Next, the company returned to all the employees their personal matching contributions. This really helped boost employee morale.

With the benefit of hindsight, Kirby reflects, "We were crazy to allow ourselves to grow as rapidly as we did. But how can you say, 'No' when somebody calls on the phone and says: 'This is Whirlpool—or Armco Steel or Merck—calling, and we want you to be a major investment manager for our pension fund.' We didn't say, 'No.' We said, 'Let's go!'"[16] But with all this opportunity, Capital Guardian's portfolio managers were not managing their clients' portfolios: They were out winning new business—lots of new business.

As the new business piled up, Capital Guardian very nearly self-destructed. Several factors were at work. Many of the senior portfolio managers were new to Capital—and to each other. And in looking for independent people, Capital Guardian couldn't have picked a more disparate group of portfolio managers. Each managed portfolios in a very different way. Even worse, they got separated from Capital's great strength—its own research—and, instead, bought Wall Street's favorite hot stocks like Sterling Homex and Mohawk Data Systems, taking increased market risk, hoping to get higher returns without recognizing the difference between luck and skill. Capital Guardian's portfolio managers were almost *looking* for trouble if the market ever turned down. And when the market did turn down, they didn't have to look for trouble: Trouble came looking for them!

Contributing to the trouble was a clumsy adaptation of the multiple counselor system without the rigorous process planning

[16] *Institutional Investor,* interview by Heidi S. Fiske, June 1987, pp. 35–37.

and administrative care that had characterized each stage of the system's development within the mutual fund company. Managers were simply paired: Portfolios were just bolted together. There was much too much differentiation in investment styles and far too little communication and coordination among portfolio managers. There was no consistency, no disciplined investment process, and no unifying concept of investment management. If two clients compared their investment results, they could be significantly and inexplicably different.

The worst of times at Capital Guardian may have been when Kirby, who was 100 percent invested in the portion of a pension fund that he managed, arrived at a client meeting only to discover the total account was actually 30 percent in cash because his comanager had an enormous cash reserve of 60 percent in his portion of the total portfolio.

As Kirby recalls, "While one guy was deep into all the zingy hot stocks, another guy was mostly in cash, holed up like Chicken Little, scared to death that the world was coming to an end. Anyway, we did everything wrong that was conceivable to do. During the stock market's 1970 to 1974 'adjustment phase,' our numbers were just *awful*," particularly in 1973 and 1974. In mid-1974, ITT invited a group of institutional investors to go on a two-week tour of its operations in Europe. "That tour had us running around so frantically," recalls Kirby, "I hadn't looked at the prices of anything for two weeks. When we got back from that trip, I couldn't believe how much prices had changed. When I punched out my portfolio on the Quotron machine, I turned to Ned Bailey and said, 'Gee, look at that: All my stocks split 2-for-1 while I was in Europe!' "

Capital Guardian nearly imploded as assets went from $1.5 billion all the way down to $600 million, caused partly by the stock market's falloff in 1973 and 1974, but primarily by clients departing, often abruptly. Capital Guardian was in serious trouble—and deserved to be.

Trouble was at least as serious a matter at a major client like General Mills: The year 1972 brought sudden change—not just in the *rate* of change, but in the *direction* of change. The market was down sharply and headed lower. Unexpectedly, General Mills was told by its actuaries that it had to make a major cash "contribution" to the pension fund: a direct charge to earnings. Significantly and without warning, it broke up General Mills' historic pattern of moderately, but consistently, rising earnings. This was a major negative event for an acquisition-oriented company whose stock price, or "acquisition currency," depended on a relatively high Price/Earnings multiple and that in turn depended on investors' confidence in General Mills' steady growth in earnings. That confidence was now history.

With the stock market declining substantially and repeatedly, a formal motion was brought by one of General Mills' directors to own *zero* equities in the pension fund. In this disturbing environment, Capital Guardian's internal problems made its termination clearly inevitable. Other clients were terminating too.

One particularly harrowing meeting was with Ford Motor. Ford routinely prepared a slide show review of each manager's record. Bob White, the Assistant Treasurer, gave a deliberately monotone review of the particulars of the portfolio and then a slide flashed on the screen showing where the manager's results came in: Outstanding, Good, Satisfactory, or Unsatisfactory. After a careful and detailed review of Capital Guardian's portfolio for the past two years, a slide went up. It said: "*Un*satisfactory." Then for one year: "*Un*satisfactory." Then for six months: "*Un*satisfactory." And for three months: "*Un*satisfactory." Shanahan leaned over to Kirby to say: "All they're going to do is fire us, for crissake. Why didn't they just call us in L.A.?"

"But they didn't fire us," says Kirby. "In fact, Ford is today one of the longest and best clients we have. Still, after that meeting we got on the plane in Detroit and staggered off in California so drunk we left our car at the airport and took a cab home."

"I discovered during that period that I'm a fatalist," recalls Kirby, shaking his head. "I gradually became numbed to the whole thing and just walked woodenly into the office every day to take my medicine—or out to the airplane to talk to clients and have them say 'Good-bye.' "

The nadir for Capital Guardian was reached on June 30, 1973.[17] At that moment, one account, the Kettering Foundation, had underperformed the market by an astounding 32 percentage points in just 18 months. One benefit of investment results getting so bad so fast was that some clients would say, as Kettering did, "There's no way we're going to fire them *now*.[18] The only way we'll ever get back to where we started is if we keep the yo-yos and hope they keep their crazy portfolios."

The problems at Capital Guardian were not limited to being committed to value stocks that were out of favor in a growth-oriented stock market nor even to the way portfolio managers ignored in-house research as they tried to outperform by chasing Wall Street's "story stocks." No matter how disconcerting the difficulties of being—for several painful years—in the wrong place at the wrong time as investors, these problems were only temporary. The real and long-term problems were organizational, both structural and personal.[19] In May of 1972, Bob Kirby and Howard

[17] "In June of 1973, Capital Guardian Trust lost ten accounts—and won six—all for the very same reason: our commitment to *value* investing!" ruefully recalls Mike Shanahan.

[18] Ray Miller, chief financial officer of the Kettering Foundation, performed a key role in maintaining the relationship during this period.

[19] *Not* assimilating individuals into Capital continues to be a challenge as the "other side of the coin" for the informal person-to-person collegiality so prized by Capital people. Bill Hurt explains, "I've been at Capital 28 years—but I still think of myself as an outsider. (That's *my* perception—hopefully, not others.') Almost all the other folks here essentially know only Capital. I'd been head of Marketing & Research and part of the executive committee at Dean Witter. It was a much different culture: essentially a sales organization, not an investment management one. Capital's value system, priorities, and personalities are focused exclusively on *objectively* trying to divine the shape of the future and its positives and negatives, like them or not. Dean Witter's focus, like the rest of Wall Street's, was on *persuading* its customers that they knew the future and that what their investment banking clients wanted to sell belonged in their portfolios. It was crisply hierarchical with all the perks that go with being near the top of the pyramid: secretaries in N.Y. and L.A., limos, private dining rooms—the whole shooting match; all the accoutrements that arm the broker to write the ticket. At Capital, I'm still adjusting to the culture shock: getting my own coffee, having just part of an assistant to type reports, and ordering pastrami sandwiches for lunch."

Schow knew something major had to be done and had gone to see Jon Lovelace[20] to see if he would object to Mike Shanahan being put in charge. Lovelace said he understood, and Shanahan was soon made chairman of the Trust Company.

After relinquishing his position as research manager to David Fisher, Shanahan went into the Trust Company to correct the mess. His objective was to provide much-needed leadership to a group of individualists who were not only new to Capital, but also were in a business fundamentally different from the mutual fund business in its economics, its competition, and its market.

Shanahan was certainly not without resources: Brilliant and clear-minded, he is strong-willed and tenacious. Having earned the strong confidence of Jon Lovelace over many years, Shanahan also knew he had the necessary support to prevail if there were any serious confrontation. Shanahan made few visible waves in restoring order: Portfolio managers were obliged to meet together so they would share ideas and information and learn to communicate with each other about investments. Under Shanahan's leadership, Capital Guardian's portfolio managers were soon buying the cheap blue chips: Exxon and Du Pont and AT&T, while most other firms owned highfliers like Xerox, Avon, and Polaroid in the era of the "two-tier" stock market.[21] Portfolios at Capital Guardian were increasingly concentrated in the companies followed by Capital's own analysts, while freelance ideas from Wall Street were avoided. Portfolio turnover was greatly reduced. Each portfolio manager's investment results were reported regularly and frequently. Soon, a classic reform was underway with Shanahan the clearly recognized leader. But the obvious question about Capital Guardian's hurtful separation from the disciplines and research of Capital remained unanswered: Why had it been allowed to happen? Why had it been allowed to continue for so long? There was no obvious answer, only a promise: "Never again!"

---

[20] Lovelace and his family were on the island of Majorca in the second month of his four-month sabbatical.

[21] Enshrined in stock market history by Carol J. Loomis of *Fortune*.

On one level, the issue for Capital Guardian became how to deal with the "two-tier market." When an *Institutional Investor* reporter asked Kirby what they were going to do, since continuing on the present path, Capital Guardian would soon be going out of business, he replied, "Well, yeah, maybe we are. But I can tell you this: The one thing we are *not* going to do is fade back into our own end-zone and throw a Hail Mary pass, hoping that somebody's going to catch it and save our bacon. Sooner or later, people are not going to pay 80 times earnings for Polaroid, while they pay six times for International Paper. And if we've got any clients left when that happens, they'll be okay."

Then in 1974, the call came from Mobil. Shanahan knew what was going to happen: "Why make us go all the way to New York City just to get fired? Why can't they just do it over the telephone?" But they had to go. They went—and marched silently into the client's[22] office, where he said, "These results are *abominable!* What are you going to do?" The answer was meekly stated: No change was planned. The client's answer was a surprise: "Okay! That's exactly what I wanted to hear!" And, surprisingly, Capital Guardian was retained.

Simultaneously, Shanahan's professional disciplines were taking hold. It took time and money to convert from simple fiat to a true process-based way of multiple-manager investing—and disciplines had to be enforced. Converting from independence to coordination in managing institutional accounts—with each account having different amounts and different timing of cash flows—was difficult and sometimes painful. "It was pretty ugly work for the next year or so," says Rothenberg. "Mike still carries some of the scars from that period of stress. As he once put it, he was sent to Purgatory in the Trust Company."

About the time that Shanahan had the most important organizational restructuring done, the stocks of the companies Capital Group usually invests in—large-cap value stocks—were beginning to have their time in the sun. "It sure helps to have luck running with you!

[22] Charles Clune.

We'd been like the proverbial voice calling out in the wilderness, while the one decision, Nifty Fifty stocks created the famous two-tier market. Then the Nifty Fifty took a plunge and Lady Luck smiled on us. Capital Guardian did much better than the market: 1977 to 1978 saved us. We had very strong *relative* results, and our business really took off." Considerable effort was also put into building stronger relationships with clients, including regular client research conferences.[23]

From the mid-1970s, Capital Guardian enjoyed a double win with institutional clients: While most other managers were still too cautious on stocks, Capital Guardian was consistently fully invested, and the stocks that Capital most likes to invest in were achieving strong results. Kirby described investing in 1977, the year in which the firm won more new accounts than any other manager, this way: "It's been a long time since there was such a clear-cut advantage of equities over bonds. Stocks are now cheap enough so that, looking ahead a couple of years, the market will definitely be higher than it is now. And the fact that everyone is buying fixed income just reinforces our feeling that equities are about to enter a giant and extended catch-up phase.

"Our definition of value is to think as though we are buying a whole company, not just a stock certificate. And when Halliburton, which two years ago sold in the 40-plus P/E range, is suddenly selling for just 10 times earnings and still growing at 12 to 15 percent a year, that's *value*. After all, we'd much rather have a growth company than a cyclical—just like any other sensible investor.

"Remember the Kettering Foundation, for whom we had underperformed the market by a full 32 percentage points in just 18 months?" asks Kirby. "It took only two-and-a-half years more before, over the life of the account, they were *ahead* of the market." With good results based on Capital's own research and a commitment to client service, Capital Guardian's assets under management were, in

---

[23] Initiated in 1974, these biannual conferences require extensive preparation by Capital Group's analysts and significant time commitment by clients.

the late 1970s, almost 50 percent larger than the assets in the mutual funds: $7 billion versus $5 billion.

Capital Guardian has two significant business tilts. First, it is much larger in equities than fixed-income investing. And second, the organization's business is dominated by defined-benefit pension funds, while employee benefit plans are shifting toward defined-contribution funds, and particularly to 401(k) plans, which involve lots of record keeping and other participant services.

In recent years—even with good investment results and relatively low fees—Capital Guardian has found itself fighting a rearguard action against the unrelenting challenge of index funds, a particularly significant challenge with very large clients, who often use passive investing as a default alternative when unable to identify enough active investors to manage their enormous equity assets or have simply despaired of ever finding reliably exceptional active managers. Capital Guardian was losing domestic equity business fairly steadily—offset by its gains in international business—until the turbulent markets around the turn of the century once again provided a target-rich environment for Capital's research-based approach to investing and its long-term focus on achieving superior results.

In addition to producing good investment results with a disciplined process based squarely on Capital's proprietary research, Capital Guardian has made a major commitment to developing complementary strength in high-level relationship management. This commitment did not come easily or naturally: Years ago, such a commitment was scoffed at. In the mid-1970s, Shanahan famously observed: "We have calculated how much clients lose by insisting on portfolio managers leaving their duty stations and making presentations at review meetings with clients. Here's what we learned: It costs nearly one quarter of 1 percent in annual investment results per meeting! So, we're asking: Just how many personal meetings with your portfolio manager do you really want?" From this low base—and more slowly than most institutional investment managers—Capital Guardian came to recognize that strong working relationships and

superior investor services are important complements to good investment results—so clients understand just how good results have been
and will be achieved.

Strong relationship managers are increasingly valuable to clients
as the size and, even more importantly, the complexity of investment
management mandates increase. A large institutional client can have
Capital Guardian managing several different kinds of investments—
from high-yield bonds to emerging market equities—and a multinational corporation may have funds being managed in several different countries. It is very hard for a portfolio counselor who specializes
in one kind of investing to stay on top of the portfolio he is managing
and know all about the portfolios he's not managing. But an effective
relationship manager can know several different portfolios well
enough to explain, to a client's full satisfaction, how they are structured and why. Such a manager can be so well informed about each
client that the explanations will fit well with the client's overall investment guidelines and its objectives for a successful long-term
working relationship with Capital. As usual at Capital, change came
slowly and deliberately—but decisively. High-level relationship management efforts began when Dick Barker and Bob Kirby, both more
marketing oriented, came into leadership roles. The change began
with just one dedicated person and then expanded as its benefits were
demonstrated.[24] Capital Guardian now has two dozen professional
relationship managers.

To develop unusually strong and mutually beneficial relationships, relationship management Discovery Meetings are conducted
each year with every client—and with most major prospects. With
each client's fund executive, Capital Guardian's relationship manager

[24] John Seiter was the first senior who concentrated entirely on client relationship management. He grew up in California, married his high school sweetheart, and studied at the University of the Redlands. On his father's advice, he got into institutional investing at Scudder,
Stevens & Clark's Los Angeles office, where he met Bob Kirby; went to WE Hutton, and
then to Lionel D. Edie. He was about to join Chase Manhattan Bank when he got a call,
after six months of consideration, from Bill Hurt, inviting him to join Capital in 1986.

goes through an extensive list of specific components of a first-rate working relationship, item by item, to identify current strengths and areas where improvement is needed and specific ways to be of greater service. While always interested in more business, the real focus in these Discovery Meetings is on better business, and on working more successfully with each client. Capital Guardian now manages assets for more than half of U.S. institutions with over $10 billion in assets. In the United States, it wins 40 percent of all the new business competitions it participates in. Overseas, it is closing 60 percent.

Another helpful development has involved changing compensation. In any organization, compensation dissonance interferes with the smooth implementation of strategy. This was, until recently, something of a problem at Capital Guardian. With substantial past growth in the number of institutional clients served, particularly in the United States, the business priority has shifted from obtaining more new clients to keeping current clients. The organization's goal is to grow with them and gain share of assets by cross-selling more and more of Capital's different investing capabilities.

In the past, financial incentives emphasized new business development and focused on getting new accounts more than on serving and building up existing relationships. The old compensation plan was made up of a relatively high percentage payout based on the fees paid for the first two years, but it dropped to a low level thereafter. This meant that relationship managers were financially motivated to win more new accounts than they were able to serve well. Now, the relationship manager receives a smaller, but continuing payout, based on a percentage of the annual fees paid by clients served. That payout varies with three factors: quality of client service; business developed with established clients or with new clients; and internal teamwork.

The third part of the client service strategy is a series of in-depth, semiannual reviews with each relationship manager of all his or her clients and all serious prospects, to assure that the specific action plans developed for each client and each prospect are being fully realized. Any relationship managers not able to implement all plans fully will have their list of prospects and clients reduced until commitments and fulfillment are back in alignment.

With good balance in relationship management and investment management, plus an increasingly full and balanced line of investment capabilities and a major presence in each of the world's major institutional investment markets, Capital has developed a model institutional investment business on a worldwide basis and is gaining market share in each of the world's major national markets.

CHAPTER 10

GLOBAL INVESTING

NOTES FOR READERS

Time used effectively, particularly when favored by the fertile unfolding of events and opportunities—what we cheerfully call "luck" or "timing"—is often the decisive resource in the successful development of corporate strategy. (As General Douglas MacArthur said, "The history of warfare can be written in just nine letters: *Not in time!*") Time and timing have both been important factors in Capital's growth in international investing.[1]

The key factors in the overall story of Capital Group Companies are also key in the story of international investing at Capital. Strong Lovelace support was crucial for the realization of an abstract concept of a differentiating venture that was "rationally irrational" at the beginning, when both the external and internal data gave little reason to push boldly forward. There was ample reason not to proceed:

---

[1] With 40 percent of its research analysts born outside the United States, Capital increasingly uses the term "non-U.S." instead of "international" and includes U.S. investing in "global."

The venture would depend on innovators who were "outsiders," and operating losses would have to be absorbed for many years. In addition, despite deeply felt and sincerely articulated resistance, the Capital organization would have to move forward at a moderate but persistent pace, adapting to developing opportunities over two long decades.

Capital's international investing began back in the mid-1950s. Time and again, the reasons for restraint or retreat were credible. In the beginning, international investing was a very small business—for the industry and for Capital—and no investment manager was doing very well in that business. Demand from individual or institutional investors was virtually nil—and prospects for change dour. Some key individuals were difficult in personality and distant in location. In the nadir years of the late 1960s and early 1970s, when Capital kept losing money in its international business and was only moderately profitable in its domestic business, the cost of closing down the fledgling international operation must have appeared quite small.

For many years, the only reason for going forward was steady support from both Lovelaces on a very personal level, apparently based on little more than inspired intuition. (Short-term rationality often focuses on data dominated by the recent past, whereas long-term rationality is often hard to document or prove.)

Jon Lovelace's continuing personal commitment to global investing was crucial for what, to the amazement of most observers inside and outside Capital, has become a very big business and a very large part of Capital. By the end of the twentieth century, international was nearly half as large as domestic Capital.

Looking ahead, international's continuing challenges are classic: how to be sufficiently local and also sufficiently global; how to sink deep roots into each national market without making its key contributors geographic prisoners of their own past successes—unable to move up or laterally because they are irreplaceable where they have done so very well; how to understand and deal effectively with the substantial differences in business ethics that exist from one country to another, particularly in the many emerging market countries; how to keep the central organization open for the "returning hero" who has loyally invested many years of her or his career serving in a distant market; and how to sustain fairness in personal and professional growth and in compensation for everyone when hundreds of professionals are working in many countries with real differences in compensation norms, taxes, and changing rates of exchange—and very different business and professional challenges and opportunities. Capital recognizes that it must meet all these challenges to become a truly One-Firm firm worldwide.

"WHY DOES A West Coast . . . domestic . . . value manager . . . need to continue losing money on international research and investing?"

Good question, particularly in the mid-1970s when the history of international investing was consistently negative. In the United States, out of several hundred investment management organizations, only two other firms—Templeton and Scudder, Stevens & Clark—were regularly investing internationally. And neither was enjoying any real business success.[2]

After nearly two decades of moderate, but steady operating losses in its Geneva operations business, Capital faced several serious problems: Capital Guardian Trust was hemorrhaging institutional business badly; mutual fund sales were at a 20-year low and AFD was losing money and most of its wholesalers (see Chapter 5);

---

[2] Morgan Guaranty would, in 1974, announce its decision to invest up to 5 percent of pension equities internationally. Fidelity and Putnam were also early, but only occasional buyers of "foreign" stocks. The money invested internationally in those early days was invested primarily in England and the Netherlands. In most countries in Europe and in all countries in Latin America and Asia, accounting was opaque and unreliable.

the outlook for the investment management business was grim; and Capital as a whole had lost money in one recent quarter.[3]

"Most of our portfolio managers were quite negative on international investing—and with good reasons, as they saw them," acknowledges David Fisher,[4] who would soon become a leader for this orphan business.

International investing had started at Capital when Coleman Morton with support from Jonathan Bell Lovelace established a small international investment staff in 1955[5]—three full decades before such an idea would even start to become generally popular in the United States. Intrigued by the Paley Report that projected serious U.S. shortages of important raw materials, JBL decided to back Morton and give it a try.

Capital's prior experience with international investing had been far from encouraging. Just two years before, in 1952, Morton had been intrigued with foreign investing. Deciding to focus on Latin America, he arranged visits[6] during the next year to all the major

---

[3] The first quarter of 1975.

[4] David Fisher grew up in modest circumstances, living with his parents in an apartment in their small motel in Palm Springs. "Everything in life is accidental," says Fisher of the early steps in his career. Only 10 of 100 in his high school class went on to college. Fisher went to the University of California-Berkley on an ROTC scholarship and, after graduation, went into uniform at Ft. Leonard Wood in Missouri. Learning that his military obligation could be shortened if he were in graduate school and that the nearby University of Missouri Business School had a program in marketing, he said "Sign me up!" and off he went. Along the way, Fisher took the one course offered on investing. After graduation, Fisher worked under Jack Welch in polymer plastics at General Electric. After three years at General Electric, he was recruited to be an analyst in electrical equipment at Smith Barney. "I'd never heard of Smith Barney," Fisher confesses. "In 1968, I made my first research call on an institutional investor: It was Capital and their analyst was Mike Shanahan. Then, another break for me, Mike asked me to help him train a new analyst. This gave Mike and me a chance to get to know each other pretty well." When Shanahan got promoted to research director, Fisher got invited to join Capital to cover electrical equipment—which he did from 1969 to 1972. Coverage was expanded to include consumer electronics just when the Japanese were fast expanding with names like Sony, Panasonic, and Hitachi. "So the obvious thing for me to do was to head for Japan. Except for one quick visit to Tijuana, this would be my first trip outside America."

[5] Capital's first international investment was made by ICA in 1954: Royal Dutch Petroleum.

[6] Through Arthur Andersen and the Chase Manhattan Bank.

cities and made plans[7] to launch the Pan-American Fund. There was *no* investor interest and *no* broker interest, so he soon abandoned that idea. "Actually, of course, as we all know today," chuckles Morton, recalling the ironic good fortune of an early, quick failure, "that was *very* lucky." South American countries were just then entering a long, dark era of totalitarian governments and seriously constricted economies. It would be more than a generation before investors would realize good profits from the potentialities of Latin America—even though the possibilities were as exciting then as they are now.[8]

[7] With Hardy Hall, who ran the New York office.

[8] "The Pan-American venture got us in touch with Leo Model of Model Roland," recalls Morton. "We got together in a project involving Borax Consolidated with Leo Model and Eddie Webster of Kidder Peabody. It didn't last very long. We'd bought an initial position of 10 percent of Borax's stock and were expecting to offer to buy the rest—but the stock ran up *three*-fold. So we accepted 'defeat'—with some grace and some pleasure—and took our profit."

By then, Capital was at least linked with "international." "Borax Consolidated was a foreign company and we'd been involved. The Pan-American Fund was international—or at least would have been. That meant, of course," laughs Morton, "that we must be great experts at international investing! The Paley Report, forecasting severe shortages in various minerals, had just come out and was attracting attention to investing in natural resources—globally. So with solid support from Ward Bishop, in 1961 we took over International Resources Fund (which was a combination of several small natural resource funds) and added what we euphemistically were then calling 'Human Resources'—and got into international investing." Morton shakes his head and smiles ruefully, "Our adventure was not to last very long."

Hired to work with Coleman Morton on International Resources Fund, Harry G.A. Seggerman played a key role in the initial period. As an oil analyst, he was soon covering the international oil companies, including the Dutch and British internationals. Attracted by the long-term investment opportunities of investing internationally, he migrated easily from being an oil analyst to being an international analyst. Seggerman covered Japanese companies and contributed importantly to Capital's being, in 1959, the first institutional investor—via International Resources Fund—to invest significantly in Japanese stocks. His initial coup was to recognize that Japanese insurance companies were significantly overstating reserves—and therefore substantially understating earnings. This was when Japanese bank shares sold at 3 times earnings and their dividends yielded 9 percent, and Nomura's salespeople were on such tight expense budgets that Capital would buy them lunch. Difficult to work with, Seggerman left Capital "well known and well recognized," and for many years successfully ran The Japan Fund (a joint venture of Prudential Bache, Paine Webber, and Nikko Securities). In 1969, he joined Fidelity Investments where he started Fidelity Pacific Fund, that company's first overseas investment venture, and was Vice Chairman of Fidelity until 2001. (He died later that

In 1955, with the International Resources Fund, Capital became one of the first American institutions to invest internationally. At Morton's[9] urging, Capital acquired the management company of Natural Resources Fund and its companion, Natural Resources of Canada, and merged them together. Unfortunately, Capital failed to study the shareholder base, which included large numbers of very small shareholdings. This made the fund very expensive to administer and service.

Small as it was—and despite its persistent losses—JL would insist on keeping the international effort going through the long, lean years that followed. As Fisher explains with obvious appreciation, "Jon fought the battle for international in the early sixties."

Capital International began with Ken Mathysen-Gerst,[10] a Dutchman wanting to focus on international investing as a way to become personally and professionally independent. In the spring of 1962,[11] the decision was made to establish an office in Europe,[12] primarily to monitor the international operations of U.S. corporations, but also to track their European competitors. The Geneva office was expected to find international stocks that Capital's U.S.

year, at 73, while serving as president of International Investment Advisors, a hedge fund investing in South Korean securities.)

[9] In 1968, Morton left Capital again to try a venture: International Geo Marine—aimed at capitalizing on the "hot holes" discovered in the Red Sea. It was liquidated in 1970 because of continuing war risks in the Middle East.

[10] Ken Mathysen-Gerst began with a 1958 summer job offered in this way by Jim Fullerton, "If you can make your way out here to California on your own, you're hired—for the summer" and then joined Capital full time in 1959. Born and raised in Indonesia, where his father worked for Royal Dutch Shell (and was imprisoned by the Japanese during World War II), he had lived for awhile in Mexico and served in the U.S. Marine Corps. As a result, he was entitled to hold Dutch, Swiss, and American passports simultaneously. This gave him assurance that he would be able to survive no matter what developed in the world.

[11] JBL and Coleman Morton participated in this meeting in New York City.

[12] Mathysen-Gerst had ruled out London as "too obvious and not really Europe" and both Germany and France because "the other country would not like it"; and although he was Dutch, he rejected the Netherlands; Belgium would not do since his French was inadequate; but he could improve his French in Geneva and the city was centrally located, so Geneva it was. (Some said it was the proximity to good skiing that convinced Mathysen-Gerst to pick Geneva. Others point out that the airport was close to the city.)

mutual funds could invest in. Investment Company of America had more than 10 percent of its portfolio invested outside the United States in the early 1960s—a full 25 years before such investing was considered "okay." This was a level far higher than most mutual funds would even consider, so Capital was developing what would later be a unique record of investing internationally *and* getting good results.

Unusual as it was, the conceptual foundation supporting Capital's early commitment to international investing and international research was strong. Price/Earnings multiples abroad were obviously lower, particularly in early 1962 when the U.S. stock market was at a high level. This valuation bargain was attractive to a long-term value investor like Capital. In addition, the decisive competitive advantage for more and more American companies was coming from their business outside the United States.[13] And, as international competitiveness increased, Capital's research analysts wanted to know the foreign competitors firsthand to gauge the long-term prospects for American corporations competing in global markets.

Ken Mathysen-Gerst, with Jon Lovelace's support, initiated Capital International.[14] "Both loved numbers," recalls Nilly Sikorsky, "but they were never close personal friends. Mathysen-Gerst was almost incapable of showing his feelings for others or making normal personal attachments."

---

[13] For example, today, Wal-Mart is no. 1 in São Paulo, Brazil, and no. 2 in Buenos Aires, Argentina.

[14] After his heart attack, JBL made an annual trip with his wife to the UK, France, and Italy; so he added Geneva, often staying long enough for at least three sequential dinners: one at Ken Mathysen-Gerst's home, one at Thierry Vandeventer's home, and one in a hotel where JBL would be host. Not only could these small dinners include everyone, there was considerable interim telephone and correspondence contact.

Thierry Vandeventer joined Capital in 1963 after graduating from Harvard Business School. He set aside offers from J.P. Morgan and Chase, which gave his father cause for concern—as did the unsavory general reputation of "financial Californians." Jon Lovelace and Jim Fullerton impressed Vandeventer, who had only one half-hour interview with Ken Mathysen-Gerst. It took place in a cab ride from New York City's midtown Yale Club to La Guardia, where Ken was catching a plane to Washington.

Initially, the Geneva "office" was in Mathysen-Gerst's garage.[15] A real office finally opened in 1963—the same year that the new Interest Equalization Tax snuffed out all hope of any American interest in international investing. The dismal outlook for international investing was symbolized by International Resources Fund being quietly merged into Investment Company of America.

Jon Lovelace sustained Capital's strategic commitment to its international business despite more than 20 years of continuous losses[16] plus a lot of dissatisfaction from those in Los Angeles who couldn't see the merit of staying committed to global investing. Lovelace gave Capital the vital and irreplaceable advantage of time in place as an international investor with what became a real record of results. Although his leadership may not have seemed entirely rational, in retrospect, it made all the difference: Lovelace had a strong sense of the potential importance of international investing. David Fisher was the energetic entrepreneur needed to build the business, particularly for investing in the emerging markets (see Chapter 11).

Capital's international commitment led it to develop in the late 1960s what soon became the global standard for measuring international investment results: the EAFE Index (EAFE is an acronym for the combined stock markets of Europe, Australia, and the Far East). The original initiative to develop the requisite database came from Chuck Schimpff, who believed that to invest internationally in a responsible, fiduciary manner and know whether portfolio counselors were truly adding value, Capital must have an objective and impartial

---

[15] To provide enough capital for operating expenses, Morton and Lovelace authorized and solemnly signed a $50,000 Letter of Credit—but they were not officially authorized signatories, so Hardy Hall and his secretary, Hazel Lazell, signed the official authorization. With that "authorization," Mathysen-Gerst was off to Geneva. Waiting in line to open the initial bank account in June 1962, he could hear the wails of others ahead of him in the line: They were closing their accounts and bemoaning their large market losses. Over and over, the same question kept coming to his mind: "What am I *doing* and what have I gotten Capital into?"

[16] While operating losses were real, measuring them would have conflicted with Lovelace's determination to stay away from "profit-center accounting." He preferred to consider these expenditures "investments."

standard for comparison. EAFE was created for that purpose. Most of the necessary data had never been collected or organized before.

In addition to providing an objective measurement of results for Capital's internal management, in 1970 the firm would distribute the EAFE index and the supporting data externally as *Capital International Perspective*[17] to help cover the large costs being incurred in Geneva. "It's doubtful that Ken really trusted Jon to continue to support the company's paying for the Geneva office expenses year after year," acknowledges Shanahan, who recalls another pragmatic reason for establishing the EAFE index: "Composing and compiling the data

---

[17] "In the very early years, local stockbrokers were used to provide custody for the mutual funds' securities. Later, since Chase Manhattan Bank was Capital's European custodian and key people on both sides had personal ties, it was only natural that Chase would be invited to co-venture *Capital International S.A.,*" explains Thierry Vandeventer. Mike Shanahan continues, "Chase was our international custodian and, in those days, our stockbroker, too. With their custody fees plus 'courtage' (a trading tax which Chase could benefit from), the business we were doing was more profitable to them than it was to us."

Nilly Sikorsky would soon be doing most of the often-laborious work of finding, collecting, and organizing the extensive data required and was principally responsible for producing what became widely known and respected as *Capital International Perspective*. Nilly Sikorsky was born in Egypt. As a Jew, her father had had to leave Egypt when tensions between Arabs and Jews became more and more serious in the 1950s. In Switzerland, he became a leading dealer in Iraqi rugs. "Before we were forced to leave Egypt," explains Sikorsky, "our family was very wealthy. Then we had nothing. As a university student in the early 1960s, I was, of course, very leftist and quite interested in socialism. We all were. I needed a job to stay in the university. Only one advertisement for part-time work appeared in the newspaper, so I was going to take it." Sikorsky planned to start working after the New Year, but Mathysen-Gerst, who was not above using people, said, "Given your religion, December 25th has no meaning for you. Why not start that day? We have urgent work to get done before year-end!"

"The vision of how to develop the EAFE index was all Ken's," recalls Nilly Sikorsky. "I took care of the details." Thierry Vandeventer understood the necessary mathematics and conceptualized an effective way to design the EAFE Index based on structured sampling of the major stock markets of the world, matching the sample to the Universe on such characteristics as size, industry, and country. (Battelle Memorial Institute consultants also assisted.) Sikorsky continues, "Ken was a true visionary—and made a practice of explaining things to others as a way of working out and clarifying his own thought process. Everything I know, I learned from Ken. He could see that China would be a great power, and that gold would not stay at $40. And Ken was the first to *know* that the economies of the world would all necessarily become interrelated and then integrated—so investors and investing *must* become global."

for the EAFE Index was done, as much as anything, to keep the Capital analysts in Geneva occupied."

Looking for help in developing the business, Bob Egelston invited Chase Manhattan Bank to become a 50/50 owner of Capital International in 1972. The invitation was accepted, but the arrangement never worked well. Chase and Capital each made important assumptions—and both were wrong. Chase expected to get enhanced international credibility, and Capital expected to get substantial help with international distribution. But there was no compensation incentive for the individual branch managers at Chase to help Capital, so they did very little—and a joint venture company that invested in equities did little to strengthen the international stature of a large commercial bank.[18] (In 1986, David Fisher would arrange the sale to Morgan Stanley of the marketing rights to the international stockmarket index business and the publication of *Capital International Perspective*.[19] The price agreed on more than recovered Capital's accumulated losses and provided a good return on the capital invested in developing the business.)

Capital has faced and surely will continue to face formidable problems as it expands globally, particularly in working through joint ventures. One of Capital's oldest and strongest joint venture relationships, the Capital Italia Fund in Italy, began when visitors came to the New York office in the early 1970s, wanting to start a mutual fund that would be 50 percent invested in Italy and 50 percent outside Italy, which would be key to attracting Italian investors.[20] A significant business developed in the early 1970s: Capital Italia Fund's non-Italian portfolio and the Capital International

---

[18] In frustration because Chase did not sell the services of the joint venture as vigorously as it sold its own capabilities, Capital Group bought it back in 1980.

[19] Thereafter known as *Morgan Stanley Capital International Perspective*. Capital Group continues to hold a minority interest.

[20] The Agnellis knew Chase Manhattan's David Rockefeller, so Capital was one of several mutual fund organizations evaluated.

Fund—both distributed entirely outside the United States—have been managed by Capital out of Geneva for over 30 years.[21]

JL turned his attention to developing Capital's global investment management business, with a particular focus on designing and launching an appropriate mutual fund for U.S. investors. One of his key actions in 1973 was recruiting Walter Stern,[22] who was Research Director at Burnham & Co., to serve as chairman of the New Perspective Fund. Among the retail stockbrokers who might sell Capital's new fund to their customers, Stern would be recognized as "knowing something about international investing," and this was important because its prospectus authorized New Perspective to invest up to 25 percent of its portfolio outside the United States.[23] (When New Perspective Fund was underwritten in 1973, it was the second largest mutual fund offering ever made[24]—and was a major step in the visible development of Capital's global and international business.)

Mathysen-Gerst wanted autonomy and sought to make Geneva a profit center[25] that could stand on its own, but Lovelace and Shanahan were strongly opposed to separate business units—at least in part because Greenwich Management had failed. So there was an unavoidable test of views and wills and the inevitable result was that Mathysen-Gerst left and went to Lombard Odier. He left, in part, for higher pay and the perceived prestige of partnership in a leading

---

[21] Until the Italian bank acquired Boston's Pioneer Funds in 2000. In Canada, the Bank of Nova Scotia distributes several mutual fund products, including funds for defined contribution employee benefit funds.

[22] Stern was particularly interested in international research and investing. Burnham & Co. was one of the few U.S. securities organizations with experience or capability in "foreign stocks," as international investing was then known. Stern was a graduate of Williams College, where he had known Howard Schow, and Harvard Business School. Low-key, but widely recognized and well respected as a leader in the development of securities analysis as a profession, he has been a strongly supportive leader in Capital's international development for three decades.

[23] This was raised to 30 percent when the Interest Equalization Tax was terminated—and then to 50 percent when, at the director's initiative, it was made a global fund.

[24] Gerald Tsai's Manhattan Fund, at $162 million, had been larger.

[25] The Geneva operations were separate for legal and regulatory reasons.

Swiss banque d'affairs; in part, because Capital would not agree to accept a large Saudi account at a "special fee" of 0.10 percent; and in part because he privately worried that his difficult personal relationships with others would constrict his career.

Meanwhile, Lovelace became so convinced of the long-range importance of international investing that he made a gutsy commitment: He offered to cover all the losses of Capital International, which had never made a profit, out of his own pocket if that was what it would take to carry on, saying simply: "We *must* do it!"

By then, it was well established within Capital that research coverage of industries should be done on a global basis with analysts calling on corporations and developing research sources worldwide. In addition to one- and two-week research trips, many Associates took advantage of Capital's offer to finance six-month and yearlong stays in foreign countries—with their families—to gain immersion experiences and understanding.

Meanwhile, in the U.S. institutional business, Capital advanced from a modest entry position to decisive leadership as an international equity manager and capitalized on a 25-year transformation in demand. In 1975, almost no pensions or endowments invested in foreign stocks; but by 2000 most large funds invested internationally, and the typical international allocation had increased to nearly 10 percent of equity assets. International investing was well established and Capital had moved past all others to become the clear market leader.

When Capital's EuroPacific Growth Fund was introduced in 1984, the combined value of stock markets outside the United States was under $1.5 trillion; by 2000, their combined value would be eight times larger: $12 trillion. (The number of U.S.-managed international mutual funds has proliferated over the same period from 11 to over 550.) Now, EuroPacific, with nearly one million shareholder accounts, is by far America's largest international growth fund.

International's business building targeted four spheres: First, steadily building up Capital's international investment business with

U.S. institutions and with individuals through the American Funds; second, developing Capital's worldwide leadership in emerging markets investing; third, developing Capital's domestic investment business in such major markets as Japan, the United Kingdom, and Continental Europe; and fourth, establishing joint ventures in specific countries such as India, Brazil, Canada, and Italy (particularly to access their consumer markets).

In aggregate, it would be a massive buildup—achieved in just two decades—from a very low initial base. "David Fisher inherited International as an orphan in the early 1980s," explains Rothenberg. "When he became its informal, adoptive parent, it was small—with less than $500 million in assets—and was losing money.[26] It sure *appeared* to be dead in the water."

Fisher's inheriting International came about in a dramatic way that shows his colleagues' strong commitment to him. In 1981, Fisher felt he was not advancing his career after a decade as research director and feared he would never get the chance to have the entrepreneurial responsibility of developing the international business, which he so wanted to do. In frustration, he "took the call" from Alvin Shoemaker, CEO of First Boston, a leading Wall Street firm. After a whirlwind courtship, Fisher was offered and nearly accepted the role of being the head of First Boston's rapidly expanding global institutional stock-brokerage business—at very high pay. Lovelace was dumbfounded. Shanahan walked into Newton's office and closed the door: "David just quit!" Newton was startled: "What can we do?" Shanahan said: "I *think* we can save him. If you'll go talk with him now, we may be able to work it out."

Newton went immediately to see Fisher, and they talked all afternoon. So he could gain some quiet time with his friend to work out an effective solution, Shanahan persuaded a colleague[27] to substitute

---

[26] The Geneva office also performed important work for all of Capital, particularly New Perspective Fund, so even though International might be losing money, the Geneva office was profitable.

[27] Mike Johnston.

for Fisher, who had been slated to make a speech in Tokyo. This enabled Shanahan and Fisher to get together for the candid talk that was only possible between friends of many years. Simultaneously, Jim Freeman, then a senior officer of First Boston and director of research, advised Fisher, as a friend, about the "palace politics" perils he would be facing and cautioned him not to take the offer.

Hoping to convince Fisher to remain at Capital, Lovelace invited David and his wife Marianna to join him for an evening walk. Fisher didn't go: He stayed at home preparing a barbecue dinner, but Marianna—who had once been a Capital Associate and appreciated the opportunity to spend time with JL, even in such delicate circumstances—did go.

They stopped to watch a local high school football game, and as they watched the game together in silence, recollections of Lovelace's many years of thoughtfulness sent a clearer message than words ever could. And through Marianna, David Fisher soon received that "message"—very directly. Marianna Fisher spoke with her husband after the ball game: "You can't be so impatient, David. Not with JL!"

"What did he say?"

"About your discussion?"

"Yes. What did Jon say?"

"David, he never mentioned it."

Fisher knew then and there that Lovelace understood—and was signaling.

Next day, Fisher went to see Lovelace. JL spoke first: "I didn't realize I was keeping you away from International! David, it's all yours!"

After the announcement of Fisher's new role, worried telephone calls came in from Geneva, and Lovelace realized that not everyone was comfortable with Fisher's leading International. To calm the immediate concerns, Lovelace offered to call Geneva every day to keep up with any problems so he could help work them out. After a week, Lovelace was asked to stop calling so frequently; and not long after, it was suggested that he discontinue the calls entirely.

Today, the move to international investing helps Capital with an asset size limit problem[28] that could otherwise become more and more restrictive as managed assets increase. First, investing in the international markets *doubles* the total securities market available to Capital's analysts and portfolio counselors—so regulatory constraints on size of holdings are not as binding or confining. Even more important for a research-centered organization like Capital, the best way to beat indexing is to maximize the availability of information that can be used effectively. As Fisher says, "More proprietary information can be developed internationally through our own research—often with substantial advantage."

Capital spends heavily on developing local investment knowledge and expertise all over the world, recognizing that all too many international investment "experts" have seen too few countries in far too little depth to realize that they really don't know all that they should know. Travel is important because regular visitors can literally *see* change. As far back as the 1960s, to increase the organization's overall worldwide knowledge, each investment professional was assigned a region about which to become well informed. The typical assignment would be to go for two or three weeks of company visits—two or three times every year—with the weekends and, perhaps, an extra week devoted to learning the countries' cultural life: concerts, dance, theater, historical sites, and so on. Fisher readily acknowledges his personal interest in going *everywhere,* saying, "The more different the place, the more interesting."

Capital's international business has been developed in each of the major national markets around the world. In the United Kingdom, after over two decades of industry consolidation, a larger and larger proportion of that nation's pension funds were being managed by a

---

[28] An individual mutual fund can't own more than 10 percent of a Federal Reserve regulated bank without becoming a controlling shareholder and subject to special regulations. And if a fund invests over 5 percent of its assets at cost in a public company, it becomes subject to different regulations as a "specialist" investment company.

smaller and smaller group of British investment managers. Back in the 1970s, 20 investment managers had been considered among the leaders in England and Scotland. One after another, however, managers turned in such poor investment results that they effectively took themselves out of the institutional business. (The process of eliminating investment managers was accelerated by the concentrated power of four dominant consulting actuaries, who were the leaders in the business of recommending investment managers to large British pension funds.) By 1985, the institutional managers still standing as major competitors numbered only a dozen. By 2000, the list of qualified competitors had shrunk to less than six.

Capital's first London office was opened in 1979.[29] New business came only gradually for several years. Mobil, a major U.S. client, became Capital's first U.K. client in 1984. During the 1980s, Capital became the leader in emerging markets and, in the 1990s, developed a strong *domestic* U.K. capability.

In the 1990s, Capital had a choice of two strategies: concentrate on being an international specialist *or* reach for the larger part of the U.K. assets by winning domestic mandates. The specialist route was surer given Capital's obvious strengths in international and particularly emerging markets investing, but the generalist route could lead to winning much larger accounts—and Capital had been proving itself as a domestic U.K. manager. Some at Capital had reservations about trying to win domestic mandates from new clients because this would require convincing prospects that an American firm would be more effective at investing in British stocks than the traditional British managers. The better strategy, they thought, would be to win larger international specialist

[29] By David Beevers and Shirley Pearton. Beevers did not want to move his family from London to Geneva, so Mathysen-Gerst suggested he open an office in London. Beevers replied: "That's ridiculous! We can't open a London office just because I don't want to move to Geneva." In the early 1980s, Capital's research analysts began using the London office when on trips to Europe.

mandates from Capital's existing clients in emerging markets. In the end, Capital's chosen strategy was to concentrate on becoming a principal *global* manager—including managing domestic assets—for British *and* Continental institutions, not just an international specialist.

Capital's initial new business development goal in the United Kingdom was to get the British investment consultants' serious attention by winning a few showpiece mandates. After winning some bellwether accounts, the new business focus shifted to working with and selling through the four largest investment consultants who advise most major funds on the selection of investment managers. The circumstances were favorable: More and more large British funds were looking for new investment managers and were becoming open to non-British firms as managers of British assets in the United Kingdom. This meant, of course, that they would be considering managers they did not already know, and this increased the importance of the consultants' information and evaluations. This, in turn, worked to Capital's considerable advantage. Today, it is increasingly accepted as a major global manager—managing both domestic and international assets—in the United Kingdom and has built an increasingly strong franchise. While not yet accepted as a leader for U.K.-only domestic mandates, Capital is one of the five leading managers for British funds.

Similarly, on the Continent, Capital is both a global and a pan-European manager. It had won over 150 institutional clients in Europe by 2000—and doubled that number in the next three years. Longer term, the economic integration of Europe will put the traditional single-country managers and single-country pension funds at a real comparative disadvantage. European funds will need to diversify away from their past emphasis on one home country—and investment managers will need to have multinational investing capabilities. These changes will benefit Capital and other managers with established multinational and global investing capabilities.

Another major business development opportunity is in Japan,[30] where by 2000, Capital had nearly 100 institutional accounts and was gaining market momentum. Beginning as an emerging markets specialist, Capital expanded into broadly defined international mandates and then into domestic accounts. In the restructuring now occurring in Japan's huge pension system, Capital has an opportunity to establish itself as a major domestic investment manager in Japan. (Most European and American professionals who go to Japan don't stay long enough to become truly proficient in the complexities of Japanese companies and industries, and this gives Capital, with its career-in-research orientation, a major competitive advantage.)

In Australia, Capital is the leading American manager. In Singapore, it is the largest international investment manager.

Overall, Capital's international experience has been very encouraging. "If we screw it up," says Fisher, "it will be due to arrogance and believing our own press." Recognizing that over the past 10 years, Capital and other organizations have raised substantial amounts of money in the developed world for investment into the developing world, Fisher expects significant future growth will come from the developing world.

Given Capital's international commitment, Rothenberg expects, "Some of our very best people will not only not be American, but they will be hired in other countries and will know they won't ever need to work in the United States to have very successful careers and to be important leaders in Capital." Currently, most revenues still come from the United States, and there's always the risk of a "HQ syndrome" with everything orbiting around Los Angeles. As Fisher recognizes, "Developing a truly global organization will be a grand challenge for Capital."

[30] Parker Simes leads the team in Japan. His father was a lawyer with the Occupation Forces and stayed on as a civilian with the U.S. Army and married. Japanese was the first language Simes learned before going to school in the United States, where he graduated from Harvard Business School before joining Capital. For many years, superior investment records were less important than Keiretsu links, reciprocal business relationships, or the very low prices (set by an inner circle of managers).

"We know it can be hard for the 'returning hero' to fit back into a hierarchy that has moved on—with those in the continuing organization having received promotions and having had many bonding experiences together. Still, our intention is to have our best people go abroad for a career with many never coming back to L.A. as they go forward, because we will have become a truly global organization."[31]

Capital has come a long way from the days of early 1979, when Bob Kirby made his wonderful statement: "I will run naked through Pershing Square, if 10 years from now, direct foreign investments account for anywhere near 5 percent of our assets!" The humor of history is not lost on Fisher, who later gave Kirby a carefully doctored photograph, framed with the text of his never-to-be-forgotten statement, cleverly contrived in a way sure to be remembered: Kirby is seen in the buff, cheerfully fulfilling his pledge.

[31] The 36th floor of Rockefeller Center's International Building, where Capital has its New York City office, has a discreet plaque that suits a global research-based organization—a reminder of an earlier research-based organization that made a major contribution to the Allies' success in World War II: "From 1940 to 1945, this floor was used by British Security Coordination. It was the hub of the largest intelligence organization in the world, and its director, William Stephenson, was the man Winston Churchill called Intrepid."

CHAPTER 11

EMERGING
MARKETS

NOTES FOR READERS

Powerful and favorable changes were developing in the world as the Cold War wound down. Authoritarian regimes gave way to free markets, technology, and more open societies; and restrictive regulations on outside investors were reduced, relaxed, or removed. Capital's traditions in research and individual decision making prepared it unusually well for what became a major, global opportunity. And Capital's presence in all the major developed markets and its increasingly recognized and valued integrity made it the institutions' worldwide firm of choice for investing in the emerging markets.

Capital is, by far, the leading manager of investments in the emerging markets, managing more investments than the next 10 managers *combined*. Yet, despite its strength, Capital is also the first to raise serious questions about the validity of the term "emerging markets," such as: How appropriate is it to make a "set" out of such obviously different markets as Jordan, Thailand, Greece, and Korea?

Economists looking at nations moving up the scale from general poverty toward middle-class affluence would want to invest in consumer products where prosperity's impact will first be strong. But the companies that sell those products in the emerging markets—Coca-Cola, Cadbury Schweppes, PepsiCo, Colgate, Procter & Gamble, Nestle, Sony, Hitachi, Honda, Wal-Mart, and General Motors—are all headquartered in the *developed* nations.

Experienced investors also recognize that the transition from poverty to affluence can be even more favorable to bonds than to stocks.

Managing emerging market investments has been a very big, fast-growing, and profitable business for Capital, and the organization has continuously reinvested in its on-the-ground research capabilities. In addition, Capital's reputation of successful investing in the emerging markets gives it an advantage when competing for new business as an emerging markets specialist or as an overall international specialist. At least as important, as shown in Chapter 10, these specialist mandates can develop into global mandates, including *domestic* investing in the client's home market—even when that means Japan, the United Kingdom, or Europe.

The emerging markets story is a Capital classic. An individual with conviction was given room to pursue his vision, and the organization provided large support resources as the business was built up. In addition, luck played a key role: Capital got the initial call only because one person outside Capital, and—without Capital's awareness—urged its inclusion in the selection process. Emerging markets investing became accepted by giant institutions worldwide as one emerging market country after another opened up its stock market to international investors. Being in the right place at the right time certainly was important, but so also was the unrelenting commitment and drive of one individual, David Fisher.

E MERGING MARKETS INVESTING, where Capital is far and away the world leader[1] came *very* close to never happening.

"David Fisher is the one who said, 'This is where the future lies. Let's go for it!'" explains Bob Kirby. "David almost *invented* investing in emerging markets."[2]

Opportunity can come unexpectedly and from unexpected sources. Capital's remarkable experience with emerging markets investing began, without its knowledge, far away from Capital or Los Angeles. A young Dutchman, Antoine van Agtmael, with degrees in economics and Russian studies, went from Yale[3] to Bankers Trust, to pursue a career as an "internationalist." After doing well in the bank's training program, he was given his choice of assignments, presumably a very easy choice: Either he would go to Paris, where the bank's office was located amidst the urbane pleasures of the City of Light, or to a modest outpost in remote Bangkok, Thailand. His swift and unexpected choice: Bangkok.

During his four-year tour in Thailand,[4] van Agtmael became convinced that some first-rate companies were operating in this Third World country. Returning to the United States, he transferred to the private sector arm of the World Bank, the International Finance

---

[1] This reality is not widely known because most of the assets have been raised privately in three similar, closed-end *institutional* funds: one for Japanese clients domiciled for regulatory purposes in Luxembourg, one in Europe, and one in North America. Capital manages emerging markets assets that are equal to Capital's total assets under management just 25 years ago.

[2] Walter Stern's support was vital during the difficult years from 1994 to 1998 when the total return on the emerging market index was *negative*.

[3] At Yale, he earned an M.A. He earned his B.A. at the Netherlands School of Economics and an M.B.A. at New York University.

[4] Managing a small investment bank that comprised the country's leading stockbroker, underwriter, research house, and investment manager.

Corporation (IFC), whose mission was to stimulate private capital flows into the world's developing countries. At the IFC, van Agtmael worked in the capital markets department on a voluntary "extra-hours" study team, developing a database to show that very good companies could be found in the Third World.

The study team soon became convinced that they were onto something, maybe something big. The first step was to create a database for a new IFC Emerging Markets Index—with the same rationale as Capital's EAFE Index: the need for an objective measure. Despite initial skepticism and resistance within the World Bank— where experienced old hands had grave doubts about the usefulness of trying to develop public stock markets in underdeveloped countries—the idea of organizing a fund for just such investments eventually prevailed.

The IFC hoped the fund would become an effective conduit for portfolio investments on favorable terms for both investors and the host countries by stimulating the flow of funds from large institutional investors; encouraging more companies to issue securities; widen public ownership of major corporations; improving the operation of local capital markets; increasing the range of financial instruments available; raising the standards of reporting information to investors; bringing more equity capital into the local markets without interfering with local control; and providing linkage between national markets and the global capital market.

Worrying that the World Bank would be seen as too political and bureaucratic for such adventurous investing—or worse, would be labeled as naïve ivory tower do-gooders—the advocates decided that only a commercial entity from the private sector could legitimize their concept. One successful profit-making example would be far more persuasive than a series of academic research papers. So, the original prospectus[5] for a Third World Equity Fund was both

---

[5] The litany of benefits concluded with a candid statement: "There can, of course, be no assurance that any of the foregoing expectations will be realized."

an offering memorandum to prospective investors and an appeal to underdeveloped countries to improve their standards of disclosure or transparency and make their markets more open to external investors. The idea for the new fund was first floated by van Agtmael and his World Bank cohorts at a Salomon Brothers conference in New York City.

An experienced international investor gravely cautioned the World Bankers:[6] "You speak of investing in underdeveloped countries as though it were our solemn moral responsibility to do this. It is *not*.

"No right-minded professional investor will have *any* interest— ever—in 'investing' in Godforsaken countries with no hopes or prospects that they can *ever* get up out of their long-established miseries, corruption, defaults—and expropriations!"

Then, surprising the World Bankers, he continued: "Candidly, I believe we are discussing a major investment opportunity for serious, long-term investors. The growth potential in these countries is enormous. Many of the companies are very well run. But you will never get serious investors to put real money into this fund or any other fund that has an albatross around its neck such as the one you're putting on this one by calling it a 'Third-World' or 'Underdeveloped Countries' fund.

"At least give yourselves half a chance by giving it a better name!"

Over the weekend, the World Bankers did exactly that. By Monday, they agreed never again to use or allow the use of such terms as "underdeveloped countries" or "Third World." Now, they would always use the term "emerging markets," and they set out to develop a plan for establishing a new, closed-end investment company that would invest in those unfamiliar and undeveloped markets.

The initial plan was simple: Get 12 very large institutional investors—one from each of a dozen major countries—to invest just

---

[6] By J.P. Morgan's Francis Finlay, a leader in international investing: first at J.P. Morgan; then at Lazard Frères; and later with his own firm, Clay, Finlay.

$5 million apiece,[7] for a total of $60 million. This amount would qualify the fund for listing on the New York Stock Exchange, where it would have visibility. The plan seemed simple, but actual implementation—after a quick start—became very hard. IBM came in early. So did PGGM, a leading institutional investor in Holland. Then Paribas in France agreed. But funds in Japan never did.

Germany's participation would depend on a fortuitous accident. By luck, a few months earlier, van Agtmael sat next to Deutsche Bank's charismatic CEO Alfred Herhausen on a seven-hour flight to Frankfurt, and they spoke briefly about investing in Southeast Asia. That pretext was enough for van Agtmael to place a call from the World Bank to Herr Herhausen. While Herhausen probably had no recollection of the airborne chat, the amount of $5 million was so small and the proposition so grand that he agreed on the phone that the idea "had merit"—and soon one of his assistants confirmed the financial commitment.

Another key step was to select investment managers.[8] Capital was not even on the list. But Capital was lucky—very lucky. An investment professional at TIAA-CREF, disappointed with her own organization's decision to pass up the new opportunity, suggested to the IFC that they consider Capital—where she hoped to get a job.[9]

What would later be recognized as Capital's big break came without fanfare and was met, initially, with great skepticism. "In August 1985, we got a call from the IFC, an arm of the World Bank," recalls Fisher. "They wanted to talk about our managing investments in

[7] A $5 million investment commitment entitled the investor to a seat on the board of directors.
[8] John Templeton was considered the leading international investor in the United States. (Templeton established the first NYSE listed retail fund for the emerging markets in 1987.) So his firm was invited, as well as Boston's Grantham, Mayo, van Otterloo. Scudder, Stevens & Clark was not invited because it had already participated with the IFC in the development of The Korea Fund. TIAA-CREF (the manager of academic retirement funds originated by Andrew Carnegie) was also invited, but turned down the invitation.
[9] Her hopes were not realized.

what they called 'emerging markets,'" because Capital was one of the very few investment managers that had established a record of investing internationally and had at least some investments in the emerging markets.

For all the conventional reasons, Fisher initially thought emerging markets investing would be a poor idea for Capital, but he decided to take a look. The more he learned, the more interested he became. After careful review of the investment opportunities, he was convinced that Capital should commit to emerging markets investing. When Fisher first advocated investing in the emerging markets and doing this in a big way, "The idea of going global was not at all a clear winner."

At Capital, the lines were fairly quickly drawn between those for and those against a commitment to emerging markets investing. The arguments against commitment included *economic* questions about comparing the modest business opportunities expected for this unusual kind of investing against the cost of organizing the strong on-the-ground research that Capital was known for. "We knew the costs had to be high because we would not compromise on our concepts of quality," recalls Fisher. "And to some, the business opportunity looked much too small. But to others, the business opportunity was significant. Demand was clearly strong." (The strength of demand caused some closed-end country funds[10] then managed by other investment organizations to sell at significant premium prices—even though most of those funds' assets were actually invested temporarily in U.S. Treasury bills while the managers looked for possible investments.)

Professional questions were also substantial. Accounting and disclosure standards were low. Stock markets were neither open nor transparent. Capital would be competing as an outsider in markets where "insider" deals had always predominated. Concerned observers cautioned that the emerging markets would blow up—again—for reasons outsiders couldn't even begin to anticipate or understand, and

---

[10] Such as the Korea Fund.

this would hurt investors *and* hurt Capital. Moreover, those countries, their economies, and their markets—and their attitudes toward investors—would differ substantially from one to another.[11] "So the obvious question," says Fisher, "was 'Why put our professional reputation at risk by investing in a country like Brazil—or Indonesia or Greece?'"

"The positive case was less clear, but we thought stronger," says Fisher. Capital's approach to investing in the emerging markets would be based on the view that major societal change was taking place in these countries. These changes would create opportunities for many companies; some of these companies would achieve great growth; and the decisive way for Capital to add value was to select the companies with the most potential by knowing them firsthand and early, through Capital's own on-the-ground research.

Investing at low prices in the emerging markets could be a very good deal for patient investors, particularly when buying into rapidly growing, truly world-class companies at the low P/E multiples that characterized the emerging markets. Continues Fisher: "This would be a wonderful opportunity for us to learn important lessons. And in business strategy terms, by being early leaders, we could raise the cost barriers against future competition."

In October 1985, Fisher went to Capital's board of directors to get authorization to go ahead. The division within the board was clear and strong. So, instead of bringing the question to a vote, which could have polarized the two sides, Lovelace shrewdly delayed the vote until the next month's meeting, knowing that it would give Fisher a month to lobby for the go-ahead. Fisher lobbied effectively, and at the next meeting,[12] he was authorized to join the competition to manage the IFC's new emerging markets fund.

---

[11] The individual countries differ greatly in size, economics, politics, resources, and cultures. "In fact, the differences from country to country are so important," says Fisher, "at Capital, we are very likely to stop using the aggregate term 'emerging markets.'"

[12] Strong views on whether to invest in emerging markets were certainly not confined to those at Capital. When the Ford Foundation later put $5 million into Capital's Emerging

In their presentation to the IFC, Fisher and Egelston explained Capital's history of international investing and its willingness to commit to a loss-making proposition and sustain that commitment for many years.

In January 1986, the IFC selected Capital to manage a closed-end fund expected to have assets of over $50 million, which would meet the minimum size requirement for being listed on the New York Stock Exchange. But to the disappointment of its sponsors at the World Bank, the fund failed to reach the $50 million minimum and never got listed.[13] To some observers, the fund appeared to be "walking wounded": not public, so not visible; not large enough to be profitable; not large enough to make a difference in the various emerging markets—and, worse, not "gone away."

Having made the commitment to the IFC, Capital knew the costs of conducting extensive on-the-ground research would be much more than the $450,000 fee it would earn from the IFC's fund. A lot more business would be needed just to cover costs, and that business would have to come from U.S. corporate pension funds. So Capital Guardian started knocking on doors, and the telephone companies[14]—AT&T, PacTel, Bell Atlantic, NYNEX—became the first clients.

The external campaign to convince institutions to invest in the emerging markets presented internal challenges to Capital and to its leadership, particularly to Lovelace and Fisher. Great personal closeness had developed between these two men, despite the apparent mismatch in their personalities: Fisher is an ever-optimistic visionary and a bold enthusiast on decisions; Lovelace is conservative and

---

Markets Growth Fund, Robert S. McNamara, formerly head of the World Bank, pronounced it, "The stupidest idea I've ever heard of!"

[13] Trying to achieve the size objective, Fisher called Kent Damon at the ARCO pension fund, saying, "I have a $5 million favor to ask of you!" The IPO only raised $44 million—including $4 million from the IFC itself—too little for the hoped-for NYSE listing. This was actually a lucky break. If the fund had been listed for public trading, it probably would have soon sold in the market at a discount from net asset value—like closed-end funds.

[14] Advised by Professor Roger Murray of Columbia University.

cautious. Fisher would make a cluster of entrepreneurial decisions, accepting some mistakes as inevitable, but correctable, and move on; Lovelace would seek to avoid any mistakes by taking the time to consider fully all possible outcomes before making deliberate, long-term commitments.

Fisher wanted to move boldly ahead on developing Capital's program of investing in emerging markets and was chafing because Lovelace wanted to go slowly. He hoped Fisher would instead concentrate on building up the mutual fund business. Fisher recognized that Lovelace saw his plan as a major opportunity and a great compliment. Even so, Fisher declined. "Jon, I respect your intention greatly, but everyone will think I'm just your bag carrier if I work in mutual funds."

Over the decade following its winning the IFC mandate, Capital's emerging markets assets grew at an average annual rate of 27 percent and were up to $13 billion. And after 15 years, assets were over $25 billion with clients in 29 different countries, and people from 30 different countries working on the investing team. On his way to London and then on to Moscow, Fisher observed: "If just 15 years ago, we'd had the gall to project the emerging market countries would be where they are today—and their companies and securities valued as they are today—we would have been derided with peals of laughter!"

Today, Capital is by far, the world's largest investor in the emerging markets, but it still has not developed a pure emerging markets equity mutual fund for retail markets. Explains Fisher, "We wouldn't want an emerging markets equity mutual fund to be mis-sold to investors. It's dangerously easy to focus on *returns* and not pay sufficient attention to *risk*. Also, market liquidity is a real concern.[15] Those emerging markets can go up or down a lot on very little volume, and we want to be able to move the investors' money from one area to another so we can hope to avoid some of the problems."

---

[15] Liquidity constraints are a major reason Capital refuses to offer "single country" or "regional" emerging market funds, but the main reason for not offering specialized funds is the conviction that fully managed mandates are inevitably in the client's best interests.

To provide managed growth—in the best interests of both current and prospective institutional shareholders—the Emerging Markets Growth Fund, which is offered primarily to large institutional investors, limits new share sales to 25 percent of the outstanding shares at prior year-end. Rothenberg explains, "Our objective as an organization is not to gather the most assets it's possible to manage. Instead, our objective is always to do what makes sense for the shareholder who is already invested in our funds."

In 1994, the New World Fund[16] was finally introduced for individual investors. It participates in emerging market economies, but is *not* a fund of emerging market stocks. To make the fund suitable for individual investors—with more market-price stability and greater liquidity—the fund is designed as a hybrid of emerging market debt and the stocks of corporations headquartered in the developed world that are doing extensive business in the emerging markets.

Capital has faced and will face numerous challenges in developing its emerging markets business. One type of challenge was illustrated when an Indian insurance company, which had a joint venture investment company with Capital, linked up with Sun Life of Canada. Sun Life insisted that all of the Indian company's asset management businesses be included in the link-up, so the 60:40 joint venture[17] with Capital had to be terminated in 1998.

A joint venture in Brazil with Banco BBA Creditanstalt S.A. was terminated—partly because the anticipated buildup of pension assets seeking equity investment management failed to materialize,[18] and partly because portfolio managers of fixed-income funds at the joint venture breached their guidelines to use leverage and derivatives. The joint venture covered all client losses, so no lawsuits or regulatory problems developed, but it cost Capital $10 million. Leverage was explicitly prohibited in the official prospectus. A falling market's impact

---

[16] The fund was designed under the leadership of Rob Lovelace.
[17] Organized in 1994.
[18] With only very small amounts invested in equities, the expectation of a substantial increase was understandable, but did not develop.

was multiplied by the same derivatives' leverage that had produced the apparently strong gains that attracted business during the rising market. Once again, business practices were shown to differ from one country to another, and assumptions about how others will think and behave were again proven to be dangerous. (After absorbing this problem, the working relationship with Banco BBA Creditanstalt continues.) Because Capital's internal standards are set so high, it has learned the importance of establishing its own procedures and cultural norms from the ground up instead of trying to jump-start a venture by combining with another firm.

Building Capital's very large business as an emerging markets investor was never smooth or easy: A major opportunity in Singapore faltered before it flourished. Fisher was one of several institutional investors on a 1985 tour of Southeast Asia that had been arranged by Morgan Stanley, when he met Ng Kog Song—then the new head of marketable securities investing at Singapore's Government Investment Corporation. The GIC is one of the world's largest funds with well over $100 billion invested "for future generations." At first, Ng wondered about Fisher: "If he's really serious about investing, why does he laugh so much?" But, as he got to know Fisher over several days, he developed a different view: "David showed how inquisitive he really is. He asks to learn and he would ask anybody anything. I was impressed."

A few weeks later, Fisher called to say: "Let's do something together." While other investment managers proudly assured the GIC that they could do great things *for* the Singaporeans because their firms had such great capabilities, Fisher wanted to work *together*. He said: "We think we may be able to be helpful to you, but we *know* we could learn a lot from you as we try to increase our ability to understand this important region of the world, which you know and understand so well." For Ng, this was a completely different approach from that of all the other firms. Fisher proposed a global equity fund being introduced in Japan that would be advised by Capital. Ng agreed.

It was a disaster.[19] The Japanese brokers churned the portfolio, and when investors wanted to redeem, the brokers paid them out in kind, peeling off the liquid, high-grade holdings. As a result, the GIC and other long-term investors got stuck with illiquid leftovers. Even with this dreadful start, Fisher and Ng were developing a strong personal-professional relationship. Now, Capital is the GIC's largest manager, and the GIC is one of Capital's largest clients.

But, it took a lot of understanding and persistence on both sides. The progression from disastrous beginning to a great relationship began with Fisher's confessing: "Ouch! That's not the right way to do things!" and Ng's ability to focus on the long term. Their first step was to set up a separate account for the GIC. Investment results were good right from the start, but Ng wanted more than a normal client relationship: He wanted a special relationship—and Capital's commitment to locate in Singapore.

Singapore, which had catapulted itself from third-world to first-world economic status in a single generation through imaginative central planning, rigorous implementation, and strict rules, had decided that it should become a major financial center for Asia, in direct competition with Hong Kong and Tokyo. A key component would be creating itself as a center for investment management by attracting the major investment organizations of the Western world to open branch offices—hopefully their principal Asian office—in Singapore. With a long history of successful trading, the government of Singapore had special things to offer: a several-year tax holiday and a large starter account from the GIC, typically $100 million. And it wanted special things in return, particularly professional training for young Singaporeans.

Fisher was willing to innovate as part of a major relationship, and the GIC had enormous assets. Still, if Ng wanted a "special"

---

[19] Nearly 20 years later, Capital is still licking its wounds over this experience, which began with solemn promises that were soon mocked by the promisers' own misbehavior. Some at Capital still have doubts about doing business with stockbrokers in Japan.

relationship, it would have to be an informal understanding because special contractual arrangements were not acceptable at Capital: Every client should get all the same services any other client was getting. So the two men agreed to try a special relationship step-by-step on the basis of a gentleman's agreement.

The next step was Capital's opening an office in Singapore in 1989. Even this was not easy. Capital believed it would need at least two senior people to conduct its Singaporean operation, so a $50 million starter account—which other managers found more than ample—would be too small, unless the GIC would pay higher fees. Mark Denning's family had previously lived in Singapore[20] so he was glad to return to open Capital's office. (Capital also hired Denning's father's personal assistant, Queenie Chin, as office manager.) Rob Lovelace,[21] who had started in 1985, opened the office with Denning.

A hitch came when Capital wanted to move its Asian securities trading unit to Singapore so traders could work closely with the portfolio counselors based there. This fit well with the government's plan to build up Singapore as a financial center. But bureaucrats refused to allow any trading unless Capital got a securities dealers license for its trading operation, which would have involved all sorts of regulations and a cash deposit with the authorities. Capital demurred: As an investment manager, it would only be placing orders on behalf of clients, not making markets and taking risks as a trader. Always sensitive to global consistency in its operations, applying for such a license would not do because Capital had a policy of not subjecting itself to local securities regulators in other jurisdictions. It took several years to work out the semantic differences between two kinds of "trader"—

---

[20] Denning's father had been regional distributor for Martell Liquors.

[21] Rob Lovelace studied mineral economics at Princeton, where he graduated summa cum laude and Phi Beta Kappa. Lovelace was a mining analyst from 1985 to 1986. Then, appealing to Fisher for a chance in emerging markets, he had followed Mexican companies—in part because he could speak Spanish. He is a trustee at Claremont Graduate University.

a dealer who makes markets versus an institutional investor who executes orders for clients—and sort out the snarls of red tape.[22]

In another temporary misunderstanding, the GIC wanted to establish a special account to invest in Thailand. This conflicted with Capital's policy against narrowly specialized portfolios—until the two parties agreed that the GIC was large enough to "own" the risk of illiquidity.

Over time, Capital and the GIC have developed an extensive and harmonious relationship. The GIC's portfolio managers can call Capital's analysts and participate in research conference calls—except, of course, calls that involve any discussions of buy or sell decisions. Recently, GIC analysts and portfolio managers jointly conducted a two-day research conference near San Diego with Capital's analysts and portfolio counselors.

[22] The Simex derivatives fiasco created by Baring's rogue trader, Nick Leason, came later. If it had come before, the time to resolve the semantics would have been much longer.

CHAPTER 12

MANAGING PEOPLE

NOTES FOR READERS

In the history of the world, there has never been a group of individuals so extraordinarily well informed about companies, economies, technologies, or governments as are today's institutional investors. They meet routinely with corporate CEOs, senior government officials, and economic and industry experts. They have command of the largest-ever library of information accessible by powerful technological devices that display all sorts of data in convenient arrays, almost instantly. They work long hours networking with other similarly privileged professionals and are treated deferentially by the powerful and wealthy because they control vast sums of other people's money.

Among themselves, investment managers joke informally about the obvious irony that, while they sit in judgment on corporations and freely criticize managements, their own firms could never meet the management standards they require of others.

"It's a *people* business" is the most frequently repeated shibboleth in the investment world, but its salience is seldom demonstrated by what investment firms and individuals actually do. Most organizations are loose and improvisational. Recruiting is typically haphazard and opportunistic. Career development is left to the individual and constructive feedback is rare. Compensation—usually with little explanation or interpretation—is the main tool for communication to individuals about their progress in their organizations.

In most investment organizations, individual careers are affected, positively or negatively, as their organization's business changes with changing markets, new products, and strategic developments. As a result, very capable people often feel the need to change employers to advance their own careers.

Capital knows that success in managing investments and providing services to investors depends on its ability to attract, develop, organize, and motivate talented individuals who can work effectively with others to develop and deliver superior investment results and superior services to investors.

Capital is one of the world's largest aggregations of talented and motivated knowledge workers, but what makes Capital so eminently worthy of careful study is not quantitative, but qualitative:

- The rigor and care and the unusual amount of time invested in recruiting.
- The regular and thorough reviewing-evaluating-coaching process by which each Associate can continue learning how best to improve.
- The constant search for optimal alignment between the capabilities and interests of each individual and the design of the role that each individual can best perform as part of the overall organization.
- The search for any constraints that might restrict achievement by individuals or groups so those constraints can be removed.
- The systematic removal of hierarchical symbols that might distort or interfere with the organization's sustained commitment to rational decision making.

- Regular redesigning of teams and groups so the mix and number of coworkers engaged in a working unit is optimal for productivity and professional and personal fulfillment.

- The pervasive tone of trust, mutual respect, and interpersonal enjoyment that minimizes "frictional" interference with good communication.

- The genuine modesty that comes of never needing to make promises or claims because actual results are visible and will determine reward and recognition.

Capital's way of managing "knowledge workers" is unusual in an industry that traditionally celebrates individual achievers and stars; where self-centered arrogance is common; where individual compensation is high; and egotism can so easily be provoked by the intensity of competition in the pursuit of superior investment results.

Capital Group Companies' managerial challenges will continue to increase geometrically as assets managed get larger and larger; the number and diversity of Associates proliferate; the differences in markets served become increasingly significant; *and* the number, variety, and complexity of major decisions—about people, investments, and businesses—expands.

As always, the managerial challenge will be to expand and improve the organization's decision-making capacity more rapidly than the need for that capacity increases.

"D O WHAT YOU really like to do—and don't do things you don't enjoy. Enjoy yourself!"

Sounds simple, but it certainly does not mean "do your own thing."[1] No one at Capital would make such a mistake. And anyone

[1] Lovelace's direct experience with serious health problems may contribute to his overall existentialist perspective.

who takes such a simplistic, superficial view will miss the depth and complexity—and will be disappointed by *and* be a disappointment to Capital.

The primary management challenge at Capital is not managing investments or serving investors, as important as these two functions obviously are. Like all professional organizations, Capital's main challenge is finding, developing, and organizing talented professionals into an effective team that will continuously achieve superior results. So, the right dimension on which to measure Capital's growth—or the growth of any professional firm—is in the number of its consistently first-rate professional people and how effectively they are organized.[2] At Capital, that means attracting superbly talented, highly motivated people who are carefully organized to produce together their best possible long-term investment results and services to investors.

"People like to do what they do well," reflects Bill Hurt. "*Very* able people like to concentrate on what they do *very* well. And they don't much like to do what they do only fairly well." That is why Associates[3] at Capital are encouraged to focus on doing what they do best—and really like to do. And that's why young analysts are encouraged to make investment decisions when they feel personally ready. "If over time, you're not doing more and more of what you *want* to do, you'll wind up doing lots of things you *don't* want to do," advises Hurt. "You only live once."

Lovelace refuses to look for people to fill the boxes in a "set" organization. Instead, he starts with individuals and then develops a structure that will enable them to concentrate on what they do best

---

[2] There is considerable concern at Capital over having underestimated the growth in the business that would come over the past two decades. This led, back in the 1970s, to underinvesting in developing investment professionals when the stock market and mutual fund sales were both at very low levels. "Actually," Jim Dunton explains, "We were interested in hiring. But with the grim industry outlook for investment management—and particularly the mutual fund business—very few of our job offers were accepted! So now we're investing heavily to catch up."

[3] Use of the term Associates began with the formation of Capital Group (see Chapter 6).

and to excel in that realm. (Associates are cautioned that others may form an opinion of what they do best and give them more and more of only that same type of work.) So continuous change and personal growth are encouraged to help Associates learn more about themselves *and* about things they don't know much about, but might actually be just right for them.

Careers are developed around individuals and the *changes* in their capabilities and interests. This means adapting to individual professionals continuously, so Associates get to know from direct, personal experience that there will always be a "right" place for them at Capital—where they'll feel continuously challenged to grow and contribute.

Capital strives to enable every Associate do his or her best—not by controls, but by removing impediments. "But," concedes Shanahan, "this is damned hard to execute successfully." Two unusual examples: Bill Newton worked out of his office-home in Jackson Hole, Wyoming, and Mike Shanahan worked out of his home in Palm Desert after 30 years in the Los Angeles office.

The focus on recruiting talented people goes all the way back to JBL in the 1920s—before Capital began. "In the final analysis," explains JL,[4] "the main reason our organization has grown into one of the world's largest and most successful investment management firms is the quality of our people."[5]

Another priority is organizational design, which rationalizes and harmonizes all aspects of Capital's working environment. It encompasses financial and nonfinancial compensation; professional challenges and personal growth opportunities for each individual; and communication of investment information and ideas—with the emphasis always on effectiveness—never on "efficiency."

[4] Speech to Chinese Academy of Social Sciences, delivered in Beijing, China, on April 22, 1983.
[5] Capital has tried various hiring practices. Through the 1960s, Capital used a consulting psychologist in addition to its rigorous recruiting interviews to help evaluate candidates. Going through Dr. Ed Sanford's evaluations became known as being "Sanfordized."

When strong growth leads to lots of hiring, average tenure declines significantly. So growth makes it hard to maintain clear-channel communications among investment professionals and very hard to sustain the best personal aspects of a firm's culture, which are so often subtle and delicate. Passing an organization's culture on to new people without diluting or distorting its real meaning is never easy. And the accuracy of institutional memory falls off. The process of decline may seem gradual, but the consequences are cumulative and almost always negative. (To help offset the problems of rapid expansion and many new hires, Capital has developed a novel Senior Partner program that encourages key seniors to stay several years after the normal retirement age.)

These problems are particularly serious in a rapidly expanding organization with new people coming from many national cultures to work in many countries—some of which are far away and very different from the United States—and who have different jobs with different kinds of responsibilities. Capital faces all these challenges simultaneously. In 1975, over 80 percent of Capital's investment professionals were located in downtown Los Angeles; today, that proportion is down to just 15 percent. With international expansion, 40 percent of Capital analysts now come from 32 countries other than the United States. Capital operates out of 19 offices in eight countries. The number of Associates has surged from 304 in 1975 to over 6,000 in 2003.

Managing at Capital starts with the individual and stays with the individual. And that means that managing really begins with the recruiting of both experienced people and new prospects at graduate schools. Tim Armour[6] sizes the magnitude of the recruiting challenge: "Twenty years ago, we had a total of less than 30 investment professionals. Now, just to keep up with the growth in our business,

---

[6] Tim Armour graduated from Middlebury in 1981 and then, with Capital's blessing, went into business—running a windsurfing operation in Florida for a year—before joining Capital in the initial round of The Associates Program or TAP.

we need to add 20 new professionals *every* year—a major challenge for all of us."

In addition to the considerable time spent interviewing M.B.A.s on campus, Capital interviews over 50 experienced professionals each year—even though less than 1 in 10 will eventually be invited to join. Capital never goes after experienced people with aggressive recruiting. "Instead, we'll let them know that if they ever feel interested in coming and want to talk, we'll be glad to see them. This helps set the right tone."[7] Capital has learned from experience that it's helpful to have at least two Associates each interview any new candidate twice before asking lots of others to make time for a full series of interviews. "We think of hiring a lot like getting married—and if the marriage breaks up, we think that's *our* fault."

In recruiting, Capital deliberately seeks unusual diversity in national, cultural, and career backgrounds of Associates. The firm likes to mix people from four different backgrounds: new M.B.A.s; those with industry experience; professionals from other investment firms; and people from its own TAP Program, which brings college graduates through a special in-house training program. The Associates Program (TAP)[8] for outstanding college graduates began as an experiment and has worked so well that it has become an important part of Capital's constant search for capable young people. "Over its 20 years, TAP has seen a majority of its participants make important contributions," according to Fisher. During the two years of the formal training program—which gives equal emphasis to both the administration and the investment sides of the organization—each TAPer spends four months in six areas, such as administration, marketing, and investing. Each position gives the TAPer enough time to go from *in*competent to competent—and appreciate firsthand what

---

[7] Paul Haaga.

[8] TAP was originated by Joe Higdon, who also opened the Washington office in the garage of his home. Early TAPers included Tim Armour, Jim Lovelace (who was hired without his father's knowing about it), and Shaw Wagener. Among those most widely expected to provide leadership in the future, easily half are TAPers.

it takes to do each job well. More than one in six eventually goes into investing.[9] The conceptual basis for TAP initiative can be traced back to JBL who represented in what he did the best of two great values that are all too often in conflict at other firms: tradition *and* commitment to creativity.

Capital is explicitly committed to hiring ahead of need so the firm will be prepared with ample resources to accommodate whatever growth develops. During the bear market at the start of this century, while other firms were laying off people, Capital not only had zero layoffs, but *hired* several hundred new Associates, including 16 senior professionals.

Capital always wants to recruit and add people during industry downturns, because that's a "win" for everybody: Capital gets some very good people; they're leaving troubled firms, so their former employers often feel relieved to have them safely and well placed; and they come to a place that really wants them. It takes courage and long-term vision, but as a private firm with a strong financial position, Capital can budget reserves, at least philosophically,[10] for this sort of initiative and invest in itself for the long term—just as it does for clients.

Holding on-campus interviews with 20 to 30 candidates at several business schools leads to inviting strong candidates to Capital. "Of course," explains Karin Larson,[11] "you have to be cautious these

[9] Of 223 investment professionals surveyed in 1999, 47 percent had had investment experience before coming to Capital, 36 percent joined after earning M.B.A.s, and 17 percent were TAPers or former assistants.

[10] Accountants, of course, keep the books on a year-to-year basis and are unable to make the reserves explicit.

[11] Karin Larson started with Capital as a secretary and studied at night school. "With a name like mine, it's no surprise I'm from Minnesota! After earning a B.A. at the University of Minnesota in 1961, I came to work at Capital in Los Angeles as Cecil Bessell's secretary. I could type and take shorthand—still do in company meetings—and, once a bit of a secret, my aunt was JBL's secretary, Florence Oxnard Jarvis. Later, I went to New York City for four and a half years as an analyst—covering Food, Advertising, and Consumer Goods—and then back to L.A. in '68. In 1973, I went to Japan for a week or so, visiting companies. I was back again in '75 because the group developed real internal conflict and tension and I got known as 'our man in Japan.' In 1988, I became U.S. Director of Research for Capital Guardian Trust and then Global Research Director—with Andy Barth covering the U.S.,

days because many young people are attracted to investment management by the compensation, not the nature of the work itself."

Interviews are exhaustive—and exhausting—as interviewers probe for such personal qualities as integrity, work ethic, humor, and perspective. "We look for a group of 'C' words," says Larson, "common sense, curiosity, caution without being stubborn, creativity, and confidence without arrogance." Then begins the search for a match between the individual and the industry they will do their research in. Such an alignment really matters, but is something most people cannot do well for themselves. An IBM engineer's résumé said he'd published some short stories that he described as being imaginative science fiction. This creative flair was key to his being a successful analyst of companies dependent on creativity—not high-tech companies, but *retailers*.

To avoid the risk of insufficient care and rigor in recruiting, Capital typically schedules 15 to 20 interviews for each candidate over a 2-day visit. Each Associate seeks different insights into the individual's capacity to invest successfully. "We know a high IQ is no guarantee that a person will be an effective securities analyst," says Larson. "Being too smart and always looking for just one more detail can really get in the way of good decision making and superior understanding of what will really drive an investment. On the other hand, we strive to avoid the easy trap of locking someone out just because he's never owned a stock. Maybe they just never happened to get involved before; maybe they will be very good when they do get involved."

Given the amount of time spent, some Associates wonder about the productivity of having so many people interview each serious candidate as well as the obvious risk that selection by consensus may eliminate the genuine outlier who might just be an investment genius. But most feel it gives candidates a chance to see for themselves whether

---

Ursula Van Almsick covering Europe, and Victor Kohn covering the emerging markets." Today, entirely undaunted by being confined to a wheelchair, she continues to travel the world conducting interviews and doing annual reviews.

Capital is right for them, and self-selection is always part of an effective recruiting process. Some people keep performing better as they do more interviews, but others get overconfident and let up and coast. Some candidates find the process just too long—and toss it in.

But in selecting people, as in making investments, says Larson, "If you ever feel you need to hurry to jump aboard, subsequent experience says: Stop! Take all the time and care you need to make your very best decision. People will be with the organization for a long, long time, so it's easy to see why investing substantial time in making the really right decision at the beginning is always a rewarding investment."

Today, women and men are treated as equals in responsibilities, respect, and compensation. It was not always so. Acknowledging the differences so evident in the United States 50 years ago, Marj Fisher believes today's reality had early roots: "JBL had two very capable daughters, and his experience with them may have contributed to his strong belief that women should be given ample opportunities to demonstrate their capabilities. When I joined Capital in 1951, there were only 19 employees, and I was our first professional woman. When one of our analysts came back from a meeting of the Los Angeles Analysts Society and announced that the first woman had just been made a member, the clear implication was that I should apply, too." Mari Fisher did apply and became the second woman in the society and the first woman to serve as president. Today, numerous women fill major leadership roles as research directors, portfolio counselors, relationship managers, and managers of business units throughout the organization.

Nobody grooms a successor at Capital because each person has his or her own particular strengths and ways to contribute, and no capable Associate will want to have exactly the same job that was just right for someone else. If a job is carefully redesigned around a new holder's particular strengths and interests, that individual will be much happier and much more productive. Appropriately, the framed Zen Buddhist text hanging on the wall in David Fisher's small, cheerfully cluttered office in West Los Angeles says: "The master in the art of living makes little distinction between his work and his play; his labor and his leisure."[12]

Since the key to organizational success is getting talented and ambitious people to work together effectively, management's first task and responsibility is to attract effective individuals who will want to work together because they like to work together. If people are capable, energetic, moral, and collegial, others will soon be saying: "We didn't know how much we needed them until they came aboard."[13] And management's next task is to continuously adapt organizational design to its people so they will achieve collegial effectiveness.

Personalizing job definitions gets harder as the organization grows in size, particularly in areas where the work is more traditional or operational. "It's not clear to us that we will always be able to take the same approach to organization and to values as our size increases," acknowledges Cody. "But we'll be very interested in doing all we can to make it feasible for as long as possible." The hallmark of Capital as an organization is its remarkable flexibility on how people choose to do their jobs, but sooner or later, everyone is measured by their results. Capital's flat organizational structure enables key people to take up, change, and leave significant roles without disruption to the organization, such as when Gordon Crawford, a senior analyst, served as the second non-executive board chairman of the parent company for a two-year term—and then returned to full-time research.

"What's really different about Capital is reflected in what's got to be the lowest employee turnover in this business—by a ton," says Bob Kirby. "Basically, people stay because it's the best working environment in the business. You have just an awesome amount of freedom

---

[12] The whole passage reads: "The Master in the art of living makes little distinction between his work and his play, his labor and his leisure, his mind and his body, his education and his recreation, his love and his religion. He hardly knows which is which. He simply pursues his vision of excellence in whatever he does, leaving others to decide whether he is working or playing. To him he is always doing both." The passage came from Osman Akiman, a Turkish Associate in London.

[13] Paul Haaga.

and flexibility to determine how you'll do your job. And everyone is measured on a results-related basis."

Only 2 percent of investment professionals leave Capital in a typical year and most of these departures are retirements. Part of the explanation for low turnover is the care with which individuals are recruited; part is due to the substantial compensation; and part is the perceived fairness and objectivity of annual personal reviews.[14] (Capital lost three technology analysts during the Internet start-ups boom—two to hedge funds and one to venture capital—because they felt "constrained" at Capital. Now, with the bloom off Internet start-ups, if they wanted to return, they could not: They have shown that money matters too much to them. Besides, it is widely agreed that leaving Capital should never be a riskless decision.)

The individual review process covers 10 standard criteria that have been identified over many years as the factors that really make a difference in achieving superior long-term results. Each analyst will have 10 or more portfolio counselors rating that analyst—and each counselor will be evaluated by as many analysts. Evaluations include open-end commentary on any other dimensions that reviewers think might be important for the individual, plus specific insights obtained through follow-up interviews. The results provide systematic feedback that is fair and balanced to each Associate.

Everybody is encouraged to rate everybody they work with: Analysts evaluate each other and analysts rate portfolio counselors, so the process is truly balanced. All evaluations are compiled—with scores reported in quintiles—and then shared with the individual in a personal review session that takes an hour or more and is specific. "Associates want to know all they can learn about how well they are doing and how they can improve, even when they are already doing very, very well," says Larson. "We find this really helps to foster interpersonal objectivity. Objectivity is the dominant factor at Capital in *every* area." All inputs matter and are followed up.

[14] An internal study completed several years ago concluded that Capital rarely lost people for dollars, but occasionally for lack of attention from those they wanted attention from. They didn't feel important enough.

Annual self-appraisals and careful development of each individual's "Franchise Plan" are combined with the personal review process to give each individual all the supportive help possible in finding the role that the Associate can perform best and most effectively. Explains Shanahan, "The recurring key question is: 'Do you want to be as good as you possibly can be?' We know we don't know what you should do, but we will help. We want each person to know they are being treated as a unique individual—even when there are 100 others at least as good as they are." (Recently, over 50 leaders within Capital were asked to evaluate each other as part of a continuing and systematic search for the future leadership of Capital Group Companies.)

Unusually long careers as analysts enable Capital's researchers not only to develop detailed knowledge of companies, products, managers, and technologies, but also to understand the probable impact of current developments. Long careers also enable Capital's professionals to develop greater understanding of themselves and of each other—which, in turn, enables them to communicate more effectively with each other on complex investment decisions.

When experienced professionals leave an investment organization, the firm loses more than one person; it also loses a network of relationships and experience in communication with and understanding of every person in that network. It is not just the parts; it includes all the myriad interconnections. So Capital's extremely low turnover is a major advantage.

Searching for interpersonal collaboration and cooperation does not mean that Capital does not hire highly competitive, aggressive risk takers: They do. Capital is filled with smart, rational professional people who are highly competitive and never sentimental. But to maximize results and collaboration, Capital structures its organization to channel competition outside, against the markets and competitors, instead of inside among professionals—and it has a deliberately low-key culture.

If such ambitious people were in some other cultural environment, the resulting behavior would surely be *very* different. But Capital is organized to prevent Associates from rubbing against each other. Capital's continuously changing organizational structure, the people it selects in recruiting, and its organizational culture or climate deliberately foster a comfortable commitment to competition—where Associates always play to win, but not to beat others within the organization.[15]

"It would be hard to find an environment where you are really so free to be all you are able to be—if you want it," says Parker Simes in Japan. "It's fun and exhilarating. Not that Capital's perfect, but we do believe in continuous improvement. With virtually no politics or bureaucracy, we strive to be a true meritocracy."

"Objectivity is a god at Capital," says Hurt. "In Wall Street, you want bright, articulate, motivated people, but you *need* people who will precipitate transactions because they are socially dominant and other people will *act* on their recommendations—whether good or bad. At Capital, we really don't want socially dominant people because that would get in the way of objectivity." The clearest evidence of the importance of objectivity is in compensation where the largest driver is a moving average of investment results achieved. Competition is controlled and made neither personal nor event-driven by using a four-year moving average measurement—with yearly weights of 40, 30, 20, and 10—of each person's investment results versus external benchmarks (see Chapter 14).

"Managing a group of equity analysts is a lot like parenting teenagers," says Larson, who recognizes that it is important to give each person clear goals and to set limits on their behavior—such as not saying things that might be personally hurtful. At the same time, it's important to give individuals lots of freedom. And it's *very* important to listen well. Managers learn to ask many open-ended questions and then listen very carefully to what is said and what is not said—

---

[15] Even at Capital, "politics" can be part of reality so it's important to have an arbiter of decisions with a very long-term perspective. Jon Lovelace has performed this role for many years; today, there are several other decision arbiters, including Jim Rothenberg, David Fisher, Mike Shanahan, and Larry Clemenson, Capital Group Companies' chief operating officer. In the Capital tradition, each would deflect the importance of his role, and point out that at Capital virtually no one ever gets exactly what he or she originally wanted.

and just how things are said. Larson continues, "It's important not to hear everything *or* remember everything that's said."

Capital looks for people who have thought carefully about themselves and like themselves, because in investing, they are often going to be wrong. "And they are going to be wrong *visibly,*" explains Fullerton, "to themselves, to Associates, and to clients. People who aren't comfortable with themselves tend to freeze up when they're wrong. They won't want to make another decision and be wrong again, so they'll get 'caught in the headlights.' Only those people who are self-aware—and *like* who they are—will be truly successful in investing."

Because Capital wants professionals who can and will learn from their mistakes, it is emotionally supportive to those who have made mistakes. Investors who have been through a few ups and downs themselves appreciate and understand what others are going through when their downs come along. A significant characteristic of Capital is its capacity to understand the extraordinary irregularity of investment results and so to give timely support to individuals during their own particular periods of great stress. Explaining that when his investment performance was unsatisfactory during the early 1960s, he had received a lot of reassuring support, senior portfolio manager Bill Newton says simply, "I'll never forget it."[16]

The secret to being truly tolerant during difficult times is, of course, to be very careful in recruiting—so everyone will *know* they want to give the individual time to get back on his horse and demonstrate the capabilities they know he has.

"We treasure the major, innovative idea," says Fullerton. "But even the best idea is only valuable to the extent it is *used.* If you like someone, you'll listen to his or her ideas. If you like each other a lot, you'll listen often and pay close attention. There is perhaps no business in which good communication of soft, emerging ideas is more important than in the investment management business." In communications, particularly in sharing information and ideas that

---

[16] Newton's career-long investment record, while never made public because of the anonymity of the multiple-counselor system, was one of the very best in the industry—and he is not alone.

might coalesce into a great investment decision, good listening is essential—and the keys to good listening are trust and confidence in each other. Of course, good communication depends on both the sender and the receiver—because when he's not listening, the receiver is really in complete control of "communication."

Good investment ideas are fragile and hard to explain *and* hard to buy—so it's important that professionals enjoy each other and feed off each other. Capital doesn't hire people just because they're likable, but it does avoid hiring people who are abrasive—no matter how bright they are. Howard Schow taught the organization what is now called Schow's Law: Hire only people who are very bright—and who are at least *possible* to like.

Associates are never put down in public, because hurt feelings will inevitably distort and inhibit communication. In a way that is characteristic of the organization's continuous self-examination, some now ask, "Is Capital *too* nice?" when some investment professionals seem to feel obliged to acknowledge, or even emphasize, their own past mistakes, saying: "I got XYZ really wrong last year, so I'm wondering about ABC. Did you consider . . . ?"

Lovelace understands that the manufacturing floor is crucial—and at Capital, that means investment research. "Research always was and always will be the core of Capital," says Cody. Lovelace, Fisher, Rothenberg, and Shanahan all began as analysts—and today devote more time and energy as *investors* than as *managers* of the organization. Around its research core, Capital has built a well-rounded business with all components recognized and treated as important because of the work they do for investors. The structure of the whole organization is horizontal and is all about mutual respect and organizational leveling. If you were blindfolded at a typical investment meeting, it would not be obvious who the 20-year veteran senior portfolio manager was and who was the recently hired analyst.[17]

---

[17] Victor Kohn and Andrew Capon, "The Capital Group Reveals Its Winning Hand," *Global Investor,* March 1, 1997.

A typical Capital innovation came with the recognition that there could be an alternative to the traditional investment career progression from junior analyst to analyst, followed by the switch in channels to portfolio manager. Researchers instead could be offered a comparable progression in responsibilities from junior analyst to analyst to *senior analyst*—with comparable advances in compensation, ownership, and stature. Likewise, an Associate could be both an analyst and a portfolio counselor. Gordon Crawford, a senior professional and firm leader, was a full-time analyst for over 20 years and then—at his choice—became both an analyst and a portfolio counselor. Crawford also served on Capital Group Companies' board of directors for nearly 20 years—the last two as non-executive chairman. The impact on young analysts of seeing this choice of career and progression in operation can be profound.

Understanding that significant actions come from individual people with a passion for an idea—not from top-down mandates "launched from Corporate"—Capital encourages entrepreneurship with retreats to stimulate and encourage new ideas. In addition, it provides generous financial and organizational support for developing initiatives. To continue being innovative as the organization gets larger and larger, Capital celebrates "wild ducks" who do not fit a mold and protect the culture from becoming too homogeneous. It also looks for people who are different from those already in the organization.

"Capital is clearly a culture of strong individuals," says Rothenberg, "set in an industry notoriously afflicted with egotism. Yet we accept, and quietly seek, anonymity as individuals in the work we do. Jon sets the example for all of us: He simply never uses the word 'I.' And we prize the reality that even among our professional peers, Capital as an organization is underappreciated, not fully recognized."

Avoiding personal publicity or recognition is deeply entrenched in Capital's culture and important to the organization. Capital people are discouraged from talking to the press and don't care—or learn not to care—about external recognition or fame. Having no names in the newspapers means something special to Associates as individuals and as a group.

Capital's "no-stars" commitment means that there's no place for anyone who psychologically needs to be a star. (They don't join, and if they do join, they soon leave.) Having no stars has important advantages for a professional organization: It avoids the divisiveness and politics that can arise between winners and losers—zero-sum games at best.

A few years ago, a top business magazine wanted to do an article on the success of the EuroPacific fund. John Lawrence, the public relations director, took the call: "We don't want to participate, thank you."

"But," the reporter insisted, "we want to call it one of the *best* funds!" To which Lawrence replied: "All the more reason we're not interested. We're not interested in publicity for our funds, especially for those things that are 'hot,' because that usually turns out to be the *worst* time to put money in."

A short time later, the reporter called back: "I don't think you understand," he said, "We want to make it a *cover* story." Lawrence gave the decisive reply: "Oh, then we're *definitely* not interested."

Since the physical environment can make important differences to people—either positive or negative—Capital strives to avoid *any* indicator of status or structure that might conflict with its deliberately egalitarian respect for each individual. Offices in Tokyo, New York, London, Singapore, Los Angeles, and Geneva are consistent in tone or feel as well as in layout and size. Light-gray walls are typically highlighted with blond woodwork. Pictures on the walls,[18] selected by an internal committee, are typically abstract and contemporary, but always conservative. Inside walls of external offices are made of glass so staff members on the inside have natural light and can always see out. (One uncontrollable sign of individual

---

[18] Including a striking series of Ansel Adams photographs (acquired by Bob Egelston) that reflect JL's work with conservancy organizations in California.

independence at Capital is notoriously evident in every office around the world: piles of memos, reports, and magazines, stacked high on credenzas and shelves.) Corners, which would inevitably project an occupant's higher status, are never used for individual offices: They are either trading rooms or conference rooms.

The careful consistency of Capital Group's facilities is a great temptation for jokesters. While opening an office in Singapore in 1989, Mark Denning had some fun with Don Conlan,[19] a determined internationalist, who was respectful of local ways and also had a strong commitment to Capital's egalitarian cultural norms. The latter, of course, called for no corner offices. In Chinese society, where superstitions are both rampant and respected, experts on Feng Shui routinely inspect new offices (and homes, gravesites, etc.) to advise the owners on ways to avoid problems with evil spirits. Sensing an opportunity to tease Conlan, Denning sent him a mock-serious telex seeking advice. Alleging that the local Feng Shui expert was insistent that Denning's own office be located in a particular corner—with a glorious view of Singapore harbor—Denning cheerfully proposed that Conlan, out of respect for local ways, would surely want an exception made to an L.A.-centric practice. Carefully positioned by Denning on the classic horns of a dilemma, Conlan sputtered until Denning burst into laughter and acknowledged the setup.

Fifteen years ago, Capital took over several floors of a prominent Los Angeles office tower that had been occupied by the senior executives of Security Pacific National Bank. This proud group of corporate executives had climbed to the top of that large bank's extensive hierarchy and understandably wanted to have "destination" offices. Their headquarters complex was lavishly designed with cathedral

---

[19] After taking a series of degrees at Michigan, Conlan joined Chemical Bank in New York as an economist. Several years later, Bill Hurt recruited him first to Dean Witter, and then to Capital. Then John Dunlop recruited him to the Cost of Living Council in the early 1970s—and Capital agreed to a year's "sabbatical" before he settled into his role as economist and Washington monitor—and then into internal management. At retirement, he was president of The Capital Group Company.

ceilings and a magnificently wide internal central stairway that rose from the 53rd floor to the 54th floor. Prospective corporate borrowers would regularly climb it when submitting their loan requests to the great bank's senior lenders. When Capital took over the space, it removed all this grand ostentation: Ceilings were lowered to a more normal height and offices were substantially reduced in size.[20] Capital installed more than four *times* as many executives and staff as the bank had housed in the same space.

In keeping with the Los Angeles practice of prestige office towers having a large, well-lighted, colorful "statement" rendition of the primary tenant's corporate logo, the landlord offered to put the appropriate Capital signage on the top of the tall building. Capital, however, quickly declined the offer: "No, thank you. No signage. We wouldn't want anything like that." Only anonymity would do for Capital.

Despite the inherent complexity of investing on a global basis, having many right-sized working units is central to Capital's organizational effectiveness. Capital moves again and again to smaller working units so everyone will know their fellow workers well and will see the impact of their own contributions. While covering the full spectrum of global investing may require more than 30 participants, the optimal size of a professional working group of analysts and portfolio counselors is usually less than 30 participants. Similarly, the ideal working limit on the size of service centers in shareholder services is approximately 500 Associates, so the senior manager will know all the people who work there.

With increasing asset size and a large organization of diverse people, communication could have become a serious problem for Capital, but communications technology—e-mail, video conferencing, and so on—has improved even more rapidly. Conference calls that link units from various parts of the world are scheduled

---

[20] Because a table in the bank's boardroom was so enormous that it simply could not be moved out, Capital kept it, but had skilled carpenters cut it way down in size and put it in a small board room.

regularly; extensive information on analysts' visits to companies is shared continuously via Internet; several daily Internet newsletters have wide internal circulation; and research "jamborees" bring large groups together to exchange information. Perhaps most illustrative, a video conference facility is used so often at Capital that the telephone company came up with a unique usage-pricing arrangement—for a flat fee, it is left on all the time.

To foster information sharing among analysts with overlapping interests and responsibilities, Capital has many "cluster[21] groups" like the Tech Zeppelin—20 technology analysts who get together by weekly conference call to share information and insights. This same group, from bases all over the world, will meet together in, say, Europe for joint calls on companies and to share knowledge on different aspects of their industries. Such a group was visiting tech companies in Mexico when they got the first clues that a worldwide slowdown was beginning to develop in telecom—months before any impact on stock prices.

---

[21] Reminding listeners of *The Graduate* and the scene where Dustin Hoffman is given *the* tip—"Plastics!"—Fisher smiles and enunciates his tip: "Clusters!"

CHAPTER 13

MANAGEMENT

NOTES FOR READERS

Every effective organization has—explicitly or implicitly—its own primary mission. The central responsibility of senior management is to make that mission clear and show how the strategy will accomplish that mission. Ideally, every aspect of an organization's strategy and structure will stream logically back from the organization's own "horizon model" of itself, validating the strategy by which it intends to achieve its primary mission.

Most small investment organizations have a simply stated mission: Achieve superior investment results and win business because of those results. But as investment firms become larger and larger, clarity of focus often gets muddled. However unintentionally, most large investment organizations have somehow shifted their focus from *professional* priorities to *business* priorities. In particular, the large organization's interest in investment results typically shifts from being "among the best" to being "good enough." From a business perspective, the optimizing strategy is to have acceptable investment products and concentrate organizational resources on selling to expand the assets under management and increase profits.

Most organizations in the investment management industry will, at least privately, acknowledge that they are primarily an asset-gathering business and that management's top priority is to run that business profitably. An uncomfortably large number of investment organizations have *two* primary missions: One is internal and real; the other is external and only for prospects and customers. The latter often involves mouthing platitudes about striving for superior investment results, while the *real* mission, maximizing owners' profits, drives all the important decisions and actions.

Capital is different. It has designed every aspect of its organization to achieve consistently superior long-term investment results for clients. Capital seeks clients who really want superior *long-term* investment results—not just saying (as everyone always says) that they seek long-term results—and, over time, has developed a sizable constituency of individual and institutional investors who understand the organization's capabilities and its commitment to produce such results consistently.

So its *structure* will never constrict its strategy,[1] Capital deliberately has almost no visible organizational structure. Similarly, leadership at Capital is always evolving: Because individual decision makers are each learning and developing, responsibilities are kept flexible and fluid so the overall organization will always be dynamic and growing as individuals develop.

Capital may appear conservative or "defensive" to a casual observer, but such a perception would be a serious misreading of a deliberate and rational thought process. To recoin the familiar phrase: For Capital, a strong defense is the best offense, just as the solid foundation for favorable long-term returns is careful research—first to limit the risk of serious loss; and then second, to search for major gains.

Capital's decision-making process is extensively consultative. But while decision-making authority is widespread throughout the

---

[1] See Alfred D. Chandler's *Strategy & Structure: Chapters in the History of the American Industrial Enterprise.* MIT Press, Cambridge, MA (1969).

organization and decision makers are certainly expected to consult appropriately and carefully with all who might contribute to or could be affected by a particular decision, the actual decisions are not made by consensus. On both organizational and investment matters, the appropriate decision makers—and there are over 250 significant decisions makers in the organization—are expected to *consult, decide,* and take *action*—and *communicate the decision.*

Since no free market is quite so free as the market for good ideas, Capital keeps its internal "market" for ideas as free as possible. It assures objectivity and rationality in decision making; maximizes the clarity and volume of useful communications; and recruits, develops, rewards, and empowers individuals who will make effective decisions.

Great leaders not only make their own breaks, they also make the most from their breaks. The number of action decisions is important, but the scale and duration of decisions are far more important—and easy to underestimate. Building the organization's capacity and capability to perform is the task-focus of the great leader, while the good leader executes and transacts well, the great leader builds the organization's *capacity* to act. The old maxim holds: The good leader will focus on doing things the right way; the great leader will focus on doing the right things.

Of course, the complement of doing the right things is the discipline to avoid doing the wrong things. Capital is unusually capable of deciding *not* to take action. For many organizations, extensive investigation of possible alternatives can develop so much internal momentum that a decision to act is almost irresistible. The most important decisions and contributions of the great leader-builders are often unknown because "nothing happened." But decisions *not* to do—*not* to go along with the industry; *not* to go along with convincingly articulated internal pressures; *not* to take a risk others don't recognize—are often decisive to an organization's long-term success, particularly in a highly competitive market.

Making constructive *negative* decisions may sound oxymoronic, but Capital has steadily improved its ability to concentrate its considerable capabilities on achieving its most important objectives. It has built trust with stockbrokers, investors, and Associates by thinking through and talking out "What could go wrong?" and by repeatedly deciding not to do popular things and thereby not get diverted from its long-term priorities.

Favorable balance is sought between exercising caution when deciding how to act on new "opportunities" that might later sour versus encouraging bold action on initiatives that can provide the foundation for important growth. These decisions have included international investing; emerging markets investing; business development in the major "country" markets; implementing the multiple-counselor system; developing innovative ways of sharing the distribution of financial rewards and ownership; having no "employees" because even those who work in conventionally routine administrative jobs are known, respected, and rewarded as Associates; keeping a conscientiously flat organizational structure; continuously changing titles so many Associates have opportunities for leadership and so nobody inside or outside takes any title too seriously; and finally, assuring an egalitarian way of relating to one another and a confident commitment to meritocracy in determining responsibilities and compensation.

"WE WANT TO be known by our clients as the best investment management firm in the world," says David Fisher. "Those words are carefully chosen. I said the *best*. I didn't say the biggest. And known by our *clients*—not by everyone. That's our objective."

Fisher goes on to explain that he means best as clients see it because even though investment results always come first at Capital, most institutional clients also care a lot about their working relationships with the professionals at Capital and most individual investors also care about informative, helpful service. So Capital strives to provide strong service, but is first and foremost an *investment* organization with a clearly understood mission: achieving consistently superior long-term investment results. As Jim Rothenberg says, "This drives how we think about our organization and how we try to manage our investment people, structure, and reward systems in pursuing a bottom-up approach to managing investments."[2]

Being private, Capital can take a long-term view of its mission and never needs to compromise by laying off workers or cutting back bonuses to boost short-term profits to please public shareholders. Quite the contrary at Capital: During tough times, the firm *adds* people and is ready to take bold strategic initiatives. Fisher adds, "Being private is important because it serves the interests of our *clients*."

"Management in investment firms is custom built," explains Rothenberg. "It is designed around the goals each individual firm establishes and its desired organizational ambiance. We have long believed that if we do our job well over time, as measured in rolling ten-year time frames, prospective clients will find out who we are. Historically, that's proven a good approach to the world. We may be the only major organization that thinks about the business this way, but from our perspective, to think otherwise is to treat investment management as a commodity and be just an asset-gatherer."

There literally is no organizational structure at Capital in the conventional meaning of the term. What little *formal* structure there is, is almost invisible. "We've never had an organization chart around here," explains Bob Cody. "It would be against the way we like to work." Smiling, Cody recalls, "Once we had a management consultant who tried rather diligently to work one out, but after several attempts, he gave it up."[3]

---

[2] "Managing Investment Firms: People and Culture." Conference sponsored by the Association for Investment Management and Research (AIMR) in 1997.

[3] At American Funds Service Company (AFS), necessarily a traditionally structured operation because of its high-volume, accuracy-dependent work, Tim Weiss admits to having an organizational chart, but smiling, says it's seldom used. "We have a pretty flat organizational structure here, too."

In Capital's remarkably flat structure, many Associates have direct decision-making responsibilities. Several hundred people carry out operational management while five committees work on long-term policies and organizational design. Two are operating committees (one for Strategy and Plans, and one for Operations) and two are management groups (one for the mutual fund business and one for the worldwide institutional business). Both meet weekly. Finally, the Finance Committee—which decides both total compensation and share ownership issues—is a particular long-term power center.

Asked directly who runs the company, Mike Shanahan responds indirectly, "It all depends on the topic. It's always somebody different. And sometimes it's 10 people at once.[4] This is a people business, and we don't manage this honeycomb with anybody in charge in the sense that you normally think of as 'in charge.' Management at Capital is a *process.* To ask who is in charge, you have to define the problem, and then we can probably identify the three or four people who would be involved.[5] Our approach to management builds on consensus, much like the Japanese."

Tim Armour illustrates the proposition with this description of what would happen if someone came to JL with a recommendation for action: "He'd reply, 'You should really run this by this person, that person, that person and that person, and think about its impact on that person, that person and that person.' "[6]

Managerial processes at Capital are constantly adjusted, tweaked, and altered. If there has not been a significant organizational change in several years, Associates will expect that a change must be right around the corner. Although most people usually don't like change, change in structure is the best way to preempt rigidity. "Change is good and powerful and allows us to move toward our goals—and our

[4] *Forbes,* August 28, 1995, p. 143.
[5] *Wall Street Journal,* July 9, 1992, "Capital Group Isn't a Household Name," Randall Smith.
[6] "Capital Appreciation" by Christopher Oster, *SmartMoney,* March 1999, p. 3.

fantasies," says Fisher. "Of course, we sometimes need to battle for change because many obstacles to change do exist."

At any given time, a dozen or more committees will be examining areas of interest, partly to develop consensus and partly to preempt subsequent second-guessing by addressing significant questions thoroughly and early—often very early. "We are always asking a broad group of our people what they most want to do," says Shanahan. "We want to capture their changing sense of passion and the nuances as they develop" to create opportunities and challenges that will meet Associates' needs and expectations.

"As an organization, Capital is best understood not as a structure of boxes connected by straight lines of authority, but as a living organism," explains Rothenberg. "It works due to the people. With over 6,000 people, we are not small so we have to battle the normal tendencies of the bureaucracy to grow and get in the way."

Explains Jason Pilalas (see Chapter 15): "Power is the power to change, and in an investment management organization, that means the power to change investments. At Capital, a remarkable share of that real power goes to the young professionals who are doing the basic research—and are learning all the time how to use that power to make real investment decisions."

To avoid intrusion on individuals making crisp decisions, Capital wants to be on the alert for any problems with bureaucracy—particularly as the organization has gotten larger. "There's lots of 'anti-bureaucracy' talk around Capital," says Fisher, "and we recognize that a creep toward bureaucracy is hard to catch early. But to say 'There's no hierarchy at Capital' or 'No one's in charge' or 'We have no controls' is simple baloney. We want to have just enough structure to get our real jobs done well."

"There is no 'one way' at Capital—and we want to keep it that way," says Fisher. "There is no one great 'Truth,' so there must be no risk to raising questions." Rigorous inquiry and examination—which could feel like being jumped on to someone who's new—is instead recognized by experienced Associates as a compliment. "Tolerance for, and active encouragement of, differences of opinion *and* the preparedness to make decisions and take individual responsibility for the consequences of those decisions are two great strengths of Capital," observes Mark Denning. "These two go together with the remarkable absence of hierarchy in the organization."

Capital's obvious challenge is how to structure and manage one of the world's largest global investment organizations for optimal investment decision making.[7] Fisher says: "I have formed several opinions about what works and what does not work in today's rapidly changing environment: The most *efficient* answer to an organizational issue is often not the most *effective*. When a conflict arises between efficiency and effectiveness, [we always] choose the latter.

"To be successful, a global organization must know what is going on locally in terms of clients and markets—which can only be accomplished by *proximity*. At the same time, the organization must be able to *distance* itself from what is going on in any particular locality to achieve investment perspective. So both proximity and distance are necessary to make effective investment decisions.

"Globalization is also creating the need for greater diversity of people. Today, more than 40 percent of our analysts are *not* Americans. Our analysts and portfolio counselors were born in 38 different countries. If you walk down the hall, the order of people you'll meet are Canadian, Chilean, French, German, American, Brazilian, French, Chinese, Argentinean, and Indian. We speak 40 languages in this organization. And we believe to be a global investment organization, you have to be multicultural and multilingual."

Maximizing the interpersonal effectiveness of the informal organization is at least as important as minimizing the constraints on communication that the formal organizational structure may cause. Years ago, to increase open expression of different views and perspectives, Jon Lovelace organized several multiday retreats for investment professionals. One evening during these retreats, Lovelace would sit

---

[7] "Managing Investment Firms," sponsored by AIMR.

unobtrusively in a corner and throw out a series of possible "bitch topics" for open discussion and encourage candor—with no recrimination later on. Capital continues to hold frequent three-day retreats to encourage the cross-fertilization of ideas, information, and new ways of thinking about investments or organizational policies.

Capital celebrates decision makers who add to its overall effectiveness by thinking differently: Often they see problems differently because they are significantly unlike in personality. Jon Lovelace is gentle, tentative, and tangential, while Mike Shanahan is blunt, bold, and direct. Despite their considerable personality differences, Shanahan and Lovelace work well together. "When I first got here," says Shanahan ruefully, "I could tell right off that Jon didn't know *any*thing. Years later, I realized he'd been right all along." Explains Don Conlan: "Very few organizations can handle more than one genius. Since both of these guys are clearly geniuses, Capital is uniquely a 'two-genius' outfit."

When a complicated subject comes up for decision, colleagues can see both Lovelace and Shanahan working the matter over in their minds, thinking way out ahead of the discussion.[8] Each of them, separately and silently, will have gone through a whole series of "what-if" sequences, reaching into the possible or probable future. Both men are very rational and can stay focused on what really matters, not getting distracted by the current emotional aspects of an issue. They guide by asking questions—lots of questions.

---

[8] "Jon's a human calculator," says his friend John Maguire, past president of Claremont Graduate University. "He can run numbers in his head like no one you ever saw. 'January 17, 1995,' Jon will say, 'Hmm, that'll be Tuesday.' He knows that six months from now he has a meeting with so-and-so at 4:00 P.M. And he can compound numbers over time in his head." Says Olin Robison, president emeritus of Middlebury College: "Jon has an encyclopedic memory of markets in this country. He can discuss the current situation and say, 'This is a lot like what happened in October 1927 and January 1939, but August 1954 was different because . . .' of such and such reasons." "Jon is a baseball statistician—with a sideline called investing," chuckles Edus Warren. "The humility with which he conducts himself—it's just watching grace at work. For anybody who might know him, he's a hero," says TV producer Norman Lear, who knew Lovelace via Claremont.

Shanahan and Lovelace almost always work in the background, combining the best thinking of others into a superior whole. (Ironically, their style of management makes it hard for most people to appreciate exactly what they have done and are doing for Capital.) Shanahan is philosophical: "Over the long term, a balanced middle way may not be very exciting or inspirational. But when combined with close attention to people as individuals—and *both* are needed— it can work very, very well." But, as will soon be seen, it doesn't *always* work well.

Building through and with as well as for the next generation is an essential characteristic of great professional firm leadership. Shared learning on specific decisions provides vehicles for genuine sharing and passing forward a firm's culture or beliefs.[9] Young Associates learn best by seeing real people doing real things and thinking their way through all the uncertainty, complexity, and conflicting values and data that characterize decision making on important issues—and making real decisions, sometimes unsuccessfully.

Management can foster an organization's agility and flexibility by moving toward centralization if the firm is highly decentralized *or* by moving toward decentralization if it is highly centralized. Having moved toward smaller subgroups during the 1960s, Lovelace felt the time had come in the 1980s to move toward greater sharing of information and ideas. This effort would show dramatically how hard it can be to accommodate gifted individualists within an organization that is designed to avoid dependence on specific individuals.

Howard Schow, one of Capital's leading portfolio counselors, had been in full agreement with the earlier movement toward small working units that suited his personal style and enabled him to develop a close-knit and highly effective unit. He could not, however, support Lovelace in assuring open sharing of ideas and information, which would mean sharing his group's investment insights. During 1981 and

[9] Paul Haaga.

1982, Schow's small group had produced remarkable investment results due in large part to an astute and early negative call[10] on energy stocks. Lovelace wanted to be sure all of Capital would benefit from such important insights.

Schow, who had agreed with Lovelace on the effectiveness of working in small units, didn't see why he should now be obliged to make sure everyone else understood all his best ideas. He worried about having coattail followers and wanted his own separate unit to continue running AMCAP Fund as well as his portions of ICA and American Mutual. This arrangement conflicted with the commitment to extensive sharing of ideas and information that Lovelace was working toward. For Schow, this total sharing of creative ideas made no sense at all.

Disagreement on such a consequential matter between two such major figures in the organization had been going on so long that it was becoming disruptive to the whole organization and needed to get resolved. Lovelace believed that systems were essential in developing a major organization and that everyone should contribute to those systems; Schow believed in the preeminence of the unique, talented individual. Schow would develop the organization around stellar individuals; Lovelace also sought unusually talented individuals, but he wanted to design an organization that was not dependent on any specific people.

While Lovelace continued to explore possible solutions to this philosophical dilemma and made what he believed were extraordinary efforts to persuade Schow to be patient, Schow felt increasing doubt about anyone's ability to find an effective resolution. He had begun thinking about developing an alternative: a firm of his own, organized in the way he believed would work most effectively. His reputation and his investment record made the prospect of launching a new firm attractive, but he had not yet discussed the nascent idea with those who might join with him—nor with any prospective clients.

[10] By Dave Richards.

After working closely together for 27 successful years, Schow and Lovelace had great professional respect for each other and strong interpersonal bonds. Both men knew the other had been thinking long and hard on this most important question. Lovelace knew he would have to find a solution that would also be acceptable to the other Associates who had clear and strong views that seemed incompatible with Schow's. Some had found it difficult to work with Schow; some were aware that Schow's leaving would open up more shares of stock for redistribution; and some were concerned about what they felt or feared was favoritism toward Schow.

Characteristically, Lovelace was patiently looking for a resolution that would work well for everyone. He had been looking for a long time—nearly a year. Both men knew that Lovelace had much greater patience than anyone else for developing managerial decisions, whereas Schow found the time devoted to exploring all aspects of all alternatives—as Lovelace habitually did on important matters—"interminable." Both men knew that Schow was keen to get the matter resolved.

Schow approached Lovelace at a family wedding reception: "Jon, how are you coming on working it out?"

"Howie, I still haven't been able to find a way we can make this work out together."

"Well, are you saying, in effect, that it can't be made to work? Because we do need to resolve things. Do you think you're close to a solution?"

"I wish I could say so. I'm still working on it, but quite frankly, right now I don't see just how to do it. I hope you aren't under serious time pressure and can be patient so we can work it out."

"Well, if that's the situation, Jon, I don't feel we can all just keep waiting—waiting to see without knowing what we're waiting for or when we'll see something." The conversation was suspended in silence.

Not having a resolution became a resolution. The following week, Schow began to develop plans for what became his new firm,

PRIMECAP,[11] and Lovelace continued working toward an organization with no indispensable individuals.

Over and over again, after extensive and visible investigation—and often, the development of strong advocates—Capital has made wise decisions *not* to do something that "everyone else" was doing. At least 80 percent of Capital's most important decisions have been 'No' decisions: active, carefully thought-through decisions *not* to take a specific action. That's why one of the hallmarks of Capital is how seldom it makes major mistakes.

Recent key decisions include both positive decisions and decisions *not* to do things. Among *positive* decisions, two stand out: the commitment in 1985 to the emerging markets, and the decision in 1988 to take the lead on 12(b)-1 programs to compensate brokers for long-term mutual fund sales. Discussions of 12(b)-1 generated considerable debate, but the resolution Capital worked out is now widely accepted across the industry.

Decisions *not* to take action include not offering high-yield bond funds when that market was too dependent on just one dealer; not offering an emerging markets mutual fund when retail interest was very high; and not offering "Government-Plus" bond funds in the mid-1980s when so many other mutual fund groups were offering

[11] Recollections continue to differ regarding the factors that resulted in Schow's leaving. Those who remained typically feel that Schow wanted too much to run his own show too separately from the rest of the organization and wanted to invest in stocks that would not fit into Investment Company of America or Washington Mutual. Another contributing factor was probably the narrow defeat of his earlier proposal to divide up Capital. "Howard was and is a superb investor, but the decision was not just about Howard," explains JL. "It also had to be about how others felt, and Howard could and would be rather confrontational. If Howard had been able to find the patience to stay longer and keep working on it," says Lovelace, "I know I would have had the patience—and with persistence, so we should have been able to find a way out of the dilemma." Friends say Schow didn't want to leave Capital and might well have stayed if Lovelace had put his arm around his shoulder and said, "Howie, this is so important to us that we're just going to find a way—because we *must* work it out." Lovelace, who does not like confrontation, had asked Shanahan to work on it, and Schow interpreted this, unfortunately and incorrectly, as a lack of direct, personal interest by Lovelace. PRIMECAP has achieved strong investment results and now manages over $25 billion. Schow is recognized widely as a great investor.

them. (The other fund groups got big sales until all those funds came unwound and hurt their investors.) Another "No" decision was to reject back-end loads on mutual funds, when the industry first turned to this structure. Now, after developing an arrangement it thinks more appropriate—including a $100,000 cap on the amounts involved in the transaction—Capital offers a full array of alternative fee structures for mutual fund sales.

"Jon's and Mike's great strength is in *not* doing things that may be wrong over the long term," says Rothenberg. "He sees long-term trends as an *investor* does, not as a sales guy would. Not doing the wrong things, as all great investors simply must know and understand, is really the key to long-term investment success. Over the long term, it's not too bad, actually, to miss the star ideas and events *if* in so doing you avoid the really bad stuff. We always want to encourage folks to try things—but *not* dumb things.

"On the other hand," he continues, "we want to be careful with 'The answer is No! . . . Now what's the question?' because you can slide over into the real risk of being too conservative and not being appropriately innovative. This would be just as dangerous as not knowing or understanding what it *really* takes to do things well and what it takes to do the really right things. If you ever *assume* the answer will be 'No,' you won't study each question fully and carefully and you'll soon fall behind on the Knowledge Curve." That's why Capital's leaders believe that decision making—whether eventually a "Yes" or a "No"—should be an active, creative engagement and that the data gathering, analysis, and evaluation should serve as preparation for making the next decision well. They are also skeptical about binary—yes or no—decisions with only two options because most issues worth deciding are too rich in complexity for such simple answers to be the best answers. The best answers usually come from a deep understanding that has been gained by studying the problems and creating new alternatives that were not even considered initially.

Capital has had some important near misses where it almost made an unfortunate negative decision, including: venture capital investing, combining American Funds Distributors into Capital Group, emerging markets investing, and even international investing as a whole. If governed by the vocal majority when first considering these decisions, serious mistakes could have been made and major opportunities missed.

Not building a robust business in bond management much earlier is now recognized as having been a mistake. But in recent years, Capital has identified sectors of the bond market where its research skills and long-term investment horizon clearly provide real advantages and has made strong progress with high-yield bonds and emerging market debt. Still, with $35 billion in bonds, it's hard to call Capital's bond business unsuccessful. After all, Investment Company of America was smaller than that after 25 years of operation, and the growth curve on bond assets is somewhat better than the asset growth curve for ICA.[12]

For several years, Capital was slow in making two important decisions: offering several types of mutual fund shares to provide investors with alternative pricing structures for different ways of investing and developing a strong relationship management program in its institutional business. Significantly, Capital has recently advanced to leadership in both areas.

If a major strategic opportunity were to present itself, Capital is prepared to take full advantage: It has ample capacity in people and capital to act boldly. Capital had accumulated nearly $1 billion of undesignated reserves by 2000, anticipating during that period of

---

[12] Capital's strength in equity research is considered increasingly important for investing in bonds. "I think the bottom-up work is a secret weapon," says Jim Mulally. "A fairly obvious advantage is that the equity analysts' work on corporates where we own the bonds helps inform our credit work. Also the work that's being done on companies helps by feeding into a matrix of information. Economic statistics are becoming less reliable, so being able to have the macro picture supplemented by the experience of specific companies is helpful. It's often 'lead' information." Mark Brett, Mulally's London-based colleague, illustrates: "In recent years, economists have had concerns about the direction of inflation and interest rates in Europe. But those concerns didn't have much of an impact on me, because our analysts were telling us that individual companies had little or no pricing power."

exuberant expectations at the likelihood of future adversity could provide important opportunities for the well-prepared organization to make strategic investments.

Another reservoir of resources for strategic action is Associates' strong identification with the organization and its core values, particularly distributive justice or fairness. Lovelace has long been almost fanatical about teamwork and treating everyone fairly. He has great tolerance for deferring decisions to gain greater understanding and will insist that while he may know what he wants decided, he doesn't know what the actual decision should be. Always nonconfrontational, he regularly uses committees and appears, even to close observers, not always to know what he wants decided.[13] When the group, after extended, even laborious, consideration, settles on the judgment he had anticipated long before, he will say quite innocently with a smile, "That's a great idea!" when he could just as well say, "Well, you've finally found it!"

Not interested in personal power or in dominating the decision process, Lovelace wants others to learn how to make wise decisions. He knows that Capital will need numerous leaders for the future and has made this awareness clear in interesting ways. In 1972, he took a four-month sabbatical with his family in southern Europe: Being away was a unique way of compelling others to share executive power. For years, Lovelace has avoided conventional, hierarchical titles and expects Associates one-third his age to call him "Jon" or "JL."

Capital is consultative in its decision-making process, seeking to achieve agreement and commitment, but Capital never *decides* by consensus. The difference is significant. In consensus decision-making organizations, most individuals don't strive to make the best rational decision so much as they look for the position

---

[13] Late in 1963, after refusing to head the firm several times, Lovelace finally agreed to accept the presidency of Capital Research and Management Company. He became chairman in 1975, four years before his father died at age 84. But, typically, Lovelace did not serve continuously as chairman. He let others try the job on for size, including Howard Schow in 1982 and 1983. Lovelace stepped down to vice chairman in 1993.

that puts them in or near the center of the crowd, near the emerging consensus where it's "safe." Not so at Capital. The firm wants to develop each person's capacity and determination to make significant decisions objectively—and to take responsibility for the consequences.

"Individuals make the decisions and live with the consequences of those decisions at Capital," says Jason Pilalas (see Chapter 15). "Associates have lots of freedom and lots of responsibility—really total freedom and total responsibility." Organizationally, Jon Lovelace pushed decision authority all the way down to the lowest possible level—for investment counselors in the 1950s and for analysts in the 1960s. Jon recognized that the primacy of the individual decision maker is, was, and always will be the one great imperative in building an investment organization. So he built the Capital investment organization by selecting and developing superior individual decision makers—and being sure they are unencumbered by the organization or managerial chores that have to get done.

"I learned something about the value attached to consensus early on in my work at Capital," recalls a senior Associate.[14] "I had what I thought was a really good idea and took it to Don Conlan, who was President. When he said, 'Sounds fine, go ahead,' I started the process of implementation—only to learn that Don had meant 'Go ahead *and* talk to people to see if they would agree.' Don sure didn't expect me to take action *before* gaining a consensus. But I'd assumed an 'okay' from the President was an action authorization. There's an important difference here, and it's linked to the respect for the many other individuals at Capital. It takes awhile for a new 'go-getter' to learn and appreciate."

"If very good people are put into an organizational structure in which they only *recommend* but others *decide,* the best of them will migrate elsewhere," says Fisher. "That's why we strive to empower

---

[14] John Lawrence, who was business editor of the *Los Angeles Times* and then served at the New York Stock Exchange before joining Capital in 1992.

individuals to take action and own the results of the actions they do take. Younger Associates are frequently asked: 'What's in your way or making it hard for you to do a better job?' If the reply is: 'Gee, I never thought of that,' it's best to say, 'Let's meet again—after you've had time to give this more thought.'"

Consultative management, with consensus developed over a long period and through many conversations, can lead to young people trying to anticipate what the leaders would think. In one sense, that's easy at Capital: It's *always* what's truly best for clients.

But trying to anticipate a leader's thoughts can be a real danger if it affects, as it surely will, how decisions are made and what decisions get made. In working with future leaders, Capital's current leaders often ask: "How would *you* handle X or Y?" This gives those future leaders experience in understanding and making decisions so their decision-making capabilities will be known before they would have the direct responsibility for making important decisions.

Experience with the multiple counselor concept contributes strongly to the way the Capital organization is managed. "The-buck-stops-here" authority for all sorts of decisions is deliberately dispersed throughout the organization. And while decision makers are both recognized and rewarded inside Capital, they get little or no individual recognition outside the organization.

"Jon studied psychology at Princeton," explains Walter Stern. "And he makes good use of PET Theory[15] and active listening to develop and demonstrate genuine understanding of another person's intended meaning. Jon nurtures the growth in competence of individuals, teams, and the overall organization as he manages on a case-by-case basis, in a gently persistent, continuously experimental way. Jon is a towering figure without towering over others." Lovelace is admired for having a great understanding of time and force and how to use time to manage or control force—and for taking a very long-term view.

[15] Tom Gordon's book, *Parent Effectiveness Training*.

Says Shanahan: "Jon's been 'retiring' for 30 years. Fortunately, his values and his approach to the managerial process were transferred to many others a long time ago."[16]

Knowing how important it is to avoid oversimplification, Lovelace has great tolerance for interim ambiguity and for keeping options open by not rushing to resolve or clarify a decision. "Jon never has—and never would—state a clear vision for Capital because he always prefers that we keep our options open," explains Rothenberg. "Business school models usually tend toward clear and decisive action-oriented approaches to management, but Jon, for all his interest in ultimate precision, is remarkably capable of muddling through a problem and keeping the problem-solving process fluid, while continuously seeking the best long-term resolution. Jon is very good at managing trade-offs to the advantage of the organization." Avoiding confrontation, particularly on a personal level, is very important to Lovelace, who will simply avoid those with whom he cannot agree.

"Jon *always* puts the interests of Capital ahead of his own interests," says Armour, "and teaches by example the importance of consistent commitment to, and even passion for, Capital's three-way mission that dates from 1963: serving clients; serving Associates; and serving shareholders."

For Lovelace, words have great meaning, and he searches diligently for the exactly right word or sentence because it could matter in the future. When a colleague commented on the firm having recurring reorganizations, Lovelace interceded: "Do you really mean *reorganization?* Wouldn't a better term be *restructuring?*" Similarly Capital Associates talk about investment *services,* not investment *products,* and about investment *results,* not *performance,*

---

[16] *Forbes,* August 28, 1995, p. 150. Recently, after declining a senior management title and role with the modest self-appraisal that he was not very good at management, Lovelace resigned from Capital's board of directors. Later, Fisher was able to persuade him to return to the board, but only with the compromise title of non-executive chairman, which he relinquished as soon as the concept of a non-executive chairman—a British usage—was accepted.

because performance is inherently ephemeral—something done by actors in Hollywood and New York.

Capital is, by design, a remarkably flat organization. "Philosophically and personally," explains Kirby, "Jon has a real aversion to being or being seen or even *thought* to be the 'boss.' He doesn't *like* it. So having a traditional CEO role is strictly *verboten*. Still, Jon does manage by veto if he feels he really must. But well before that, when he's nervous about something or feels it's inappropriate, he'll stop by your office and gently say, 'Let's talk this over together.'"

Then shifting naturally to Shanahan, Kirby continues: "Mike can make tough decisions and make them without delay. He doesn't screw around or put decisions off.[17] When he says, 'I'll let you know in a day or so,' he does. Mike's decisions are well accepted because all of us believe he always treats everyone very fairly. Rothenberg's the same kind of guy: Ready to make the tough decisions—and very fair." Still, Shanahan, who is seldom in the office, can sometimes be difficult for others to understand or agree with. This happens most when he has missed the preparatory meetings during which an idea was explored and discussed.

Overall, Shanahan is so insightful and creative in conceptualizing ways to solve or manage problems that he shares Lovelace's difficulty: People try to anticipate how he might decide. "Mike's so good at making decisions," says Graham Holloway, "he soon found too many people were bringing their problems to him and asking him what they should do. But Mike's too smart for that. His response is to ask the question that puts the problem squarely back where it belongs—with the person who came to him." Shanahan listens and then simply says: "So how are *you* going to solve that problem?" Some Associates

---

[17] Shanahan has been central to several strategically important initiatives and decisions. In 1971 (as explained in Chapter 4), he arranged for the link-up with venture capital investor Don Valentine. In 1972, when an inadequately organized and supervised Capital Guardian Trust was in serious difficulty (see Chapter 7), Shanahan took charge. Reorganizing and merging American Fund Distributors into Capital Group Companies (see Chapter 6) was another crucial contribution.

suspect he stays away from the office as much as he can[18] so others cannot become dependent on him and he can spend more of his time on what he loves to do: investing.

Leadership at Capital is an evolving, organic, natural process of selection. To help get at the core issues, senior Associates are regularly asked such direct, provocative questions as: Whom do important people at Capital respect and trust? Who will make sound decisions under serious pressure? Whom would you trust with your mother's money?

Since difficult times—not easy times—are the real test of leaders, Shanahan says, "A serious bear market will show us who can learn what from seriously unfriendly experience. I'll be interested in learning who keeps a long-term horizon and who can keep focused on people."

Shanahan is also an important worrier—pondering the long-term possibilities, several iterative sequences out into the future. In the late 1990s, while others were enthusiastically enjoying the benefits of a long bull market, he worried that too many individual investors had been seduced into *assuming* 15 to 20 percent returns were normal or even likely. The stock market had never gone so high for so long before, and it clearly couldn't continue. Shanahan worried that if and when investors lost money in a bad market environment—particularly if their losses were large and sudden—they might rush to sell out. Since today's inexperienced mutual fund investors are probably the "weakest hands" in investment history, the impact of their selling in a bad market could compound into a major market decline with increasingly serious consequences for the economy, the stock market, the mutual fund industry—and for Capital. That's the way Shanahan worries.

---

[18] Most of the time, Shanahan works out of his home in the desert near Palm Springs, California, or Lake Arrowhead, in the mountains, saying, "Personally, I like my freedom. I don't like crowds at airports—or meeting with unhappy clients." The arrangement also enables Shanahan, a serious golfer, the time for an hour a day of self-disciplined practice of his short game.

Another area for worrying about the unthinkable is the risk of any slipup in ethics and integrity. "When I joined Capital," recalls Cody, "the firm was known to all of us in the industry for having consistently high standards in every area. The one word for Capital was and still is 'integrity'—both moral integrity and intellectual integrity. That commitment goes right back to JBL."

There have been very few breaches of the organization's zero tolerance on matters of integrity over the past 70 years. One trader let it be known to Wall Street firms that he wanted "in" on promising new issues for his personal account. He was promptly dismissed. The wife of an analyst who came from a Boston mutual fund organization was trading in her personal account and "front-running" Capital's mutual funds. Although it took some time to get the facts, the analyst was obliged to resign.

In 1983, Capital learned a painful lesson when a senior administrative officer was found siphoning money from a money market fund. The amount was large: approximately $2 million, but this was determined only after an extensive in-house investigation.[19] Some felt that, while he hid as much as he could as long as he could, the only reason he was ever caught was that somehow he psychologically wanted to get caught. Others felt that, as so often happens in white-collar crime, he came to believe he was just too smart to get caught and so got careless. The SEC conducted a major investigation of the facts and imposed sanctions barring the individual from the mutual fund industry but decided not to press criminal charges. Nor did Capital.[20]

Lovelace was determined to find out what had gone wrong and why. Thoughtful questions were raised: Why had the deviation of funds not been uncovered sooner? Was Capital unwilling to believe

[19] Initially, the amount diverted was thought to be only $40,000. And it first appeared that all or most of the money was going to fund an overcommitted pledge to the Boy Scouts. Actually, most of the money was being kept by the perpetrator.

[20] A mutual fund director of the then recently acquired Anchor Group resigned, at least in part, over this decision not to press charges.

that it could ever happen—or even unwilling to see that it was happening? Were overly elaborate cross-checks at fault? Or were people concerned that if they pointed out the problem, management might "shoot the messenger"? Capital realized that assuring integrity required extra care in recruiting and training; rigorous searching out of unexpected problems; and continuous training on the important reasons for firm-wide diligence. More importantly, Capital realized that no large organization could assume that its people would not lie, steal, or cheat—so it designed a series of cross-checks into its systems.

Concern about integrity is particularly strong when Capital is defending the interests of investors. While declining to comment to the press, Gordon Crawford took a leading role with other institutional investors in protesting the 1997 plan of TV evangelist Pat Robertson to sell his super-voting Class A shares in International Family Entertainment at $40 versus the $26 price being offered to public shareholders. Robertson soon backed down and agreed that all shareholders would get the same payment: $35 per share.[21]

Business history courses teach students to think carefully about questions like: What business *are* you in? and What business do you *want* to be in? A quarter century ago, when total invested assets at Capital were $2.5 billion—$1.5 billion in mutual funds and $1 billion in Capital Guardian Trust—Bill Hurt organized a session down at Newport with several seniors[22] and asked what seemed to him to be the central, long-term question: "How will we organize to manage $10 billion?" Everybody was much too polite to say anything negative about Hurt's asking his silly question: The sum of $10 *billion* was unimaginable so they gently changed the subject. Years later, when Capital was well past $10 billion, Newton took Hurt aside and confessed he and all the others at the Newport meeting had all thought then that his question had been "one of the dumbest questions *ever* asked."

[21] *Institutional Investor,* July 1997, p. 9.
[22] Bob Egelston, David Fisher, Ed Hajim, Bob Kirby, Jon Lovelace, Bill Newton, Howard Schow, and Mike Shanahan.

"Today," says Hurt, "the question we need to ask is: 'How will we manage $1 *trillion*?!' If we're ever going to manage $1 trillion, we'll want a structure organized and designed for the future. So one of our management challenges is to conceptualize the character and design of an organization that can achieve superior long-term investment results and do this when managing very large sums of money."

Rothenberg takes a typically cautious view of projecting a linear continuation of Capital's remarkable success: "In emerging markets, we're larger than the *total* of all the managers ranked 2nd through 9th. And in overall international investments, we're larger than the next two or three active competitors *combined*. There's no way we're going to increase our market share in either. And if the investment assets supervised by Capital are adjusted or deflated to eliminate the impact of market appreciation, the underlying growth is about 7 percent. The increase in investment people is also about 7 percent. So, just as JBL once said, 'There's no leverage in the business.' That's why we ask ourselves, 'Why isn't Capital reaching its peak profitability and maximum growth rate *now*?'"

Maintaining a sense of the whole firm—and not devolving into separate units or, worse, into profit centers that would focus attention on cost allocations instead of on substantive achievements—is vital to maintaining the organizational flexibility to accommodate changing individuals, changing investment markets, and changing business opportunities.

In the early 1980s, anticipating Capital's need for more capacity to manage far greater assets, Lovelace proposed dual or even triple analytical coverage of major industry groups. Of course, this generated considerable controversy, partly because of the obvious increase in costs, but primarily because of the expected infringement on each analyst's "territory." Few, if any, other investment organizations could accommodate—or even tolerate—having three different and often conflicting researchers' opinions on major companies or industries, but Capital now does.

In recent years, Capital has quietly originated an important change in its overall organizational structure. In cooperation with the

Securities and Exchange Commission, two decision-making groups have been delineated: one for mutual funds and one for institutional clients worldwide. Centering the definition of an entity on the way investment decisions are made—instead of on organizational ownership or the way information is obtained—separates the two groups. The SEC's maximum investment limits[23] apply to each group separately, instead of to Capital Group Companies as a whole. The two carefully separated investment groups share all sorts of research information and extensively discuss themes and trends before making decisions, but they do not discuss their separately made investment decisions or actions. (Demonstrating that investing units are operationally independent in their investment decision making has not been easy for an organization that celebrates completely open communication of information.)

The organization's new name—The Capital Group Companies, Inc.—signals this disaggregation within the organization, and as usual, such semantics are taken seriously. The name Capital Group Companies—without an "of"—is important both symbolically and in reality, as experience validates the concept of disaggregation.

Capital strongly believes this structure accurately reflects the way it invests, and that the SEC's regulatory flexibility relaxes an understandable, but artificial limit. This should make an important difference in Capital's ability to invest successfully in the future. Still, size is a persistent challenge in liquidity when buying or selling large positions; in communications between increasing numbers of professionals of the delicate, detailed information that can be vital to investment decisions; and in assuring a strong personal identification with, and deep sense of responsibility for, the "we" of an organization as large as Capital Group Companies.

"Success, of course, generates challenges," acknowledges Mark Denning, "and the more success, the more challenges we will have."

---

[23] Including poison-pill "triggers" and "control" percentage ownership limits.

CHAPTER 14

COMPENSATION

NOTES FOR READERS

Compensation in investment management is very high. When combined with the interesting work; the excitement of competing with the best; the enjoyment of the remarkable people engaged in the field; the myriad information on companies, industries, countries, and markets; and the opportunities for professional self-fulfillment; the panoply of rewards for top practitioners are the highest in history for any group of professionals.

Differences in compensation between firms (particularly different types of firms)[1] and from one nation to another are large, but investment capability is a main driver of differences in compensation within a firm, and capability is easily measured by results achieved. But factors other than merit have significant impact on compensation. Three

---

[1] Banks and insurance companies—the major managers of 40 years ago had a profound problem: Their organizational compensation structure was designed for a very different business and compensation was much lower than the compensation offered by firms that specialized in investment management. As more and more investment professionals migrated from banks and insurers to investment management specialists, the clients and the business went with them. Starting as a trickle, the flow became a flood.

aspects of investment industry compensation are particularly power-ful. First, total compensation is often dominated by something as sim-ple as each individual's date of arrival at the firm: Early robins do get the best worms.

Second, most firms allow "politics" to matter, sometimes greatly. Often, the politics are personal: It pays to be well liked by those in powerful positions. Some politics reflect unit profitability: The more profit in your unit, the more reward for you. And some politics simply express the powers of ownership, particularly in the differences in di-vision of payout driven by ownership vs. contribution. Usually, the owners make the important decisions and set the rules of the game—almost always, understandably, in their own interests.

Third, current compensation is notoriously *current:* Large bonuses are typically determined by performance in the current year—which makes little sense in long-term investing and all too often accidentally rewards, often generously, what really is just luck.

A sudden change in ownership unleashes a large, "loose cannon" in long-term compensation. Although ownership is rewarding while the firm is privately owned—because industry profit margins are so large and the required capital reinvestment is so small—there always lurks a "Big Bang" when the firm gets sold or goes public. At that moment, more wealth can be created—or made known—than in all of the firm's prior years.

This large transaction reward is, of course, the main reason in-vestment firms are sold. Although the bank or insurance company that has just become the new owner always describes the transaction as a purchase, only naïve outsiders think these transactions are really purchases. Because the initiative is always with the selling investment firm, insiders all know they are sales.

The most dramatic demonstration of the founder's disproportion-ate dominance occurs when the firm is sold. All too often, a con-structive internal transfer of ownership cannot be achieved because the founder has not arranged for the orderly fair sharing of owner-ship in the years before Judgment Day. This makes a sale to the high-est bidder virtually inevitable when transaction time comes. At the crucial moment of decision and action, the market price to buy the firm is too high for the internal group to come up with enough capital to match the acquisition bid and the founder feels unable to accept any less.

Usually—not always, but usually—serious harm is done. The delicate fabric of mutual trust and collegiality that is so important in a professional firm is stretched or torn by the crude calculus of who owns what and who gets paid what. Some suddenly become so wealthy, they no longer feel the motivation to strive while others feel shortchanged and bitter over having been unfairly treated. The sale of a firm provokes a series of adverse internal changes that result in both the appearance and the reality of the firm's capabilities deteriorating—often rather rapidly. Meanwhile, the firm's future development is silently constrained to far less than might have been possible with more thoughtful and equitable sharing of ownership.

A second major reason for selling is the age of the owners: The age at which most owners sell is 60 plus or minus 5 years.

The third reason is often the dominating reason. Whether deliberately or by inattention, the early owners have not worked out a sensible scheme for gradually transferring ownership to their successors. The structure of ownership is designed to maximize the economic interests of the principals, particularly the original principals, who not only are the larger owners but also make the decisions on how ownership shares will change. Understandably, they are in no hurry to reduce their own ownership. At the risk of overgeneralizing, the typical background follows.

Three generations are discernible at most mature investment organizations: First is the *founder* generation. The founders naturally center their thinking on the importance of their essential contributions in the entrepreneurial days when they took all the risks of a start-up— and then did all the hard work of breaking into the winner's circle. Second, is the *builder* generation. It comprises the people who joined the fledgling firm and brought in a lot of the business, are often well known externally, and are increasingly the recognized internal leaders in investing and in firm management. Although they center their appraisals of significance on current contributions, they anticipate taking control—soon. Third is the *future* generation. These members of the firm are now just coming into their own, and represent, as they see it, the organization's hopes and expectations for the long-term future. Each group has its reasons for believing—particularly at the time of suddenly monetizing ownership through sale or merger—that it should own *more*.

Intense internal negotiations often occur and are usually resolved by recognizing that at current market valuations, the market value of the enterprise is too large for the internal successors to pay and the current owners see no good reason to take less than the market says the firm is worth—a valuation they understandably feel is rightfully theirs.

Almost always, the buyer thinks it is buying the future earnings, but realists know that what was sold was not the future, but the past earnings and the past accumulation of assets. This misunderstanding helps explain why so many acquisitions of investment organizations fail to meet the buyers' expectations.

The sale of a professional firm is always disruptive and sometimes destructive. The cold realities of specific economic rewards are distressful and distort personal relationships. Harmful experiences before, during, and after the sale hurt the firm's ability to do its work—with clients famously "the last to know."

Capital is intriguingly different from these industry norms in important ways. The first and strongest difference is a deep determination *never* to sell; to remain forever privately owned by the firm's major contributors. This important commitment is particularly unusual because the economic value of Capital is so very large—at least in part due to the bold reinvestment of past years' profits in developing capabilities that now generate profits at a higher level.

The second major difference is a profound commitment to objective fairness. The usual forces of power, politics, seniority, and so on are balanced at Capital by persistent objectivity based on each individual's contributions.

Capital has developed an unusually flexible and responsive structure of compensation with six levels, each determined by the individual's value-added in achieving Capital's three-constituency mission of serving Clients, Associates, and Owners.

Significantly, generosity from the top has long been a governing characteristic of Capital's process for continuously redistributing ownership. The process was begun long ago and is based on such a modest valuation for the organization that the transfer price is not allowed to distort the process.

A special strength in Capital's overall compensation is the systematic removal of all those status signals that can indicate one person's importance versus another's: title, corner office, different size office, different furnishings, and so on. Titles are notoriously peripatetic, abundant, and never considered particularly important. There are so many business units that wags say there are enough chairmanships and presidencies to "cover *all* the bases."

A strong form of compensation at Capital is the deep personal satisfaction of working with unusually bright, engaging people in an organization that has an impressive lack of politics and a pervasive commitment to designing responsibilities around individuals. Capital always takes a long-term view, particularly on ways to achieve consistently superior investment results. It is an organization that professional peers admire and clients appreciate, often with great gratitude.

" SELLING MY STOCK in Capital was the worst investment decision I ever made," Coleman Morton[2] accurately acknowledges, as he observes what has become the most valuable firm in the business.

---

[2] Morton, at one time, owned 10 percent—with options to buy up to 20 percent (see Chapter 2).

The *internal* valuation, the only basis on which Associates buy and sell shares each year, is determined by a formula that works out to about $3 to $4 billion. But this is only one-tenth of the fair market value estimated by comparing prices at which acquiring firms have been buying other investment organizations.

But of course, it doesn't matter: Capital is not for sale. Ever.

Even without the big markup to a public market valuation, investment in Capital as a private company has been very rewarding: approximately 20 percent returns, compounded annually, for nearly three decades.

Owning Capital has not always been so rewarding. Not nearly. In the early 1970s, Capital briefly lost money. And from 1931 to the end of 1954, Capital averaged only a breakeven business.[3] In loss years, JBL, then the sole owner, absorbed all the losses personally. These stringent decades taught Capital to be conservative on all forms of compensation.

During the 1960s and 1970s, investment industry pay levels rose higher and higher, but Capital continued paying only the going rate in Los Angeles, which was well below the level in New York City. JBL believed in Old School ways of compensation: Work hard and prove yourself over the long term, and then we'll take care of you. The real payout was deferred well into the future—too far out for some.[4] Associates got separate paychecks from several different units within Capital, allegedly because this complexity made it difficult to compare pay packages. (Compensation comparisons are still strongly discouraged, and it's understood that if you want to continue advancing, it's wise to remain silent on that subject.)

---

[3] The year 1954—with the stock market up over 40 percent—was Capital's first really profitable year.
[4] Contributing to the exodus of Don Smith, Steve Reynolds, and Bob Leppo in the early 1980s.

JBL was genuinely conservative.[5] His restraint on compensation came partly from his 20 years' experience of personally underwriting the small, marginal enterprise Capital had been in the 1930s and 1940s; partly from his sobering experiences at Eddie MacCrone's stockbrokerage firm in Detroit; and partly from his deeply held philosophical views of investment management as a business.

When Bill Newton joined Capital in 1959, JBL asked him how much he hoped to earn in five years. "I recognized this was *not* a casual question and that an answer was expected," recalls Newton. "So I thought as carefully and as quickly as I could and said, '$50,000'— which was pretty far up there from the $10,000 I was then making. From Mr. Lovelace's reaction, I could tell it was at least *possible.*"

When Capital finally became profitable in 1954, JBL started sharing ownership with others. "JBL took others in as partners long before he needed to," says Dave Fisher. In sharing equity, JBL was not simply being generous. He wanted to sell shares internally at a price/earnings multiple equal to the multiples of public companies he thought were comparable.[6] (With the typical company's price/earnings ratio over 20 times current earnings, this was, at least by historical standards, a fairly full price.) Two months before his 60th birthday, JBL sold, on a pricing formula based on a blend of book value and earnings, 60 percent of the shares of Capital.

JBL's secretary called Graham Holloway and said JBL wanted to meet—and that it would be over lunch. "I didn't know him and assumed he didn't know me. After all, it was my first year and I was always working in Kansas or Nebraska, not Los Angeles. Frankly, I was worried I might have done something wrong. I couldn't think what it might be, but I was sure worried. Imagine my surprise when

[5] A significant example of personal conservatism was shown by his wife, Marie Lovelace, who didn't drive and, declining to use a chauffeur, regularly took the bus into Los Angeles well into her 80s.
[6] Mr. Price had a similar idea as he shared ownership at T. Rowe Price.

I learned his purpose for that luncheon: JBL had decided to sell me my first shares of stock in Capital—from his own holding. What's more, much as I wanted to buy, he knew that coming up with the money could be a real financial strain for my family just then, so he offered to lend me the money himself. Of course, I was stunned!"

By agreement with his father, Jon Lovelace was not given—and did not inherit[7]—any of JBL's once sizable ownership[8] of shares in Capital. The stock JL later shared out to others was stock he had purchased in the 1950s. Says Fisher: "We all remind ourselves that it was just as this business started to prove so successful in the mid-1950s that JBL started to distribute ownership. Jon has done the same. I think that has given us all a special sense of obligation."

Capital's compensation program is designed to align the motivations of each individual with those of the company *and* those of the clients—and to reinforce the Capital culture. Capital tries to neutralize current compensation versus the compensation paid by competitors—so decisions to join Capital are always made for all the other factors: organizational climate and culture, professional challenges and personal growth opportunities, core values, colleagues, and so on.

Financial compensation at Capital comes in a variety of forms:

■ Salaries are set near the top of the range within the investment industry. Today, a top-ranking, investment professional at Capital can earn well over $2 million a year in salary and bonuses—when his or her investment results are strong. To encourage long-term thinking, those bonuses are based on a four-year moving average of investment results—not the short periods, such as a single year, that most other investment organizations commonly use.

[7] On graduation from Princeton at 23, he received a cash gift of $20,000 and $10,000 in the shares of American Mutual.

[8] Capital's corporate attorney, Ben Long, once wanted to assure that Jon Lovelace would continue to have majority voting control, but Lovelace refused, so his own shares never had more than 39 percent of the voting power nor more than 25 percent of the economic interest.

■ Individual bonuses differ substantially, as warranted by differences in individual contributions, and can be large in comparison with salaries particularly with superior individual performance and strong Capital earnings. "Every investment decision has a direct impact on your performance record and how much you are paid in the next four years," says a portfolio counselor. "This concentrates the mind wonderfully."

The compensation system strongly encourages sharing investment ideas among portfolio counselors; when the organization as a whole does well, it rewards all of the fund's portfolio counselors.

If investment results are good relative to competition in a down market, bonuses can increase, even though profits are down—because fees are paid as a percentage of the market value of managed assets. This approach to compensation makes great sense for a truly long-term, privately owned investment organization, but is a luxury a public company could not afford.

■ Participation in Capital's Defined Contribution employee benefit plan, which is invested in the same American Funds that over 20 million investors own, has compounded at above-market rates of appreciation. Vesting takes six years.

Restrictions on individuals' investment activities, other than investing in Capital's own mutual fund shares, are far more limiting at Capital than at most investment organizations. One result is that most of Capital's Associates do not invest actively for their own account: 80 percent make zero trades in a year, and most others do only one or two transactions. The other result is that, in a classic example of "we-eat-our-own-cooking" affirmation, Capital's 6,000 Associates are large owners of the American Funds through the Master Retirement Plan. Including the plan and all personal investments, Capital Associates currently have investments amounting to nearly $1 billion in the American Funds.

- Participation in one or another of the various bonus pools is very broad. Participation percentages vary significantly from Associate to Associate and are reset every year based on merit. Participation is based partly on such qualitative factors as contributions to the overall organization, and partly on such quantitative factors as investment results versus appropriate benchmarks for investment professionals—calculated on a four-year moving average.[9] The size of the whole pool varies with the results achieved by the whole organization.

- Participation in the Special Compensation Plan distributes a significant part of the pretax profits of Capital. Participation units are assigned at the start of each year to nearly 500 key people who have made major contributions over the longer term. The "Special Comp" Plan was developed in 1981 by Lovelace and Shanahan, because share ownership, while structured to recycle, would not recycle as rapidly as individual contributions were changing.

  Units of participation in the "Special Comp" Plan vary considerably among individuals and from year-to-year for the same individual. Payouts from all bonus plans range from less than an individual's salary up to as much as 3 to 4 times salary in a great year for both Capital and the individual Associate. "Special Comp" units are distributed after great effort is made to be sure the distribution, *if* disclosed (which it is not) would be recognized by all participants as very fair.

  One exception: Jon Lovelace, despite his major role over many years and what was then his large share ownership,[10] insisted in the initial years that only a small amount of "Special Comp" be allocated to himself—so more would be allocated to deserving younger professionals with smaller ownership.

---

[9] The averaging used to be weighted 40-30-20-10, but it was changed recently to approximately 40-20-20-20.
[10] Approximately 25 percent at that time.

- Capital has several programs designed specifically to reward unusually promising young investment professionals. Awards take several years to vest and then convert into stock ownership of Capital Group Companies. Says Shanahan: "Compensation policies at Capital focus on meeting the needs and interests of the junior guys—because they aren't in a position to absorb major fluctuations in their pay."

- Ownership of Capital[11] has been extended to over 350 key people[12] to assure that ownership and long-term reward will match long-term contributions as closely as possible. "We want the people who make up most of the payroll to own most of the shares," says Fisher. Ownership accumulates with tenure and cumulative contributions made over many past years. Shares are divided into two classes: A and B. Voting control of Capital Group Companies is concentrated in B shares,[13] which have 15 votes each, whereas A shares have only one vote apiece. The 70-plus holders of B shares are very carefully chosen. Selection criteria include many years of substantial contributions and broad

---

[11] The ownership by key employees of partial interests in subsidiaries was brought back into the parent company in the 1970s. Ed Hajim, Steve Reynolds, and others had owned 30 percent of Greenwich Capital when they launched it on the East Coast in 1967. And five seniors—Bob Kirby, Ned Bailey, Bill Newton, Chuck Schimpff, and Jim Dunton—had each owned 2 percent of Capital Guardian Trust when it was originally organized on the West Coast. In the 1970s, these shares were brought back into the parent company. (Chuck Schimpf had previously sold his shares to others—including Shanahan and Fisher.) Even more importantly, Ward Bishop, who built American Funds Distributors, had owned 100 percent of that mutual fund sales and servicing organization for 30 years. American Funds was combined into Capital Group in 1974, at a cyclical low point in the mutual fund industry.

[12] By comparison, in 1990, only 75 Associates owned stock.

[13] JL owned close to one quarter of the B shares many years ago, but has brought his total share ownership of Capital Group Companies down from 20 percent to less than 5 percent, and is now at 0 percent of B shares. Bill Newton has reduced his share from 5 percent to 0 percent. Mike Shanahan, David Fisher, and Jim Rothenberg each own 5 percent. The cohort of professionals who joined between 1958 and 1972—in part because so few professionals were hired in the 1970s and 1980s—each owns a relatively large proportion of shares. (All shares are governed by a stock restriction agreement.)

internal respect for the individual as a real leader, but the principal criterion for choosing B shareholders is that they so fully understand and care so deeply about keeping Capital privately owned that they would never even consider a sale. To keep passing voting control to younger Associates, B shares are sold back to the firm on a set formula that starts at age 65 and is completed at 72.

Shares of Capital are valued on a formula basis—based primarily on book value plus a "collar" based on assets under management plus revenues. The formula sets the value much closer to book than to current market valuations. Moreover, young shareholders are provided with generous loans by Capital[14] to facilitate their initial purchases of shares.

After extensive discussion and exploration of many alternatives with senior professionals, JBL worked out—and JL worked to develop a consensus on—a commitment to abide by a formal buyback of B shares in three tranches: one third at age 65, another third at 67, and the final third by age 72. JBL was the first to act on this commitment. (At retirement—or on leaving for another firm—owners must sell back all their B shares in 90 days.)[15]

Shareholders hold their A shares as long as they are fully active in the company—and then sell all A shares back over the six years following retirement.[16] A shareholder who joins a competing firm, must sell back all A shares immediately.

[14] This prevents the daunting impact on family finances experienced by younger shareholders in 1973 to 1974, when Capital actually lost money in a few quarters and Bank of America called their loans.

[15] They get a longer-term "claw-back" warrant to repurchase their shares if the firm were ever sold.

[16] Shareholders who were at least 65 in 1968 to 1970 are allowed to hold their shares in their families for two generations past the then-current owner; that is, for the lives of grandchildren, the youngest family members with whom the owners would have had personal contact. JBL and Ward Bishop were both large A shareholders.

In the late 1980s, Capital recognized that it had underinvested in Information Technology and committed to a program of major catch-up investments in IT that took 12 years to complete and cost even more than was expected. (IT investments continue to be very large and currently run $375 million annually.) This investment spending kept profits low for several years, but has since paid off as profits have grown substantially. "The freedom—and the discipline—to take and keep the long, long-term perspective on everything we do is an important reason we remain private," explains Rothenberg.

Central to Capital's open stock ownership program was Jon Lovelace's deciding, at his own initiative and without even discussing the matter with others, that the Lovelace family owned too much of Capital[17]—and then organizing a massive redistribution of shares.[18] This proved to be one of the seminal forces in Capital's long-term development. (While Lovelace reduced his and his family's percentage ownership, substantively, he recognizes that his family has done well financially with a smaller piece of a much larger pie.)

The value of shares in Capital has increased substantially—more than 200 times over 30 years—due to strong, favorable trends, both in the industry and in Capital's position within the industry. Seniors recognize that the rate of gain is virtually sure to slow down and, as Kirby says, "If we ever get caught in a down draft as bad as we had in '73–'74, it would cut right into our younger Associates' standard of living."

If Capital Group Companies now has a theoretical market value that outsiders' guess is over $30 billion, Lovelace has shared (colleagues would typically use the term "given") many billions of dollars with others in the organization. Each generation of Associates, it is well understood, has been and will be subsidized by prior

---

[17] Jon Lovelace owned shares with over 30 percent voting control of Capital in 1968.

[18] To increase the size of the available ownership pie, JL's two sisters agreed with him to reduce their shareholdings—an important part of their patrimony. Some others, particularly very early-year shareholders such as JBL's secretary, Mary Bauer, and Ward Bishop were "grandfathered" and invited to keep their shares for life.

generations. And each generation of Associates is expected similarly to subsidize future generations, because stock ownership is seen as a passing phenomenon and that ownership is really stewardship, endowed with more responsibilities than rights.

Jon Lovelace understands and exemplifies the real meaning of the advice his father—who knew he was near the end of his own life—gave the nurse who sought his wisdom on how to be successful in life. JBL's simple advice: "Don't be greedy."

"When I once asked Jon what he worried about, what could really hurt Capital," says Fisher, "his answer was as brief as it was swift: 'Greed!' Greed could come, of course, from individuals or from a group. Greed is always a threat."

"I recall visiting JBL in the hospital not long before his death," observes Nilly Sikorsky. "We held hands and talked for three-quarters of an hour. I well remember his concern as he alluded to our impending move to new offices: 'Don't lose your heads up there in the clouds.' He wisely worried about the temptation to extrapolate the short term—and to get carried away."

As Mark Denning says, "JL focuses on two vital words: fair and greed—always striving to be fair and always striving to avoid greed, either short-term or long-term greed."

Venture capital investing has, for many years, been an important aspect of life in California, and Capital has had a long and very successful relationship with Sequoia Capital and Don Valentine, a very successful venture capital investor.[19] During the last two decades of the twentieth century, the nearly 100 senior Capital Associates investing in parallel funds earned large returns on investments with Sequoia. At Capital's initiative, this special relationship has been discontinued on a "Caesar's wife" basis to preclude even the *possibility* of suspicion about any distraction from the absolute focus on investing for clients.[20]

---

[19] As explained in Chapter 2, Capital Associates are often investors in Sequoia Capital funds.
[20] Of course, exchanging insights into significant trends in technologies and markets continues to benefit Capital Group Companies' decisions.

Estate and tax planning can make an important difference in long-term compensation, and access to Capital's Personal Investment Management unit, which serves wealthy clients and individuals,[21] can be an important consideration. One large group of clients for Personal Investment Management consists of Capital Associates, their families, and heirs. As one of the unit's leaders says, "They set the standard for this effort and are very demanding of the competence and service value they expect," a beneficial discipline for this business unit.

Capital encourages Associates to get involved with philanthropic organizations and matches charitable gifts two-for-one up to $10,000 for each Associate and matches three-for-one for shareholders.

If a firm wants fairness, generosity, and commitment throughout the organization, then the leaders of the organization must show the way. Jim Rothenberg learned this lesson early in his career. "When I was first offered the opportunity to buy some stock in Capital, it was exciting, and I bought the stock." Little did he know that Capital was entering a very difficult period; 1974 was one of the few times that the value of Capital stock actually declined significantly. Rothenberg, describing himself as a brash young analyst, went to the research director and said, "It would be wonderful if you would give me the opportunity to buy some more stock, so I could average down." A few weeks later, the chief financial officer walked into his office and offered Rothenberg an amount of stock equivalent to his first purchase—at the lower price.[22] "The stock was sold to me by the then president of the company.[23] The lesson? Fairness, generosity, and commitment must come from the top of the organization."

---

[21] Solomon "Sonny" M. Kamm, who also serves as General Counsel of Capital Group Companies, was for 22 years a trust and estates partner of O'Melveny & Myers in Los Angeles and heads up estate planning for Personal Investment Management, which has a Nevada subsidiary for the tax-favored benefits provided by that state.

[22] When Murdoch "Bud" MacCrea, the chief financial officer, would walk into an Associate's office in the 1970s to say he or she could now buy stock, not everyone was thrilled. Some Associates would cautiously close their doors when they saw him coming down the hallway.

[23] Jon Lovelace offered the same opportunity to other key professionals.

Another important form of compensation is nonfinancial.[24] Sharing in the extraordinary panoply of information and insight into economics, technology, government, and society—and the personalities involved in these dynamic sectors—all around the world is wonderfully interesting. Being part of a widely admired and respected organization that is full of talented, committed, and interesting people doing difficult work skillfully is both fascinating and challenging. And having many opportunities for professional growth and personal self-actualization is spiritually and emotionally fulfilling.

[24] Capital also has an extensive program of distributing opportunities to travel and to participate in professional groups widely within the organization.

CHAPTER 15

INVESTING

NOTES FOR READERS

Institutional investing, as practiced today, is a remarkably intensive activity. With annual portfolio turnover across the industry now in excess of 100 percent, the average holding period for an investment is less than one year.

Serious observers must wonder—no matter how extraordinarily well informed fund managers are about current industry, company, and market conditions—how much of all this institutional activity is really *investing* and how much is only highly informed market *speculation*. Consider these simple numbers: If six investment possibilities are given serious consideration for every stock bought and an institutional portfolio typically holds 80 stocks, then at 100 percent turnover, the typical portfolio manager is making four multimillion-dollar "to-buy or not-to-buy" and "to-sell or not-to-sell" decisions every business day of the year. Can each of these decisions be given the deep thought and analytical care usually required for any serious investment?

While capable, independent thinking will always be valuable in true investing, the increasing institutionalization of the stock market[1] has reduced the scale and duration of opportunities available to *any* investor—and *every* investor—to obtain and exploit significant competitive advantage on a regular basis if their investment horizon is only one year ahead and all major competitors have constant access to the same information.

Thousands of institutional investors are interconnected by a complex web of instantaneous, continuous communications via Internet, blast fax, telephone calls and conference calls, computer terminals that provide instant access to massive databases and analytical models, conferences, meetings, and a blizzard of written reports on every aspect of corporate, industry, market, regulatory, and technological information.

The very largest stockbrokerage firms each have 300 or more research analysts providing information and evaluations on a wide range of companies and industries—all competing for the lucrative business of the institutional giants, while the institutions compete to get new information in time to take action.

This is not a fair game. The 50 most active institutional investors spend over $100 million apiece (the 10 largest spend over $1 billion apiece) in commissions and underwriting spreads to acquire the premier services provided by more than 100 stockbrokerage firms around the world. They *always* get the "first call."

Institutional investors all strive to achieve better than market returns, but with nearly 90 percent of the public trading on the New York Stock Exchange—and an even larger notional value in futures trading on the CBOE—now done by institutional investors, they collectively so dominate the stock market that they must buy from and sell to each other. Since it does cost something to trade and since most institutions manage widely diversified portfolios that are carefully matched to the composition of their benchmark portfolio—which

---

[1] Institutional trading has, as already noted, gone in one generation, from less than 20 percent of NYSE public activity to over 80 percent.

precludes really big commitments to "high-conviction" stocks—it cannot be surprising that, in this negative sum game, a large majority of institutional investors underperform the market they try so hard to beat. This reality makes it all the more important that Capital's investment professionals understand and live by the view that the secret to long term success in investing is in *not losing* and that a strong defense is more important than a strong offense.

The intensity of competition—year by year and quarter by quarter—for superior performance causes most institutional investors to do two things: (1) They hug the index to avoid getting caught out and underperforming their comparative benchmarks, and (2) they are hyperalert to the "need" to take quick action—whether buying or selling—before other institutions get to the market ahead of them. Hence, average annual turnover among institutional investors is greater than 100 percent.

Being the aggregation of billions of decisions by millions of human beings, the stock market is not perfect. Errors are made every hour of every day. And some of the major mistakes, like the dot-com bubble, have been spectacular. But information gathering and distribution are self-correcting—usually, but not always, rather quickly. That is why profiting from the abundant, but fleeting errors of others has proven notoriously difficult. And for those engaged in hyperactive investing, profiting from errors of others—however naïve—is the only hope. Long-term *investing* must be different.

In their efforts to achieve superior performance, most institutional investors strive to develop internal coherence and consistency in their investment process. Most organize their efforts around an overarching concept or philosophy of investing, typically centered on a common denominator such as growth or value that becomes the central guiding principle of "how we do things around here." Another organizing principle of most institutional investors is to develop and articulate—internally to all analysts and fund managers, and externally to all clients—an explicit investment process that is both understandable and expected to govern all investment decisions.

In contrast, Capital professionals cheerfully distance themselves from *any* comprehensive investment philosophy or *any* overall specific investment process, and candidly celebrate that each investment decision is made independently—on its own merits. Capital's professionals don't even use the word "performance," typically noting that performance is what Hollywood and Broadway are all about. They speak instead of investment *results*.

Portfolio counselors have very different ways of arriving at their investment decisions and there is no one way of investing. Capital continuously struggles with the term "value investing" because other investors often confine "value" to stocks with low price-earning ratios, high-yield dividends, and substantial assets. Instead, Capital uses value to include *all* investments—even growth stocks—that offer unusual promise of being recognized, several years into the future, as having significantly more value than is currently recognized in the stock market.

Capital is notorious in the investment industry for being very independent. This is partly because it has such strong in-house research capabilities; partly because its portfolio counselors and analysts are always looking for opportunities to be independent or contrarian; and partly because the time horizon on which its analysts and portfolio counselors concentrate extends significantly farther into the future than the focal length of most institutional investors.[2]

Capital, as a result and despite the intensive competition, is the only major investment organization that consistently produces superior long-term investment results and uniquely has done so over the past 10, 20, 30, 40, 50, *and* 70 years.

Remarkable as its record of consistently superior long-term investment results surely is, it cannot be surprising—at least in retrospect. Capital has been deliberately designed to achieve its

---

[2] On the other hand, a real drag on investment results at Capital in the 1980s and 1990s came from the sometimes large "cash reserves" held when stock markets were generally rising significantly.

three-legged objective of superior long-term results for Clients, Associates, and Owners.

"THE MARKET IS screwy most of the time," Bob Kirby announced to a large audience in April 1999. "Long ago, I began to look at the stock market as a kind of pendulum swinging back and forth—with no discernible pattern or rhythm. The pendulum swings between 3:00 on one side and 9:00 on the other. At 3:00, *fear* has taken over and it's full panic. At 9:00, *greed* has taken over and it's full manic. At 6:00, there's a point where logic and balance exist and where valuations make a lot of sense to most rational people. Unfortunately, the pendulum doesn't spend much time at 6:00—when prudent men seem to be in control. I am not sure that we are at full manic today, but we sure as heck are well past 8:30!" (The market drop over the next few years gave ample evidence that the stock market had indeed been seriously overpriced. Kirby's pendulum did not stay "well past 8:30" very long.)

Kirby didn't stop there. His next target was investment strategy, saying: "I have decided that there is a time in everyone's life when he should come clean on stuff like this. After all, I am fully vested in the company's profit sharing fund, I own all the stock in the company that I am ever going to own—and I always have Social Security to fall back on if I need to. Therefore, despite the fact that there are a number of clients here in the audience, I confess I have *never* had an investment strategy—not once in my whole career!"

After describing how traditional investment strategists set forth their view on the economy and then determine the proper economic sectors, industries, and companies to invest in on the assumption that there is a logical relationship between economic developments and the stock market, Kirby declared: "I have been managing common stock portfolios for well over 40 years. If there is *any* relationship between economic developments and stock prices that is predictable, it certainly has escaped my attention.

"We're trying to put together a portfolio that has more opportunities than risk and has diversification in the real sense, and we couldn't care less about the composition of the S&P 500. A lot of madness has developed in this business over the past few years, so that a guy who doesn't like the oil industry at all, 'underweights' it in his portfolio—to 10 percent versus 13.2 percent S&P 500 weighting. This is hokum. He *still* has 10 percent in an industry he doesn't like!"

Conceding that saying he'd never had an investment strategy was not quite true, Kirby explained that his investment strategy was not top-down, but bottom-up—the product of individual investment decisions based on identifying strong, well-managed companies in growing industries and investing in them on reasonable terms. "With a little patience and a lot of hard work, over time you are going to find 30, 40, or 50 companies that meet your investment criteria. Then, Voilà! You have a portfolio!"[3]

Capital concentrates on evaluating the future prospects of specific industries and individual companies through intensive research by its own analysts and deliberately encourages independent thinking and action. It cheerfully celebrates its eclectic approach to investment decisions and, recognizing that the organization's portfolios will often show a very "mixed" character, eschews any single overall portfolio strategy. Instead, it concentrates on making rigorous value judgments for each specific investment.

Full decision-making responsibility for each decision centers with the individual analyst and the specific investment counselor involved. And individual responsibility for each investment is made explicit by linking compensation directly to each professional's carefully measured investment results (as explained in Chapter 13).

While the focus on long-term investment *value* is consistent, there is no strict adherence to any set process or to particular screens

---

[3] *Tirade of a Dinosaur,* April 1999.

for selecting stocks for investment. Far from it. Says Mark Denning: "It's a bit like being a Christian, I suppose. You can decide for yourself whether you are a Catholic, a Baptist, or a Methodist. We're looking in every nook and cranny around the world for intriguing companies. They don't have to fit *any* preconceived pattern or description. The only thing in common is that the stocks must offer good value and the opportunity to make money over the long run. There is absolutely no one way to invest at Capital. We want and need the diversity of independent thinking—by many different professionals working in very different ways. I like to look at free cash flow. Others are very price sensitive and driven by traditional valuation criteria like price earnings multiples and price-to-book ratios.[4] Some are fascinated by the *market,* while others are fascinated by *companies.* David Fisher is far more focused on identifying good management—and is less price sensitive."

Fisher explains, "I prefer to invest in companies where *people* make a difference. I don't like investing in companies that are driven by 'macro' things like the direction of interest rates or oil prices. I love investing where people can really have an impact on the outcome, and if that's what you are going to invest in, then you'd better be right about the people. I've always believed that good people tend to make good things happen, and if you can find good people and let them work for you—work for you in the sense that you invest in their company and your interests are aligned—good things will happen."[5]

Capital's bottom-up emphasis does not mean that the macroeconomic environment is ignored, but it does mean that the "macro" is understood from the "micro"—not the other way around. "A good example is Thailand," explains Karin Larson. "We had some very big positions in Thailand beginning in the late '80s, but in early 1998, we had virtually nothing. The reason: When we called on many Thai companies, we could see they were operating in a lousy environment.

---

[4] *Dow Jones News Retrieval,* March 1, 1997.
[5] Andrew Leeming, *The Super Analysts,* New York: John Wiley & Sons, p. 124.

What the companies were telling us was signaling a major economic downturn, long before the official GNP numbers were reported. You could see what was happening in the real economy several months before the 1998 collapse in Southeast Asian stock prices."

Another example is an Italian telecom company named Stet. Capital started buying Stet when it was trading at two times cash flow, or about 2,500 lira. The Gulf War hit Italy, as a big importer of oil, and Stet's share price fell to about 1,600 lira. Capital kept buying more and more. Eight months later, the Gulf War was over, the political situation in Italy had improved, and the stock market was forging ahead. Stet went up to 6,000 lira. The language of top-down investing is so pervasive that descriptions of how Capital invests are easily misunderstood. Portfolios were "overweight Italy" only because Stet was its biggest holding. Capital protests: "We didn't get *Italy* right; we got *Stet* right."

As a helpful self-discipline in evaluating investment decisions, Capital uses the "whole company" approach (multiplying the stock price by the number of shares outstanding) to compare what the market thinks the whole company is worth with the analyst's evaluation. If you wouldn't buy the whole company for that price, then you shouldn't buy 100,000 shares, 1,000 shares, or 100 shares because you'd just be relying on a Greater Fool theory that somebody else is going to pay you even more for a piece of paper. That's not what investing at Capital is about.[6] "Investing is more an absolute than a relative valuation issue," says Jim Fullerton, "because the world is full of things that you don't have to buy. So you had better find the company absolutely attractive if you're going to invest." The lesson: Good companies are not always good investments and great companies are not always great investments.

The principal focus is on true value investing, but Capital's senior investors are not at all comfortable with the term "value" as it is conventionally used. To most other people, value means only one

[6] Leeming, p. 125.

kind of value: low-multiple, high-book value and high-yield stocks. At Capital "value" means the current price is below true, long-term value to an owner. "All our funds are really value funds—whether 'growth' or 'income' or 'growth with income,'"[7] says Lovelace, "because, with superior research-based understanding of long-term *business* value, we are always striving to buy at prices that are low compared to true long-term *investment* value."

Capital's focus on value investing and research-based rationality originated with Jonathan Bell Lovelace in the 1920s. With his interest in, and facility with, statistical information, JBL understood the cumulative power of long-term compounding and of *not losing* during the interim. The benefits of not losing led JBL to an abiding appreciation that thorough research enables investors to make long-term, value-based decisions and sustain their commitments through the inevitable interim periods of stock market distress and uncertainty. JBL recognized the harm done to individual investors when a bear market frightens them into getting out when the market is low and fearfully staying out of the market long enough to miss the early—and most rewarding—part of the market's recovery.

In investing, the highest returns often come from buying into major companies that are very much out of favor. "That's why so many truly great investment ideas are so very unpopular at the best time to make them," explains Bill Hurt. "Major change in valuation is an important factor in *every* great investment success." Most investors spend their time and energy trying to identify companies that can go from *good* to *great*. Yet, the rate of return is just as large, and often even larger, when a company goes from *awful* up to simply *poor*, and there's still plenty of room left for that company to go even farther—from *poor* up to *weak*, or even on up to *okay*. So Capital is always at least willing to look carefully at an awful company because that company may be changing for the better. If fundamental

---

[7] Capital has no "aggressive-growth" mutual funds, believing this term is just a euphemism for speculation and excessive risk taking.

research shows that it will improve, the long-term rate of return can be very large. And when a company is out of favor with most investors, that's when it's easy to acquire a large position at a favorable price.

"When everybody is 'down' on a stock, they'll know all sorts of reasons *not* to own it and certainly several good reasons *not* to buy it," adds Jim Fullerton. "And their reasons will be very well documented; clearly and compellingly expressed in a strong, coherent argument that is widely accepted and understood." The typical investment committee will be familiar with and ready to agree with the well-rehearsed line of reasoning. Against these strong defenses, the analyst with a new and different perspective, who may have seen something significant that all the rest were missing, can have great difficulty just getting heard. He or she may have a fragile idea that could easily be blown away—but, if listened to, may just be the beginning of a truly great investment. Jason Pilalas and Gordon Crawford are two examples of career analysts who have discovered great investments.

When Jason Pilalas[8] joined Capital, he was first assigned to cover the Automotive industry. But just two weeks later, a more experienced auto analyst joined, so Pilalas was switched to Pharmaceuticals—where he has specialized for 30 years. "I wanted to know a *lot* about something, not a little about many things, so I studied the nature of the drug business and what it takes to succeed, learning how the game is played and how it should be played. I wanted to

---

[8] Jason Pilalas ran away from home and joined the Navy at 17. After chipping paint for a year, he was sent to the University of Southern California on an NROTC scholarship, and then served six years as a naval officer before leaving the Navy. For a few years, he ran a tanker company and then, at 30, went to Harvard Business School. In 1972, a bridge-playing friend suggested he interview with Capital. He bought a new Hickey-Freeman suit—his first—and went to his appointment: Mike Shanahan and Bill Hurt were his interviewers. Not far into the interview, Pilalas abruptly called for a stop—and then asked Shanahan, who was proud of earning both his B.A. and M.B.A. degrees at Stanford: "How can you *possibly* succeed in investing, coming as you do from . . . the . . . Radcliffe of the West?" Shanahan was rising up from his chair when Hurt cut in: "You really *stuck* him!" Hurt was also an alum of USC, Stanford's arch rival. Shanahan quietly marked Pilalas as a risk taker who should definitely get an offer from Capital—but didn't tell Pilalas until nearly a decade later.

know all about how each company had responded to its historical experiences. Studying the industry, I got to understand how important R&D can be."

Month after month, Pilalas made no recommendations to buy any drug stocks. He was, instead, recommending against drug stocks: He was a serious seller. "I went for many *years* before I recommended anything." During the early- to mid-1970s, in the era of the two-tier stock market, growth stocks became seriously overpriced. "Drug stocks—no matter how great the companies were—got *way* overpriced." Except SmithKline.

"There are no future facts—just estimates. So I developed product-by-product analytical models of each product produced by each major company. Before computer spreadsheets, it was all done by hand on enormous big sheets of paper." SmithKline was a major company, so Pilalas included it in his product-by-product analysis. It was *not* overpriced. It was cheap—but not forever.

As Pilalas puts it: "It was decidedly *un*loved by the market." SmithKline had had lackluster earnings for 15 years as it faced more and more competition from generics, so its price/earnings ratio had come way down.

But, in the mid-1970s, SmithKline had high hopes for its new anti-ulcer drug, Tagamet—if and when it could get FDA approval for sale in the United States. Even before its introduction, Tagamet had great promise because from the ulcer patient's perspective, it was a real winner: no more bland diets, no required abstinence, no pain, and no operation.

"I try very hard to put myself inside the mind of the patient—to see how he would think. For example, before Tagamet, anti-ulcer drugs were confined to a small market. From the patient's way of seeing things, that's quite understandable. Say you fear you've got an ulcer. You know it hurts and you go to your doctor who prescribes a bland diet. Boring. As a patient, you don't like it. Your doctor doesn't seem to care about your discomfort: He is going carefully through a series of step-by-step treatments. Next, he puts you on a super-bland diet—with zero wine or booze. Now you really don't like it. Worse, he tells you to swallow a thick, tasteless 'milk'—and somehow find a way to reduce the stress in your life. Then he offers you, as the patient, an alternative: an operation that cuts the vagus nerve *and* causes perpetual constipation. So obviously, lots and lots of ulcer patients stopped going to the doctor *and* were not getting medical follow-up—and were lost to the market. And that's why the anti-ulcer drug market seemed so small to Wall Street. A big part of Tagamet's sales went to patients who had been lost to medical science, because they got so discouraged by the traditional treatment regimen, but they came back in droves when they learned about Tagamet.

"Jim Rothenberg was a big help to me. He knew I'd need help getting a serious hearing for my first buy recommendation, so he went with me from one portfolio counselor to another, getting each one to listen carefully to my analysis and my sales and earnings projections. My case for SmithKline was so simple: a cheap stock in a decent company—so no real downside risk—and a free call option on Tagamet's potentially explosive future.

"I put everything I had into making my case. As part of my internal sales campaign, I organized a dinner at the Beverly Hills Hotel with Bob Dee, SmithKline's CEO; Henry Wendt, the president; and several of our key portfolio managers. Bill Hurt, a real connoisseur, brought the wine. Bob Dee asked Bill Newton why he had come and Bill said, 'Jason would kill me if I missed.'" Over dinner, everyone relaxed while talking seriously about the company and its business. "Our guys got to like their guys," recalls Pilalas, noting, "It's easier to buy a company's stock in real size if you like the people."

Capital's portfolio counselors loaded up, buying a massive position in SmithKline—and waited. They didn't wait long. Soon, Tagamet became the world's first $1 billion product, and Capital was the #1 shareholder in the company with what became the world's #1 drug. SmithKline's earnings over the next several years beat Pilalas's estimates, which were well above Wall Street's expectations—and SmithKline was for many years a major winner for Capital.

Years later, the strategic situation was changing. Strong follow-on products were needed to protect and extend Tagamet's sales, so when the last remaining follow-up product fell away, Pilalas knew that SmithKline, for all its strengths and past successes, had come to a major, negative inflection point and that the tide was turning. So Rothenberg and Pilalas went around to each portfolio counselor again and explained what was going on. They recommended selling Capital's major position in SmithKline—a stock that had been wonderfully rewarding for Capital and a stock that all of Wall Street now loved and was recommending at its high price/earnings multiple, based on linear projections of the past. "We assembled what then was the third largest block of stock ever sold. At 66¾, Capital's holdings totaled over $150 million. Goldman Sachs bid 63 for the whole block—and got it distributed to other institutions in less than one hour.

"For the next nine years, SmithKline's stock underperformed. At Capital, we reinvested the proceeds from that sale into Glaxo—and saw Glaxo's Zantac become the new #1 seller." Such back-to-back home runs really matter.

In 1985, Pilalas had another opportunity—this time in Merck with Vasotec. Getting clearance for a new drug was easier in France than in the United States, so it would be marketed in France sooner. Pilalas flew to France and called on the French executive in charge of national distribution. He and Pilalas, an easy-to-like guy, hit it off. In a two-and-a-half-hour probing conversation, Pilalas learned all he could about every aspect of the French experience with the introduction. He was particularly interested to learn the specifics of the French ways and customs in writing and filling prescriptions so he could develop a realistic model for the subsequent introduction in the United States, where prescribing new drugs was handled differently.

A half-hour appointment turned into nearly three hours of argument and discussion, climaxed by the French executive gesturing vigorously with a stack of pink slips held high over his head and finally, to prove his point, throwing them onto the floor in exasperation.

They scattered everywhere. Pilalas joined in picking them back up and realized that they must be reorders. In medicine, new drugs are used on new patients so that their doctors can observe results. If the new drug works very well, they will switch other, older patients to it. The pink slips showed a rapid rate of substitution. Merck must have a real winner!

In the plane on his way back home, Pilalas was totally involved with his notorious spreadsheets, desperately trying to figure out exactly how the results of the French launch could be translated into the likely results of a probable American launch. An expert at modeling the demand for individual drugs, Pilalas was getting increasingly frustrated. All his numbers seemed to come out *wrong*. They appeared to be way too high.

When the plane landed, he got on the phone right away to call his contacts at Merck's U.S. headquarters: "Am I *way* off base—or are these big numbers actually possible?" Of course, Merck would never give Pilalas any real guidance, but when there was no laughter and no denial, he realized he must be in the ballpark and knew he'd found a real winner. Vasotec became Merck's #1 product and Capital became Merck's #1 shareholder. Along the way, Merck told Pilalas: "Your estimates are way over our budgets" (they were also way over Street estimates). Undaunted, Pilalas the risk taker replied, "You have your budgets—and we have our estimates."

A few months later, Merck's CEO Roy Vagelos introduced Pilalas at Merck's corporate planning conference with a command: "Listen to this man," and putting an arm around his shoulder, added, "He knows more about our company than we do." But by 1999, Merck's new product pipeline was nearly barren: The company's size was nearly $15 billion versus $4.5 billion in 1985 and Pilalas was recommending sale.

"The real work of managing information is to achieve a rational result in an irrational world," says Wally Stern. The past *is* past. Investors live in a world of future estimates. Although the future is the only realm that really matters in investing, there are no definite facts about the future; it's all estimates. "An analyst's job has two different aspects," says Pilalas. "One part is predicting the future and the farther out you can predict and the more unusual or different from consensus your prediction is, the better because, of course, it's much more profitable. The second part of an analyst's job—it's not a job really, it's a *mission*—is to understand and report accurately and clearly how the company's actual results confirm or differ from that predicted future. On the surface, portfolio managers love to be reported to on current and recent developments, but investment success depends on accurate *predictions* and that's far more important."

In recent years, Capital has invested well over $250 million each year on in-house research. "We believe in the concept of comparative advantage," says Denning. "We believe we will achieve better results than the competition if we can spend money on the best research analysts coming up with the best investment ideas." In industry surveys in the United States, Europe, and Asia, Capital's analysts are regularly voted among the best informed by corporate executives,[9] and the numbers for a recent year suggest why: Capital's analysts and portfolio counselors made close to 20,000 company visits—averaging 80 every day—in 68 different countries gathering information and insight.

Information dissemination at Capital is extensive. Three internal newspapers that share information gathered from company visits—one for the United States, one global, and a third, called "Capital Ideas," covering topics of general interest—are distributed worldwide every day via Lotus Notes.

Conference calls are the main means of communication at Capital. Some calls have set agendas and set times, and some are entirely ad hoc. For example, on a chosen day, the G Unit[10] holds conferences to discuss global issues—at 7:00 in the morning in Los Angeles, 10:00 A.M. in New York City, midnight in Tokyo, and 3:00 in the afternoon in London. And at the same times on Tuesday, changes in

[9] *Dow Jones News Retrieval,* March 1, 1997.

[10] Letters with no particular meaning are used because words might carry "baggage" of interpretation or inference.

specific company recommendations, for which a "green sheet" written recommendation will have been prepared and distributed, are discussed to see if the stock should go on the Action list. On Wednesday, the calls are on Asian investments and emerging markets, and so on, and so on. These conference calls are interactive, open discussions by professional peers, not a one-way flow from young, subordinate analysts up to senior portfolio managers. As noted, a worldwide in-house videoconferencing facility is used so frequently that AT&T has shifted from charging by the minute to simply leaving the system on 24 hours a day.

"Wall Street analysts are too often too impressed by the latest newsbreak or event," says Pilalas. "A stock will fluctuate—and it *will* be affected from time to time by short-term factors—but in the long run, the stock will be determined by the real business. So at Capital, that's where we focus our research and analysis. I try to focus on the A List of crucial, success-making factors." Pilalas's basic philosophy on investing in pharmaceutical stocks is to know the industry globally and go with the richest flow of major new products, concentrating on the larger companies with the largest and most successful research. Recent major investments include Pfizer and AstraZeneca.

"Analysts need to be genuine experts on the companies and the industry they follow," says Pilalas, "but they *cannot* be forever looking for one more fact or answering one more question. Analysts need to learn how to get to the point of decision in order to maximize the productivity of their time. Years ago, I learned[11] to focus on the *weak* aspect of any argument, so I let management spin its web—and then focus on the weak spots.

"I know we're investing the life savings and financial security of millions of other people, so it's very important to get it right and I know my limits as an analyst. The pharmaceutical business is very

[11] From Ray D'Elia, who regularly focused on the weak point of an analyst's argument—and did it so gently and graciously that every analyst would accept it as helpful.

long wavelength. Product life cycles are *long.* Just right for a slow guy like me.

"I'll only recommend a stock if I believe we should become that company's largest shareholder. So by definition, we're long-term investors and allied with the company in a true partnership with management. As I tell the companies, 'So long as you continue to make strategic progress, we'll be with you.'"

In investing, it really helps if you can be in tune with the future; feel what's going on—and sense what's coming. As JBL explained his principles long ago: "Capital is in the business of making decisions on incomplete information. This is not to be confused with making decisions on inadequate information. Those who can't tell the difference are doomed to failure. Through research, be sure you understand and can determine the true worth of the investment, then buy securities at reasonable prices relative to their prospects and hold them long term."

Pilalas continues, "My wife, Rena, and I entertain stockbroker analysts and corporate executives, often in our home[12] with the best lobsters they've ever seen. This means a lot to these good people because they're used to *taking* institutional analysts out, not being taken out *by* an analyst. The corporate execs fly into the little airport over at Groton where I'll drive out on the tarmac and meet them. But they better be in jeans and a T-shirt because if they're wearing a tie or a jacket, just as I've warned them, I'll jump back in my car and drive away without them! So it's all very relaxed. The conversation reflects that, too. Never any 'inside information,' of course, but you always improve your understanding when you understand people better.

"I'm always looking to develop strong long-term relationships based on professional as well as personal respect and confidence.

[12] From Memorial Day to Labor Day, the Pilalases live in a home they built in Connecticut that includes the carefully restored Noank lighthouse. Once in horrible condition, it is now recognized as magnificent. By agreement with a local sightseeing boat that comes close to his property, Pilalas pretends to be threatening "serious trouble"—and fires off a small cannon.

The test is easy: Do they still feel good about us *after* we've sold our stock. From the mid-80s to the mid- to late-90s, Capital was the #1 owner of Merck. Then the time came when Merck's strategic development went through a negative inflection point, and I sat down with the management and explained very carefully that we were selling and why. Naturally, that was respected—and appreciated."

Working with an unusually long-term and broadly based understanding of specific companies and industries gives experienced researchers more opportunity to sort out real problems from apparent problems and thus identify unrecognized long-term value. Usually, one or two key variables are what really matter over the long term for a particular company—but analysts also need to look at the small stuff, because a small item today can suddenly mushroom into decisive importance. So analysts have to talk to all the companies in the industry and develop a relationship with each of their managements—and then probe to see if the different strategies make sense and how well they are being implemented.

Developing these analytical skills takes time—lots of time. "It takes ten full years for a capable analyst to reach his or her top performance," says Karin Larson. "But in most organizations, the analysts just won't have the opportunity to concentrate on one industry for anywhere near that long. That means our senior analysts have a very real competitive advantage in analyzing and understanding investments."

To help young analysts, Pilalas has now agreed to travel with them as they call on the companies they cover: "If I invite them to come with me as I call on *my* companies, that would take up time they should be investing entirely in mastering *their* industries. In their first decade or so, Capital analysts really have to devote all their skill and energy to knowing—absolutely *knowing*—their industry on a worldwide basis."

As professional investors have come to dominate the world's major stock markets, market efficiency has increased, particularly in pricing shares of large companies on the basis of what is known or knowable about the near and intermediate term. Having invested more in sheer brainpower and professional talent per increment of investment results than any other investment manager, Capital's challenge is to make sure that this large talent pool is effective in achieving superior results.

The commitment to active management is challenged by passive investing,[13] particularly when serving large institutional funds. While acknowledging the wisdom of very large funds indexing part of their portfolios, David Fisher laments the pattern of funds moving into passive investing shortly after their active managers have been beaten by an unexpected surge in one sector of the Index—such as oils in the early 1980s or technology in the late 1990s. Fisher's advice: "If you are determined to index, history says do so *after* active managers have beaten the index."

In recent years, Capital has had difficulty with one particular type of investment decision: the percentage of each portfolio to hold in cash reserves. In a strong, sustained bull market, holding 7 percent[14] in cash while the stock market rose at an annual average rate of 15 percent, would produce a "performance drag" of 1 percent every year—an amount that would be difficult for any investment manager to overcome.

The open architecture of Capital Group Companies and the widely dispersed authority to make investment decisions that characterizes both the multiple counselor system and the research portfolio depend on independence in decision making and interdependence in developing the basis for making decisions. Capital strives always to be an effective loose-tight organization—loose where that helps and tight where that helps. So each investor is entirely free to make decisions,

---

[13] And by "enhanced" passive investing where the overall structure and the specific stocks in the index are accepted *except* where the manager has very strong convictions—either positive or negative—on specific stocks.

[14] Within the multiple counselor system, an overall cash position of 7 percent could be the result of one out of six counselors holding a 40 percent cash reserve while all the others were fully invested if each had an equal proportion.

but this freedom is always within a set framework, with all trading centralized and with results carefully measured and frequently reported and tied directly to compensation.

The qualitative strengths of research at Capital are illustrated by another of its several senior analysts: Gordon Crawford.[15] He has covered media (movies, newspapers, broadcasting, etc.) for more than 30 years. Notoriously conscientious and self-disciplined, Crawford is described by colleagues as "the world's nicest guy whose redeeming quality is that he's at least as smart as he is personable." After investing over 30 years in getting to know the companies and knowing 20 to 30 executives both personally and professionally at each of the major companies in his industry, Crawford is so widely respected for his detailed knowledge and understanding—as well as his objectivity and good judgment—that corporate executives often check with him on how institutional investors are thinking. Company executives know Crawford always bases his opinions on what's best over the long term for the company and its shareholders. His advice not only is free from any bias, but also is given free of charge by an expert with no axe to grind.

Crawford accepted a two-year stint as Capital Group's nonexecutive board chairman a few years ago, and relinquished it two years later so he could concentrate on his work as an analyst. "He's like a great scientist: happiest when he's doing his research and adding to his mastery of his industry." Crawford teaches beginner analysts that being nice *is* important because life is short and everyone has too little time and so must make choices of where to spend that limited time. "CEOs will, quite naturally, spend their time with those who are enjoyable to be with *and* have done their homework."

[15] Crawford was initially expected to cover insurance companies. When recruited to Capital, he claims to have been a bartender—and did have a part-time job tending bar at The Boar's Head Inn in Charlottesville, where he was earning his M.B.A. at The University of Virginia's Darden School; he had earned his B.A. in Classics at Wesleyan. After a year at Capital, he switched to cover media.

Following his own advice, Crawford has developed a unique personal-professional franchise over his three decades as an analyst and is on easy conversational terms with "Ted," "Barry," "Rupert," and "Sumner"—and 20 to 30 senior executives at each of their respective corporations.

Crawford is so widely known to be well-known in a people-intensive industry that he can tease an executive like Sumner Redstone—who recently married at 79 and has built a fabulous new home—by saying in a large gathering, "It's embarrassing to me, Sumner. I've not seen your new house!" He soon received a dinner invitation to the Redstones' home.

Crawford enjoys his intensive personal contacts with all the key players in an industry where people and personalities matter so much. "He can and will pick up the slightest vibration—long before anyone else can—so he's always way out ahead of others," says a colleague. And while he obviously makes mistakes—some quite large and visible—his long-term results have been outstanding, both as an analyst and as a portfolio counselor. Major successes have included Liberty Media and Cap Cities—which went up over 100 *times*. These big wins are more than enough to overwhelm mistakes like AOL Time-Warner.[16] Crawford, described by his brother as always having an iron-willed determination acting with others, increased the position in AOL Time-Warner from nearly 100 million shares to 300 million shares during 2001 *and* then led a four-month campaign[17] to oust Chairman Stephen Case.

Crawford's influence extends well beyond the strength of ownership he represents. A few years ago, Crawford clamped a no-trading

---

[16] "I didn't know what I didn't know," says Gordy Crawford in self-critique on how he got it wrong on AOL-Time Warner. "I didn't have enough of an understanding of the Internet. Also, there were accounting shenanigans a year or so ago that could have been a warning flag that I could have paid more attention to and dug deeper, instead of accepting management's view that it was minor and 'one-off.'"

[17] "Gordon Crawford's Bet Soured So AOL's Case Had to Go." *Bloomberg News*, January 16, 2003.

freeze or embargo on the shares of Time-Warner and a series of other media companies—and, on advice of counsel, did not explain why. Later, the other Associates at Capital would learn that Crawford had been in Bozeman, Montana, for a weekend of fishing with his friend Ted Turner when Gerald Levin of Time-Warner flew in for a surprise visit. Crawford knew Levin and knew Time-Warner[18] very well, so he immediately recognized the high probability of a merger. This made him—and anyone he spoke to at Capital—an "insider." So, after checking with Capital's lawyers, he took the proper action: no buying and no selling until the deal was announced publicly two months later.

"Being from Capital gets you off to a good start, of course, but after that first call, it's up to you as an individual and how good you are as an analyst and how well you've done your homework. Each analyst develops his own best way of doing his work so there isn't much coaching or teaching 'how' to do research. Each person should and will do it differently.

"As an analyst, it's important to be a good communicator— both with the companies you follow and within your working group at Capital. It sure helps to have a good sense of humor, because even a very good analyst will be wrong 40 percent of the time—and once in awhile, *very* wrong. To get through these negative experiences, you have to know yourself very well and be comfortable with who you are.

"There's an awful tendency for young analysts to model their reports on the reports they see coming in from Wall Street, but that means not taking advantage of Capital's main strength—our long-term orientation or focus."

Developing his personal expertise and the "media savvy" understanding among Capital's portfolio counselors is a continuous process for Crawford. He recently hosted a two-hour meeting with Sumner Redstone in Los Angeles, the week after hosting a two-day teach-in at

---

[18] Later, AOL Time-Warner.

Capital's offices in New York City for Capital analysts and portfolio counselors. At this meeting, 10 industry leaders each gave a two-hour presentation of their particular company's operating results and forward strategies *and* answered question after question. Guests included Rupert Murdoch, John Malone, Dick Parsons, and Mel Karmazona.

Crawford also organizes annual two- or three-day meetings of Capital's Media Cluster—a group of 20 analysts and portfolio counselors. He brings in well-known industry leaders for successive two-hour discussions at which traditional presentations are set aside to make time for intensive question-and-answer sessions. Similar special meetings are held for many groups or clusters within Capital.

Recently, a group of 50 Capital Guardian professionals plus 28 from the Emerging Markets team drawn from all over the world, went to Latin America—in groups of 8 to 12 per country—for a week to visit companies, government officials, and various experts in the private sector.

Another group of 30 portfolio counselors and research analysts from London, Los Angeles, Singapore, Hong Kong, Geneva, New York, and San Francisco spent a full week with their counterparts in Tokyo, meeting with companies, government officials, and various specialists on Japan. Recognizing the high costs—not simply the travel expense of each, but the opportunity cost of taking active investors off-line—few organizations would even consider such a commitment. But in the long run, the investment in developing more and more experience-based commitment to being a One-Firm Firm has great value. Crossruffing Asian and European experts into Latin America—to learn firsthand about real problems and capabilities—increases shared understanding and shared knowledge. At least as important, participating Associates' capacity to understand and communicate effectively with each other is continuously expanding. This is important for an organization that makes each investment on its own merits.

Using the eclectic, "bottom-up" approach of selecting individual securities for investment—instead of following a consistent "top-down" portfolio strategy approach—is not the only way Capital differs from other investment organizations. Another major difference is in the much lower turnover in portfolios: Capital's turnover is typically only one-third the investment industry norm. Low turnover and long-term investing are, of course, reciprocals in a virtuous, repeating cycle. Analysts have the time—and the responsibility—to develop deeper and more rigorous expertise in their particular industries and to take a longer-term perspective in appraising value. In making investment decisions, portfolio counselors have more time to develop their understanding because they make only one third as many decisions—the happy reciprocal of longer-term holding periods—and can take advantage of the analysts' greater understanding. Working with longer holding periods also means Capital is "away from the madding crowd" that is overconcerned with the short term.

"The investment business is no place for those who've never been wrong or who can't be wrong," says Jim Fullerton. "Some people psychologically just have to be right. For people like that, investing can kill them. In investing, you make lots of mistakes—and *all* those mistakes are very visible. So your internal self-confidence must be substantial and solid."

"I'm a risk taker!" says Pilalas and he is—but in a very special way that is characteristic at Capital: He makes very large investments, and this means he puts his hard-won professional reputation on the line in a few outsized commitments. Everyone at Capital knows exactly where he stands; most if not all the portfolio counselors have large investments in his stocks. So if Pilalas is wrong, or even just not really right, the total holdings at Capital in one of his recommendations are so outsized, it will be obvious to everyone in the firm. So Pilalas is a risk taker—big time. In addition to risking his professional reputation, Pilalas will cheerfully "take it to the edge" interpersonally. Once challenged about his lack of modesty, Pilalas's retort: "If you do it all the time, it ain't arrogance."

Pilalas goes on to modify his assertion: "By risk, I mean *intelligent* risk," explaining, "Capital is truly a long wavelength investor—we don't speculate on stock price movements and we intend to continue to hold the stock as long as the company is making substantive strategic progress." Even more than he is a risk taker, Pilalas is a risk avoider and a risk *minimizer*—because he drives himself unmercifully to develop and use the most complete understanding of the commercial potentials of the products being developed and marketed by his focus group of less than two dozen pharmaceutical companies worldwide. And he is determined to have absolutely the best understanding of the 5 or 6 companies Capital now owns, saying, "We extract riskiness by being at *least* as well informed as anyone else about the companies we follow." After 30 continuous years of unrelenting focus on the major companies in one industry, Pilalas drives himself to have more expertise than "anyone else on the planet."

"My ace in the hole is the set of comprehensive models I've developed product-by-product of differential profit opportunity. In pharmaceuticals, operating leverage can be a very powerful force: A 5 percent increase in sales can produce multiples of that in increased profits. A billion dollar product is significantly more profitable than five $200 million products. A major product is simpler, requires less detailing by salesmen, needs only one advertising message, is easier to support properly with follow-on R&D, etc.—so it has higher profit margins. I focus on knowing the sales, product-by-product, compared to the world's estimates. I have detailed and comprehensive models for the sales of every significant product for each of the 20-odd companies I follow. Thank God it's all on computers: Years ago, it was all by hand on huge spreadsheets."

"Success in the investment business does not come from *not* making any wrong decisions—nor even from making more right decisions than wrong ones," explains Fullerton. "Success comes from having the results of right decisions far outweigh the results of wrong ones." In a similar way, Babe Ruth struck out three times more often than he got homers. So did Maris, Mantle, and Sosa. But the results of their home runs far outweighed the results of their strikeouts.

AFTERWORD

L EARNING AND THINKING about Capital began for me in 1967 at Pebble Beach, California. I was on a bus about to head off for San Francisco's airport. As the bus slowly started pulling out of the driveway, I was surprised to see Mike Shanahan ambling slowly toward my window, waving and smiling warmly. We had met just three days before at the beginning of an intensive portfolio management seminar where my responsibility had been to provoke candid give-and-take discussion on difficult investment topics by two dozen "top-gun" portfolio managers assembled for the occasion. A blunt-spoken man, Shanahan gave as good as he took in discussion or debate, and he and I had disagreed on several questions. In those first few days of acquaintance, I knew we had come to respect each other, but this farewell warmth was quite unexpected.

Then the petite woman sitting between me and the window waved back to Mike. "Do you know him?" I asked. "Yes, he's my son. Do you know him?" "Not really. We just met a few days ago. But after three full days of intensive discussion on all aspects of investment management, I know he's one of the clearest, best thinkers I've ever met. And I know he works for an outstanding organization."

"Then maybe you can do me a favor," said Mrs. Shanahan. "Perhaps you can tell me what my son really does. He's too shy to tell me himself. Or maybe he feels I wouldn't really understand."

We had nearly two hours ahead of us, so we had ample time to talk, but I was only beginning to learn about the extraordinary intersection of individual talent, organizational design, core values, professional discipline, and person-to-person understanding that help make Capital Group Companies what it is. Over the next 35 years, I would learn much more, particularly over the past half-dozen years, when I have had the remarkable privilege—as no one else has had before because Capital has no interest in publicity and has very deliberately kept itself nearly unknown—of interviewing dozens of Capital Associates in a series of long and remarkably candid discussions. In a way, this book provides a far better answer than I could give in 1967 to Mrs. Shanahan's questions about Capital and the work of its leaders.

Readers are entitled to know and judge for themselves the basis for my views—particularly since they are strongly held. For three decades, mostly as Managing Partner of Greenwich Associates, my career has been devoted to research-based consulting with more than 200 leading institutional investment managers and securities firms—particularly in the United States, but also in Canada, Australia, Japan, and Europe. As a long-term, confidential advisor to the leaders of these organizations, I've been in an unusually privileged position to understand the challenges facing investment organizations and their leaders.

Writing this book has been a great personal experience in several ways. First, the privilege of learning how Capital Group Companies works as an organization has been professionally fascinating. While knowing the conventional wisdom that "Capital is very well managed," I've been impressed by how very well this organization is managed. Capital is the best managed investment organization among the more than one hundred leading investment organizations and another hundred professional firms in other fields that I've known as a consultant over the past 40 years. I'm confident that Capital is one of the best and quite likely *the* best designed, best staffed, and one of the best managed professional firms in the world.

I am deeply grateful for the openness with which several dozen senior Capital Associates shared their insights and understandings of the important decisions and developments in the history of this outstanding organization. Setting aside Capital's long-standing preference for absolute privacy, virtually all the senior people at Capital have made extensive time available for many detailed discussions. While all evaluations and explanations have been clearly mine to make, Capital's Associates have been remarkably helpful to me in explaining the organization's many carefully thought-through policies, as well as helping on accuracy of dates, places, and names. Working on this project has been another way to learn firsthand how this unique organization operates—and to learn again how many extraordinary professionals combine their talents and energies into Capital Group Companies, the world's best large investment organization.

Associates—and others—who know specific parts of the Capital story have been exceptionally generous in the time and candor with which they have contributed so very generously to this book's development. Several have invited me into their homes for intense discussions that have lasted many hours—and then invited me back again and again. In alphabetical order, they are:

Antoine van Agtmael · Marj Fisher · Jon Lovelace
Tim Armour · Heidi Fiske · Rob Lovelace
Bill Bagnard · Jim Fullerton · Jack McDonald
Dick Barker · Bill Grimsley · Mitch Milias
Joe Beles · Paul Haaga · George Miller
Bob Cody · Ed Hajim · Coleman Morton
Don Conlan · Graham Holloway · Bernie Nees
Gordon Crawford · Bill Hurt · Bill Newton
Mark Denning · Mike Johnston · Ng Kok Song
Jim Drasdo · Bob Kirby · Shelby Notkin
Jim Dunton · Karin Larson · Vic Parachini
Bob Egelston · John Lawrence · Jason Pilalas
David Fisher · Jim Lovelace · Henry Porter

Jim Ratzlaff	John Seiter	Ursula Van Almsick
Steve Reynolds	Mike Shanahan	Thierry Vandeventer
Claude Rosenberg	Nilly Sikorsky	Shaw Wagener
Julie Roth	Don Smith	Cathy Ward
Jim Rothenberg	Wally Stern	Edus Warren
Ted Samuels	James Stewart	Pat Woolf
Howard Schow	Don Valentine	Jim Zukor

In closing, I have three hopes. First is the obvious hope that you have enjoyed getting to know Capital and its people, concepts, practices, and values.

Second, I hope this description of Capital is as accurate and objective as Capital Associates would expect and deserve.

Third, I'm very hopeful that Capital was right to accept the proposition that it should share with seriously interested people the valuable lessons to be learned from examining this remarkable organization.

As you think back over the Capital story, I hope you will ponder the insights and lessons that I have found most meaningful:

- If you are seeking career employment, take careful note of the way in which Capital has designed itself to provide opportunities for exceptionally capable, self-disciplined individuals to contribute to an important organizational achievement and to experience personal and professional fulfillment—the ultimate aspirations of all remarkably talented and aspiring professionals.

- If you are a serious student of how best to lead and manage any contemporary professional organization, you will find inspiration in the many interlocking ways in which Capital has innovated and developed an environment for excellence and then recruited and nurtured the capable individuals who are the dominant contributors both to the environment for excellence and to results—and I hope you will agree that we can all learn much from how this professional organization, as large as it is, organizes itself around individuals.

- If you are responsible for leading an organization of what Peter Drucker wisely calls "knowledge workers," I urge caution. Tempting as it will be for managers of professional service organizations to try to adapt to or adopt a few components of Capital's process of management, it may not be possible to borrow particular components without also making a larger and much more profound commitment to the totality of the management process: devotion to achieving superior investment results and delivering superior service to individual and institutional clients; rigorous meritocracy; consistent objectivity in decision making and distribution of rewards; flexibility of organizational structure; and a results-oriented organizational culture.

  On the other hand, a wholesale adoption would be particularly daunting, since the leaders of Capital would assure any inquiring visitor that as much as every component in the system of Capital Group Companies has been developed with great care and only after extensive study, no component is ever permanent—except the twin commitments of forever striving to be among the best, and pursuing, in balanced fashion, service to Capital's three constituencies: investors, Associates, and owners.

- If you are looking for an investment manager and think Capital might be right for you or your family or an organization you care about, I urge you to consider a profound reality. If your intention is, as it should be, to find the investment manager you can stay with indefinitely, if not forever, then your selection will not be based on recent years' investment results, on current holdings, or on individual investment managers. Rather your selection will, like the selection of a spouse, be based on such enduring dimensions as character, values, beliefs, capabilities, and personality. In a business organization, these enduring characteristics are a firm's culture—the so-called soft factors that will actually sustain it over many years and through many situations while the hard factors like investment performance all too quickly come and go.

The only truly enduring factors in any investment organization are the culture or organizational values that, year after year, attract and keep those talented individuals who will do the research and make the investment decisions that will consistently achieve realistic, long-term objectives. The priority focus of the leaders of Capital Group Companies is not so much on superior investing as it is on the means to this super salient end: recruiting, developing, organizing, and rewarding those extraordinarily talented and dedicated individuals who—working effectively together—can achieve sustained superior investment results and attract, train, and reward their successors.

A final word. Every reader will know that I have the highest regard for Capital as an organization, as a culture, and as a gathering of gifted, committed individuals. After three decades of diligent searching for excellence in investment management, the strengths of Capital are all the more remarkable to me: I believe Capital is unique. That's a problem. If you were an Arapaho scout, riding alone on your pony miles ahead of your tribe as it crossed the Arizona desert, what would *you* do if you came to the rim of the Grand Canyon? Would you return to your tribe, describe what you'd seen just as you'd seen it; *or* knowing how easy it would be for others to assume you must be exaggerating, would you understate what you'd seen to make it sound more believable? But, what if your moderated description *still* seemed too good to be true? Maybe it would be better to say nothing and hope that the tribe would reach the canyon rim on its own. But what if they somehow passed it, moving perhaps parallel to the Colorado River?

I decided long ago to "call 'em as I see 'em." At 66, it's too late for me to change now. Besides, I love excellence and having found it, I believe in sharing the good news.

Capital has been designed and led for more than 70 years by two remarkable men: Jonathan Bell Lovelace and Jon Lovelace. As Capital's founder, Jonathan Bell Lovelace endowed the organization with core values: very long-term focus; keen attention to innovation and innovators; consistently high professional standards; patience in investing soundly, based on thorough research; appreciation for first-rate people and all that they can do when well organized; and the clear and consistent priority of serving investors well.

As the organization's long-time servant leader, Jon Lovelace has facilitated several important strategic advances and nurtured the interior strength of the organization during its enormous expansion in scale and international growth toward being truly global. Like his father, he shows great respect and caring for individuals with investment talent and commitment to client service; a long-term strategic perspective; a deep sense of responsibility for the welfare of individual investors; numeracy and objectivity; personal modesty—and love of baseball.

Great as their respective contributions have been, both Lovelaces would insist correctly that many people have made major contributions and that Capital's success has been and always will be the success of individuals working within and through the organization.

Servant leaders are increasingly recognized as crucial to the development of superior professional organizations. They are enablers who have a special kind of vision. Very good parents, who may have no clear idea what their kids will do with their lives, devote many years to facilitating the healthy development of their children's strengths and skills *and* deferring when appropriate to the maturing child's own decisions. Similarly, the primary focus of an organization's servant leader is usually *internal:* recruiting and developing talented people, developing culture and climate, assuring both collegiality and self-discipline, fostering accurate and objective communications, and removing inhibitors and "noise." The leader also ensures equitable financial, professional, and personal reward systems based on merit that motivate each individual and the whole organization to strive to achieve the firm's chosen *external* goals and strategies.

Servant leaders at Capital have developed a particular style best explained by reference to Aristotle's definitions of three major styles of leadership:

1. *Logos.* The rational, logical reasoning that convinces people to accept and follow a particular plan or strategy.
2. *Pathos.* The emotional, inspirational style that can induce people to commit to follow a particular individual.
3. *Ethos.* The values and worthiness of the objective or the goal of commitment that makes people loyal to a leader's values.

Aristotle recognized that most leaders rely on *one* of these three kinds of leadership. He feared leadership based on pathos and revered those rare leaders who combined logos and ethos. Capital's servant leaders are devoted to empowering individuals and enriching the organization through an affirmative mixture of *logos* and *ethos.*

The Capital story is truly an adventure story of the human spirit carried forward and upward by many capable professionals devoted explicitly to "achieving the best in everything we do." Given the scale of past achievements, it may be difficult to visualize just how Capital Group Companies will sustain its past rate of development and continue to provide great career opportunities for its many professionals. Certainly, the challenges will be great. Still, the creative capabilities of the many young professionals attracted to Capital, as well as its enabling organizational design, give promise of future success.

While readers are entitled to know my own thoughts,[1] I believe strongly that such opinions ought not be mixed in with an objective

---

[1] Readers interested in my views on investing will find them in *Winning the Loser's Game,* 4th edition, published by McGraw-Hill, New York (March 2002).

description of Capital Group Companies. This is *their* story. So each chapter has had a separate "Notes to Readers" section providing perspective on the challenges facing Capital—and all other investment organizations.

While dozens of Capital Associates contributed importantly to my understanding of the firm, I have quoted only a few Associates individually. Many important individuals are not even mentioned. Several hundred Associates perform significant leadership roles and have made major contributions to the development of The Capital Group Companies. Obviously, they could not all be fairly represented. Nor could the even larger number who will determine Capital's future. As Jon Lovelace says, "The real strength of the organization is the many, many capable and dedicated people who are not individually identified." Using a few Associates to represent a very large group of individuals is feasible because decisions at Capital are made only after full, open discussion has produced a strong, broad consensus. So individuals are quoted here as representatives of the Capital organization, which may well be the strongest major organization of professional knowledge workers anywhere in the world.

Summary Statement of Corporate Objectives and Goals

ORGANIZATIONAL HISTORY AND THE NATURE OF OUR BUSINESS

A STARTING POINT for any program of corporate planning requires consideration of the question: What business are we in? It is surprising how often this is a difficult question to answer. In the case of our organization, various individuals would probably choose to emphasize different points. The description given here has been developed with close attention to the organizational history of Capital Research and Management Company.

Our field of operation might best be described as being investment management in the field of corporate securities, with primary emphasis on common stock investment.

Our primary area of application of these business talents and abilities has been in the mutual fund field, since this offers the opportunity for (1) making clear-cut investment decisions for a limited

Approved and adopted at meetings of Board of Directors on December 17, 1963.

number of specific clients, without the administrative problems involved in an extensive investment counseling operation, while (2) allowing broad participation in the fruits of our investment efforts through the purchase and holding of Fund shares by individuals and institutions wishing to take advantage of the investment management by our group, and choosing the Fund or Funds whose investment policies most closely coincide with their own objectives.

Since the primary area of application of our investment management abilities has been in the mutual fund field, a second aspect of the business has been developed—administrative services for, and business management of, mutual funds. In contrast with most other mutual fund organizations, this has not involved direct participation in the selling effort for the Funds, with this handled by a separate organization, American Funds Distributors, Inc.

An important part of the historic development of and philosophy behind our investment management organization has been the emphasis on providing internally our own investment research of high caliber, and with considerable emphasis on direct company contacts. These investment research services have been provided by a wholly owned subsidiary, Capital Research Company.

Finally, a relatively minor but periodically important source of revenues for our organization has come from projects relating to our primary investment management services:

1. Although we have determined as a matter of policy not to offer our services as investment counsel, at their request we provide investment advisory services for a fee to a limited number of individual and institutional clients other than mutual funds; and

2. Special appraisal and financial counseling services performed individually by members of our organization; these latter functions are now grouped in terms of corporate organization under the operations of the new Capital Management Services subsidiary.

BASIC CORPORATE OBJECTIVES

It shall be the objective of Capital Research and Management Company to conduct its operations so as to achieve as fully as possible and on a continuing basis the reasonable objectives of our clients, our key personnel, and our CR&M shareholders. It is recognized that if the risk of obsolescence in a changing world is to be avoided, there must be a continuing willingness to re-examine areas of activity, services, and products.

The interests of these three groups are much in common. By meeting successfully the objectives of our clients, primarily at present the shareholders of the mutual funds for which we serve as investment advisor, we gain personal satisfaction and the ability to pay good salaries to our employees, and the opportunity to operate with growing profitability. By meeting the personal objectives of our personnel as fully as possible, we put them in a position to serve our clients better, and to attain good financial results for Capital Research and Management Company. Finally, the successful operation of Capital Research and Management allows our clients to be sure of a continuing high-caliber operation, and allows us to attract and keep capable personnel.

It might be pointed out parenthetically that many individuals in our organization are served in all three capacities—as shareholder of client funds, as employee, and as management company shareholder.

SPECIFIC CORPORATE GOALS

To measure our success in meeting our basic corporate objectives, we need to have specific goals for periodic review and measurement.

A. *Service to Mutual Fund Clients*

    1. To maximize the investment results achieved by each Fund in accordance with its own specific objectives, measuring ourselves against other funds and investment managers with similar objectives, and, where appropriate, with general market indices; to concentrate on consistency of above-average investment results over the years.

    2. To handle our business management services as efficiently and effectively as possible, measuring results by a minimum of shareholder and dealer complaints, a below-average rate of Fund redemptions, and costs which are economical relative to the services provided.

    3. To provide superior results in both of the foregoing categories at a competitive management fee.

    4. To measure over-all our results in terms of the percent of assets that we manage in relation to total mutual fund assets, recognizing that this figure derives in combination from

        a. portfolio results, and

        b. sales less redemptions.

B. *Results for Employees*—It is our objective to pay competitive salaries, with substantial performance bonuses for excellent results and achievements, with direct profit participation through a profit-sharing plan and, for key personnel, through stock ownership in CR&M, and in a working environment to achieve individual personal fulfillment to as great a degree as possible. Results here can be measured in general terms by employee morale and organizational enthusiasm.

C. *Results for Shareholders*

   1. Because our present revenues are closely tied to general movements in the stock markets, and we have a high degree of operating leverage since salaries represent a major portion of the expense ratio, it is difficult to establish realistic year-to-year earnings goals. For our per-share earnings growth objective, therefore, it is proposed that a longer time period be used with an objective of a 10 percent annual increase over any three-year period and a doubling over any six-year period; this is approximately equal to a compound growth rate of 12 percent per annum.

   2. Financial strength for the corporation sufficient to assure continuity of high-caliber operations through periods when even the most economical administration of operating expenses consonant with the basic objectives of the corporation may result in sharply reduced net profits or even in operating losses.

D. *Criteria for New Corporate Activities*—In considering new ventures and/or the extension of corporate activities, to concentrate on expanding the utilization of existing capabilities of our personnel. In such consideration, to be mindful not only of the potential opportunities, but also the risks of such new activities reducing the quality of present services, and jeopardizing rather than enhancing the achievement of the above goals.

Outline of
Basic Managerial Beliefs

The Capital Group, Inc.

12/67 SPECIAL MEETING OF THE
BOARD OF DIRECTORS

THE FOLLOWING BASIC beliefs shall guide and control the management of this company—and appropriate steps shall be taken to gain understanding and effective support for these principles throughout the entire organization.

1. The Capital Group, Inc. shall assure that the operation of its subsidiaries achieve as fully as possible, and on a continuing basis, the reasonable objectives of the clients served, the personnel of our companies, and Capital Group stockholders.

   The interests of these three groups have much in common. By meeting successfully the objectives of our clients, we are able to provide personal satisfaction, the ability to pay good salaries to our employees, and the opportunity to operate at optimum profitability. By meeting the personal objectives of our personnel as fully as possible, we put them in a position to better serve our clients and to obtain good financial results for Capital Group. Finally, the successful operation of Capital Group allows our customers/clients to be sure of a continuing high caliber operation and helps us to attract and keep capable personnel.

2. To achieve optimum results, we must perform effectively in the following key result areas:

   a. Customer/client satisfaction.

   b. Profitability.

   c. Productivity: cost effectiveness.

   d. Innovations—new and better approaches and techniques.

   e. Resources—creation, conservation, and use.

   f. Management development and performance.

   g. Employee attitudes and performance.

   h. Public responsibility.

3. The highest ethical standards will be maintained in all of our external and internal relationships.

4. The business must be kept in adjustment with environmental forces and be administered with a sense of competitive urgency.

Growth of The Capital Group Companies, Inc.

	Associates	Assets Managed
1931	8	$ 12,269,766
1935	8	18,609,832
1940	17	13,212,232
1945	23	22,336,048
1950	28	36,204,538
1955	30	146,307,522
1960	71	368,065,221
1965	106	1,010,754,319
1970	274	2,653,704,000
1975	304	4,202,831,000
1980	417	11,798,327,000
1985	612	25,985,934,000
1990	1,529	60,322,374,000
1995	3,276	218,316,393,000
2000	5,224	560,654,082,000
2003*	6,012	652,991,094,000

*June 30.

INDEX